The Land Speed Record

1930 **1939**

Compiled by R M Clarke

ISBN 1 85520 5157

BROOKLANDS BOOKS LTD.
P.O. BOX 146, COBHAM,
SURREY, KT11 1LG. UK
sales@brooklands-books.com

Printed in Hong Kong

ACKNOWLEDGEMENTS

When Sammy Cahn the great lyricist was asked which came first, the words or the music he always replied "the phone call". Its a bit like that with publishing, and the phone call that started us on our Land Speed Record series came from Brian Harvey of Grand Prix Models. He had recently acquired a box of cuttings that Cyril Postumus had collected while researching his 1971 book *'Land Speed Record'*. He agreed to put these at our disposal if we would consider compiling a book on the LSR.

Armed with Cyril's collection we turned to our own archive which yielded a great deal of post-1925 material but we were still short of articles up to 1924. We turned again to Brian and he suggested we speak to Ugo Fadini in Padova. Ugo was marvellous, he loaned us invaluable books and magazines which made it possible to consider covering the pre-1920 period.

There were still gaps however so we turned to The National Motor Museum Library in Beaulieu. Michael Ware and Annice Collett, the librarian, assisted us in every way. We left after many enjoyable hours armed with precious photocopies of relevant material.

Brian also introduced us to David Tremayne, the well known racing journalist and LSR historian, who generously volunteered to write an introduction to each period.

The next need was coloured illustrations for the covers. Arthur Benjamins had produced over the years a wonderful collection of LSR paintings and he graciously agreed to let us feature them on the covers - thanks also go to Michael Turner, who had helped us before with our Le Mans series, who came to our aid with his splendid painting of Thrust SSC.

Thanks also go to author Paul Clifton for allowing us to draw from his 1964 book the *'The Fastest Men on Earth'*, now out of print. Paul's book has brought cohesion to the magazine stories that make up the main fabric of our books. In 1964 William R Tuthill retold the story of Daytona Beach in his book *'Speed on Sand'* which was published by the Museum of Speed in Daytona. Our thanks go to both the author and the Museum for allowing us to include the early chapters of this book. Finally, our thanks go to The British Petroleum Company Limited for allowing us to quote freely from their 1963 publication - *The BP Book of Land Speed Records*.

Our books, which in the main are collections of copyright magazine articles, could not be published without the help, understanding and goodwill of the world's leading motoring journals. Our thanks go to in this instance to the publishers of *The Antique Automobile, Autocar, The Automotor and Horseless Vehicle Journal, Automotor Journal, Auto Topics, Canada Track and Traffic, Car and Driver, Car Annual, Car Life, Ford Times, Hot Rod, Hot Rod Yearbook, The Literary Digest, Motor, Old Motor, Modern Motor, Motor Racing, Motor Sport, Motor Trend, Rivista Illustrata Mensile, Road & Track, Speed, Speed Age, Sporting Motorist, La Vie Au Grande Air, The Veteran and Vintage Magazine* - with the kind permission of the National Motor Museum at Beaulieu, *Wheels* and *The World's Fastest Cars*.

We beg the indulgence of our readers with regard to the quality of reproduction of pages covering the early years. In many instances we have had to work from copies of copies and very blurred early photographs. We are publishing our Land Speed Record anthology in two ways, firstly as a single hard bound volume and secondly as five separate soft covered books.

R M Clarke

Brooklands Books

CONTENTS

FOREWORD

The land speed record. Motorsport distilled to its most fundamental elements - Distance versus Time. There is something intensely appealing about that, for it is the pure essence of speed and little else.

There is none of the visceral, adrenaline-pumping thrill of Grand Prix racing about land speed record breaking. Indeed, it is ironic that in a branch of the sport where speeds are astronomically higher than they are in Formula One, there is none of the glamour and the glitz one associates with the 16-ring circus. Instead, the speed seeker all too frequently finds himself and his dedicated team miles from anywhere, in some of the most inhospitable (yet breathtakingly beautiful) parts of the globe. He will spend his time waiting for nature to be benign, eyeing the curvature of the earth, fighting the ennui of isolation and hoping like hell that it isn't going to rain. It is a cold-blooded affair that requires a special kind of courage and determination.

To me it has always been an ultimate test, a peculiar measure of an individual, an unusual means of judging the worth of his claim to heroic status even though, almost to a man, such self-aggrandisement is never part of their personal thinking. I don't think I've met a speedking yet who wasn't a reluctant hero.

My personal fascination with the land speed record was fired even before my passion for Grand Prix racing, in the days long before I graduated to secondary school. And I give a nod of thanks to the gods of fate that I have been fortunate enough in my professional life to meet many of the people concerned intimately with record breaking, and on two occasions to have been present when Britain pushed the barriers forward. Some speak with awe of the total eclipse of the sun, but there is no sight I have encountered more impressive than that of ThrustSSC charging like a big black locomotive down the Black Rock Desert in Nevada, chased by a roostertail of dust, outrunning its own noise. Nor any sound more emotionally charging than the two sonic booms that took Andy Green and Richard Noble into the history books. As people are wont to say of events that somehow change the world, you had to be there to appreciate it. The sheer splendour and beauty of if all.

And was it ever thus. Throughout LSR history, men have savoured such pivotal moments as they have waged war on speed on public roads, racetracks, frozen lakes, beaches, salt flats and alkali playas. Long may they continue their quest.

The period covered in this third volume of Brooklands Books' Land Speed Record series came after the orgy of speed in the Twenties, and began with the tragedy of Sir Henry Segrave's death attacking the water speed record on Windermere. Perhaps subconsciously spurred by that, Captain Malcolm Campbell continued on his indefatigable course, each year creating a faster version of Bluebird, always seeking something better. In 1931 he would push Segrave's Golden Arrow record to 246 mph, but no sooner had he achieved four miles a minute than 250 became the figure with the magic ring. He achieved that the following year, and reached for 270. He attained that in 1933, and a heavily modified Bluebird's subsequent failure to add more than four miles an hour to that figure finally prompted the angered move from Daytona Beach to the Bonneville Salt Flats. There, in 1935, Campbell would achieve his final mark of 300 mph, and bring the curtain down on the old era.

In his wake would come two more Englishmen, but fellow Brooklands racers Captain George Eyston and John Cobb were different characters altogether to the brash Campbell. And different, too, were their machines. Eyston's self-designed Thunderbolt introduced twin engines and the enclosed cockpit; Cobb's brilliant Reid Railton-designed Railton Special the teardrop shape and four-wheel drive. Brute force was no longer sufficient; it was science as much as a heavy right foot that would take Eyston and Cobb through the 300s, and tantalisingly close to the magic 400 ...

DAVID TREMAYNE, Harrow, October 1999

KAYE DON'S GIANT SUNBEAM FINISHED "ON TIME"

Driver to Sail with His Car and Mechanics To-morrow.
Completed Vehicle "A Masterpiece of Engineering"

THE great Sunbeam car with which Kaye Don will set sail for Daytona to-morrow was completed to time-table by a devoted staff that worked night and day, and was shown to a distinguished gathering at the Wolverhampton works last Friday.

Grey skies and a cold north-easter could not chill the enthusiasm which the car evoked, and this found expression in spontaneous cheering when Don arrived at the wheel of his 12-cylinder Sunbeam "Tiger." Dozens of cameras and a Movietone "talkie" film apparatus recorded the greetings which followed between the man who will drive "Silver Bullet" and the man who directed its design: Mr. Louis Coatalen.

The car, which is a masterpiece of engineering skill, is even more impressive in its complete form than was the bare chassis which we examined some weeks ago, when *The Motor* published the first authentic drawing, in section, and a complete description. Although 30 ft. in length from the blunt, whale-like nose to the tail fins the car does not look ungainly; the flattened top of the bonnet above the engines is only 34 ins. from the ground, and the body is but 3 ft. wide.

Like a Submarine!

When sheet-steel covers were raised to reveal the engines we found ourselves irresistibly reminded of a submarine; there is in this "Silver Bullet" the same cramping of man and machinery into a sheath of shining metal, the same wonderful British workmanship and the same clever contriving to avoid waste of all-precious space. An inch in body width might mean the difference between success and failure. And to carry our analogy a stage further it may be remarked that the air which this car will meet at over 4 miles per minute will present as solid and wall-like a resistance as the water cleft by a submarine at a tenth of this speed! Sheet-steel carried by a structure of angle-iron and reinforced around the cockpit forms the bonnet and "body," which presents a smooth contour from the nose to the windscreen but for a pair of bulges (which enclose the long shafts of the steering gear) and a pair of shallow grooves in which fit the flattened exhaust pipes. The nose holds the

The cockpit was "made to measure"; its chief adornment is a large rev. counter reading up to 5,000 r.p.m.

ice-blocks, over which the cooling-water is pumped; behind this come the two specially built power units, each with 12 cylinders (arranged in a narrow Vee), four camshafts

A close-up view of one of the hydraulically operated front-wheel brakes, which are water cooled.

and 48 valves. So close does the bonnet fit around the engines that it almost seems as though it would short the plugs.

A huge rotary supercharger fits behind the rear engine, following which is a fireproof bulkhead to protect the cockpit. This cockpit was "made to measure," and, when seated, Mr. Don is between the two propeller shafts and just ahead of the rear axle. In front of him are the conventional clutch, brake and accelerator pedals and a centrally mounted D-shaped steering wheel; the gear lever is on the left and there is a special hand control for the "wind brake"—a hinged flap which fits between the vertical stability fins on the tail.

Prominently located near the steering column is a large revolution counter, calibrated up to 5,000 r.p.m. There are six other dials: these consist of two oil-pressure gauges, two thermometers, a pressure gauge connected to the fuel tank in the tail and a battery charge indicator.

Behind the driver's head is a padded bolster, to obviate the terrific suction which a slip-stream would create, and this merges gradually into the curving shape of the tail.

Only a short portion of the ends of each axle projects between the body and brake drum, but, even so, these portions are streamlined by fairing. Windage on the wheels is also reduced to a minimum by the use of robust triangular fairings behind each of them.

Water-cooled Brakes.

The hydraulically operated brakes are designed to fit partly within the wheel rims and are water cooled; each drum, which now weighs 45 lb., was originally a solid 4-cwt. billet, over 3½ cwt. having been machined away!

There is a prevalent impression that the engine crankshafts are coupled end to end, but this is not the case. As has already been explained in *The Motor*, each crankshaft is geared to a long layshaft which runs at about twice the engine speed, and carries the power to the clutch and gearbox. It is then distributed through further gears to the two propeller shafts and final bevel drives.

Painted externally in silver, with the crossed flags of Britain and the U.S.A. depicted on its curving bows and its name in red letters along the flanks, the car makes a brave showing. As we left the works it was about to be placed in the long packing case in which it will journey to the scene of action. May all good fortune attend it!

KAYE DON'S SUNBEAM "SILVER BUL

An impressive photograph of "Silver Bullet," with which Kaye Don is to attempt to beat the world's land-speed record anticipated that this twin-engined conception of the Sunbeam Motor Car Co., Ltd., will

Looking down upon "Silver Bullet" from the rear gives some idea of
its enormous size and the method of fairing employed.

Kaye Don, who will pilot the car, photog
has to be re

A close-up of the tail showing the ai
of the car before the brakes are a
adhesion

ch, Miami, Florida, U.S.A., next month. The present record for the flying mile is 231.362 m.p.h. and it is confidently
e. The car is over 31 ft. in length and is the most powerful racer so far created.

cockpit. Incidently, the steering wheel
to get in.

bject of which is to slow the speed
eory this should also increase the
wheels.

The front view shows the enormous length of the bonnet, while the nose
of the car shows that it has been aptly named " Silver Bullet."

KAYE DON'S TWIN-ENGINED 4,000 H.P.

Exclusive Illustrations and Details of the Actual Car, "The Silver
Ice-cooling, Hydraulic Clutch, Stabilizing Fins, Air Brake, Hyd

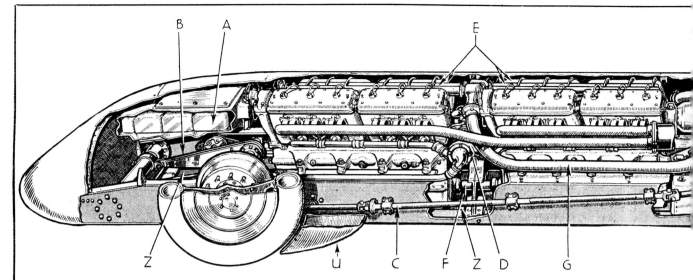

FIRST ILLUSTRATION OF THE ACTUAL CAR BUILT FOR

A part cut-away sketch of "The Silver Bullet." Other drawings that have appeared of the car have been based upon conjecture and are
inspection at the works, and is authorized by the Sunbeam Motor Car Co., Ltd., who have built it. The following key is explanatory of
drag links ; (d) cross-shaft driving the water pumps ; (e) induction manifolds ; (f) secondary shaft coupling the two 12-cylinder engines to
carburetters (one removed) ; (k) duplex Marles type steering gear ; (l) separate oil tank for dry sump lubrication ; (m) gearbox er
(q) strong cross member embracing driver's cockpit ; (r) radius arms controlling movement of rear axle and forming longitudinal locatio
to assist streamlining ; (w) stabilizing fins to help the machine to maintain a straight course ; (x) one of th

NEVER before has been seen such concentration of machinery as exists beneath the yards-long bonnet of the giant Sunbeam racer, "The Silver Bullet," with which it is hoped that Kaye Don will make a successful attack upon the world's land speed record at Daytona Beach, Florida, in a few weeks' time. Some idea of the concentration of power can be gathered from a perusal of the drawing accompanying this article, but even the apparent chock-a-block fullness of the portion forward of the driver's seat does not fully convey the extent to which packing has been resorted in order to maintain a smooth, yet not too bulky, external shell.

The driver—Mr. Kaye Don.

The great importance of shape (length does not matter so much as the cross-sectional or projected area) in a car intended for speeds of between 200 m.p.h. and 300 m.p.h. cannot be too highly stressed. Consequently, the bonnet, as it might be termed, just clears the main features of the power

units, and everything else has been accommodated in the remaining space. Yet the chassis does not appear in any way an unsightly maze of details; indeed, it seems that the very magnitude of the task has compelled neatness which might not otherwise have been present had dimensional considerations been less restricted. In actual fact the width of the frame is less than 3 ft., and the height to the top of the bonnet line less than 44 ins., dimen-

How "The Silver Bullet" w

et," Built by the Sunbeam Motor Car Co., Ltd. Features Include Four-wheel Brakes, and Other Exceptionally Ingenious Ideas

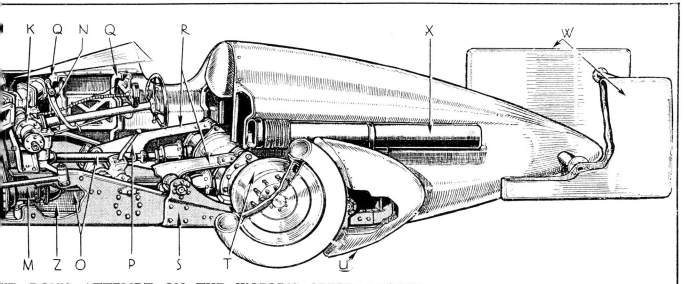

K Q N Q R X W

M Z O P S T U

E DON'S ATTEMPT ON THE WORLD'S SPEED RECORD.

urate. The drawing by "The Motor" artist reproduced above is the first and only one to be made from the actual car after long
nding features in the design : (a) Ice cooling tank ; (b) radius arms to control the movement of the front axle ; (c) one of the two 3-piece
g) pipe conveying the mixture to the forward engine ; (h) high-speed centrifugal type supercharger ; (j) breeches-pipe carrying the two
a dual drive to each rear wheel ; (n) pedal operating hydraulic control to clutch ; (o) propeller shaft ; (p) control to 3-speed gearbox ;
rengthening plate which forms the rear spring mounting ; (t) brake drums housing two pairs of side-by-side shoes ; (u) fairing for wheels
aust pipes moulded into the body shell ; (z) flat shield enclosing the whole of the underside of the chassis.

sions which, for a vehicle 30 ft. long, are astonishingly small.

There is an old saying, "Anything that looks right is right," and from a close inspection of the details of this Sunbeam racer we have no hesitation in saying that it looks a very likely "model" further to enhance with the people of the world the prestige of the British motor industry generally and that of the Sunbeam Co. in particular.

ar when finally completed.

It is a beautiful job both in conception and execution. The main frame, for example, has clean lines, is immensely strong (being not less than 11½ ins. deep around the part supporting the engines and 13½ ins. deep at the section where the transmission is divided), and fits in snugly with the rest of the major components. At intervals throughout its length there are stout tubular cross-members, which, of course, assist materially in preventing torsional movement (or lozenging) of the chassis.

Semi-elliptic springs with exceptionally thick leaves support

The designer—Mr. Louis Coatalen.

both front and rear axles, both sets being controlled by enormously powerful Andre shock absorbers. A point of interest in the design of the suspension is that the total movement of the front axle is limited to an amount less than 1 in. (i.e., within half an inch of each side of the normal static position) in order to preclude all possibility of a high-speed wheel wobble developing, or a sudden lurch, caused by some irregularity in the

The upper half of one of the 12-cylinder engines. There are four valves per cylinder with the camshafts located above each line of valves. This view shows how the sparking plugs are encased in tubular extensions which project through the valve covers.

course, setting up a pitching action, which might be helped by a sympathetic vibration.

Both front and rear axles are controlled by radius arms which are anchored to cross-members; thus the springs do not provide any measure of fore and aft location to the axle. The rear springs are inclined throughout their length, and although they sit above the top of the channels for the main frame, they are virtually underslung beneath the axle casing. At the point of attachment to the chassis, reinforcing plates have been added, which serve the dual purpose of carrying the springs and strengthening the frame at a critical point.

Much could be written concerning the design of the power units, but space considerations forbid a thoroughly detailed description of such gigantic

(Above) The assembled dual-drive rear-axle casing which, besides being immensely strong, is relatively light in weight. (Right) This photograph of one of the engines gives a good idea of the general layout of the main components. Note the cross-shaft, at each end of which is a water pump.

machinery. The two engines each have 12 cylinders set athwart common crankcases, with banks of six on each side. As might be expected in the interests of efficiency, all valves are situated "overhead," but instead of being formed in pent-roof type of cylinder heads the valve stems are all parallel to the centre lines of the cylinders. There are four valves to each cylinder, with the sparking plugs centrally located

in the best firing position. This arrangement has considerably simplified the mechanical features, because the camshafts are directly above each line of valves and, being gear driven from the front of the engine, a very neat assembly has been achieved.

These Sunbeam-Coatalen engines represent a very great advance in design, the mechanical efficiency being much higher than usual. This is due to the low friction of the roller-bearing crankshaft and the adoption of roller bearings for the big-ends. They are designed to run at 4,000 r.p.m. and can carry much higher loads than plain bearings. Each engine weighs less than 1,000 lb. and develops 2,000 h.p. This is believed to be lowest weight per horse-power yet attained.

No racing car nowadays is up to date unless the power unit is supercharged, and to supercharge 24 cylinders is a job calling for the greatest possible ingenuity in the layout of pipe lines, induction manifolds, etc. At the rear of the second engine

a drive is taken to a high-speed large-diameter centrifugal blower, which draws mixture from the carburetters and blows it out under high pressure from tangential ports formed in the rotor casing. Large-diameter pipes then lead the mixture to the induction manifolds running between the banks of cylinders of each engine.

The engines are coupled, but not, as might at first be thought, directly through the crankshafts. Actually a secondary shaft runs along the bottom of the engines, and is coupled to each crankshaft by gears in such a manner that the secondary shaft runs at rather more than twice engine speed, thereby reducing the stress in the shaft, and avoiding the necessity for the second crankshaft to transmit the torque of the first engine plus its own torque.

We now come to a consideration of the manner in which the power is transmitted to the road wheels. A multi-plate clutch with the "pot" or outer member mounted directly on to the rear of the main shaft transmits the drive to the gearbox, the casing for which is virtually a cross-member. This component contains the gears for distributing the dual drive to the back axle bevels. Plain spur gears are used and, as might be expected, they, together with the shafts which support them,

Coatalen patent—and in the event of a pipe line of the hydraulic operating system breaking the other brakes still function owing to the fact that an automatic seal is incorporated in the system.

The steering gear sets something of a new note, for although a normal type of hand wheel, steering column and Marles roller-type reduction gearing are used, there are two drag links, each consisting of three pieces, universally jointed and held in bearings attached to the outside of the frame, which operate each front wheel independently; there is, of course, no track rod.

Finally, a few words must be said concerning the streamlining. Everything has been fitted inside the body shell. Even the exhaust pipes are moulded into the sides of the body, while the steering gear, including the drag links, is enclosed The actual construction of the "body" is of more than passing interest, for all the panels are built up on an angle-iron framework, with strips of rubber interposed between the framing and the panels. In the neighbourhood of the driver's seat two especially strong 3 per cent. nickel steel cross-members are used "just in case anything untoward happens"; it is hoped that these strong members would form some sort of protection for the driver, in case of the car going into the water for it would

This photograph of the 1,000 h.p. twin-engined Sunbeam, which, driven by Major Sir Henry Segrave, was the first car to exceed 200 m.p.h., makes an interesting comparison with "The Silver Bullet."

are of really substantial dimensions. Although the overall gearing of the engine to the road wheels is something in the order of 1 to 1 (we believe it is even higher than this), the axle bevels show a reduction of nearly 3 to 1. This means to say that the propeller shafts run at a much higher speed than that of the engine, but the whole transmission line benefits by the reduction in stress caused by the increase in rotational speed.

In a car such as this Sunbeam it is essential that the brakes should be powerful and yet simple in construction. The application embraces a straightforward hydraulic system, all four drums being of the same size both in so far as diameter is concerned and the width of the shoes. These latter components, by the way, are manufactured from malleable iron castings, which are well ribbed radially (and consequently immensely strong) and equipped with fabric facings. An interesting sidelight on the braking system is that the drums are machined out of the solid, which when in billet form weighed about 4 cwt. each; they now weigh 45 lb. each.

The brakes are water-cooled—a Sunbeam-

plane like a motor boat and only sink when it lost speed.

Everything that human ingenuity can think of has been incorporated in the design so as to make the attempt as safe as possible. In this connection an air brake has been incorporated. This consists of a special contrivance fitted at the rear to slow the speed of the car before the brakes are actually applied, while if a skid occurs it will have the effect of straightening the car.

Fuel is carried in the fairing for the tail, while an ice tank in the "nose" forms the cooling medium for the engines. A special by-pass has been arranged with a controllable valve, so that the temperature of the water entering the cylinders can be regulated to suit any conditions that may arise. There is one other item of interest. A fireproof bulkhead is to be installed between the rear engine and the driver's compartment. This should, of course, form an excellent measure of protection and also tend to exclude any possibility of a flame reaching the fuel tanks.

Altogether the design and construction of this giant Sunbeam is extremely impressive.

The
Land Speed
Record

Target: 250 M.P.H.

Before Malcolm Campbell could produce a faster *Blue Bird*, however, a new British competitor appeared: the Sunbeam *Silver Bullet*. The speed this car was designed to achieve was 250 m.p.h.

The Sunbeam *Silver Bullet* was conceived in its entirety especially to win the world's land speed record. While some cars that attempted to break the record relied on aircraft engines, the engines powering the *Silver Bullet* were designed especially for the car. The combined output of these two V12 engines was stated to be about 4,000 b.h.p.—making the car an exceptionally powerful contender for the record. A single centrifugal supercharger, fitted behind the rear engine, served both engines. The two engines drove a high speed counter-shaft and had a combined capacity of 48,040 c.c. The positioning of the two engines one behind the other ahead of the driver made the overall length of the car unusually great: 31 ft. 1 in. including the two fins.

The designer was Louis Coatalen, assisted by Hugh Rose, and the objectives of the design team at the Moorfield Works, Wolverhampton, were to achieve a lower wind resistance and a better power-to-weight ratio than those of any previous competitor.

The streamlining was influenced by the results of tests in the Vickers wind tunnel, and the chassis was entirely enclosed by a streamlined body made of aluminium sheeting. Oddly enough, though, the wheels were not enclosed; however, fairings were fitted behind them. Streamlining was assisted by the low height of the body, its top being only 2 ft. 9 1/4 in. off the ground. The low placing of the driver, which also helped to cut down wind resistance, was made possible by the positioning of the two propeller shafts on either side of him. The elimination of a radiator, and the substitution of an ice tank to cool the engines, further improved the streamlining.

The driver of the *Silver Bullet* was Kaye Don, a famous Brooklands driver who had set up a lap record in the 4-litre Sunbeam. Don was faultlessly turned out in spotless white overalls, as usual, when he prepared to make his attempt to push the record still higher for Britain at Daytona in March .

The strong wind was against Don when the engines were tried out at speed for the first time on 15 March. The wind had blown the sand into ridges—and Don had a bumpy ride. Nevertheless, even though his runs were not timed, his rev-counter indicated a speed of 198 m.p.h.—although his actual speed was slower, owing to wheelspin.

A big problem that Don was up against was that the engines had not been thoroughly tested at high speed—a difficulty not faced by drivers using aircraft engines for, even though their cars may not have been tested at high speeds previously, at least their engines had been proved in flight. The engines of the *Silver Bullet* usually started up all right, employing compressed air, but, as soon as Don opened them up, they frequently misfired. The supercharger was one cause of trouble, and, on 17 March, Don had to cancel his run when the supercharger caught fire. Engine difficulties did not

diminish the following day, when the car was stopped by further misfiring. Don could not see too far ahead, owing to haze, and the sands were still bumpy. His difficulties were not eased when a fuel line burst. Nevertheless, he set up a mean two-way speed of 168 m.p.h.

The failure of the two engines to give the output for which they were designed, however, prevented Don from reaching the speed for which he was aiming. Nor did the big weight of these two engines in the centre of the car assist the problem of holding the car straight in the strong wind encountered on the bumpy sands.

Bad weather continued to cause delays, to add to the mechanical difficulties, and, even though he achieved 190 m.p.h. in one direction on 21 March, these delays were costing money. Finally, the *Silver Bullet* was sent back to Britain without breaking Segrave's record.

This British attempt to be first past 250 m.p.h. had ended in failure. Now Malcolm Campbell, in the next attempt to raise the record for Britain, set his sights on 4 miles a minute— 240 m.p.h.

Malcolm Campbell wanted Britain to keep the record. Sir Henry Segrave had stated he would not tackle the record again. Yet Campbell heard that foreign competitors were making plans to take the record away from Britain. Campbell therefore felt that everything was up to him.

More power was one way to keep the record for Britain. In the reconstructed *Blue Bird*, a supercharged Napier Lion engine giving 1,450 b.h.p. at 3,600 r.p.m. was substituted for the earlier unsupercharged version; this aircraft engine was similar to that used in the 1929 Schneider Trophy race.

Improvement of the streamlining, to cut down wind resistance, would also help to secure victory. Wind tunnel tests were therefore carried out. One result was that the propeller shaft was shifted to the left-hand side of the driver, to reduce the height of the cockpit. Wheelspin was decreased by using lead as ballast, to improve the grip of the rear tyres on the sand.

The designer was Reid A. Railton.

After J. Gurney Nutting completed the body, in six weeks, the Napier-Campbell *Blue Bird* was taken through London after dark to the Rootes showrooms in Piccadilly, where it was displayed before being shipped to the U.S. in the Homeric. Campbell reached Daytona at the end of January 1931.

He experienced a bad fright in an early run: through the mist, a big crowd suddenly appeared on the course directly in his path. His speed was just under 200 m.p.h. He immediately put on his brakes—but they did not function properly. He was still moving towards the crowd very fast. He dropped down into second, then turned the engine off. Still the car was getting closer to the people. *Blue Bird* finally stopped well under 100 yd. away from the rather frightened spectators.

On 2 February he achieved a speed of about 240 m.p.h.— but this was not officially recorded as it was set up in only one direction.

Next day everything was going well, and his speed was about 260 m.p.h. in the measured strip when, suddenly, the gear lever slipped into neutral, and the needle on the rev.-counter practically went off the clock. Throughout the following day, when he had to wait without making a run owing to the high wind, doubts about possible damage to the engine grew in his mind.

On 5 February a mist made visibility poor—and the officials warned him to keep his speed down when he made his run. He made a longer preliminary run than usual, 51 miles, to get up speed, so as to give himself more time to get used to the mist. The wind added to his problems by making it difficult for him to hold the car straight. But the mist was what really worried him. Owing to its thickness, there was not much point in sighting by the rev.-counter on the bonnet; all he had to go by were the marker flags. Finally, he aimed at the red square above the far end of the measured strip.

The thickness of the mist restricted his visibility to a few hundred yards, and, on his way back, he was suddenly alarmed to see a policeman on a motor cycle unexpectedly appear out of the haze directly in his path—heading straight towards him. There was nothing Campbell could do. Fortunately, however, the policeman swerved off the course, avoiding a nasty collision at the last moment.

The spectators rose to their feet, cheering, as soon as his speeds were made known, for he had achieved speeds much faster than were thought possible in such a thick mist: he had broken the world's land speed record by setting up a mean two-way speed for the flying mile of 245.73 m.p.h. and a mean two-way speed for the flying kilometre of 246.09 m.p.h. Malcolm Campbell had become the first man to go faster than 4 miles a minute.

But he was always moving forward towards a new goal, and, as soon as he climbed out of the cockpit of *Blue Bird*, he made an attack on a record for cars of less than 45 cu.in.

When Campbell returned to Britain he was given a victor's procession through the streets of London to Westminster Hall. Having won the world's land speed record for Britain for the fifth time, he was given a knighthood by King George V —recognition by his country that one of his principal objectives throughout had been to keep Britain ahead of the rest of the world.

But Sir Malcolm Campbell still feared that a foreign country might take the record away from Britain: he had heard that a new car was being prepared in the U.S., and he also knew that the Australian driver Norman ("Wizard") Smith was planning to attack the record in New Zealand. Campbell therefore decided to improve *Blue Bird* again, in case he had to defend the record for Britain. When the Mayor of Daytona Beach invited him to go back the following year, to make another attempt, Campbell set his sights on a new target: 250 m.p.h.

The modifications to *Blue Bird* included the increasing of the power of the engine by about 50 h.p. and the further reduction of wind resistance by the streamlining of the nose. In February 1932 Campbell was back at Daytona.

He found all his old doubts about Daytona creeping back into his mind when he looked out of the window, day after day, on waking: the wind stayed strong, making the surface rough and the car difficult to hold straight. At least, though, he had obtained permission to get up speed over a longer distance, by using the stretch of sand beyond the pier—which would enable him to tackle the longer distance records in addition to the flying mile and kilometre. Even so, the course was not really long enough, nor wide enough, and he turned over in his mind again thoughts of Ninety Mile Beach in New Zealand, a dry salt lake in the Argentine, and other venues he had considered. Total calm would be ideal; but at Daytona one was always so much at the mercy of the wind.

The wind was still strong when he finally slipped behind the wheel of the Napier-Campbell *Blue Bird* on 24 February. Owing to the strength of the wind, the plan was that his first run should be nothing more than a trial. The wind was behind him, though, and its strength persuaded him really to let the speed build up as he drove south. He had to struggle to hold the car straight, but the only other snag was the blotting out of his vision at one stage when spray splashed over the cockpit. Then he made his run back—this time against the wind.

Campbell had to wait a little while to find out his speeds: the timekeepers had not made any calculations after the first run because they thought he was making only a practice run, not a bid on the record. The speeds in opposing directions dramatically illustrated the effect of the wind: his speeds with the wind behind him were 267.45 m.p.h. for the mile and 262.24 m.p.h. for the kilometre—but facing the wind the speeds were only 241.77 m.p.h. and 241.3 m.p.h. respectively. Nevertheless, he had successfully broken the world's land speed record: his mean two-way speed for the flying kilometre was 251.34 m.p.h. and for the flying mile 253.97 m.p.h. He also set up a new world's 5 kilometres record. The shifting direction of the wind was against him on 26 February: its veering and backing made steering difficult and also blew the sand into ridges, making driving bumpy. He did not improve on his existing land speed record, but he did break the world's records for the 5 miles, 5 kilometres, and 10 kilometres distances.

Sir Malcolm Campbell had become the first man to go faster than 250 m.p.h.

Having successfully achieved one target, Campbell immediately began to consider what would be his next target. Meanwhile, though, he had to face a challenge from the other side of the world.

1930 SUNBEAM *SILVER BULLET* SPECIFICATION
COUNTRY OF MANUFACTURE. Britain.
ENGINES. 2 Sunbeam. Cylinders: 24 (2 V12). Bore: 140 mm. Stroke: 130 mm. Cubic capacity: 48,040 c.c. Valves: overhead camshafts.
Carburettors: 2 Amal. Ignition: B.T.H. distributors. Lubrication: dry sump. Cooling: ice tank, approx. 11½ cu. ft. capacity.
Countershaft driven by both engines. Single centrifugal supercharger mounted behind rear engine, 17,000 r.p.m.
TRANSMISSION. Clutch: multi-plate combined with positive drive dog type. Gearbox: 3 forward speeds, reverse.
Ratios: 1st—1.125, 2nd—1.780, 3rd—2.653, reverse—1.125. Final drive: straight tooth bevel, ratio 12/33.
CHASSIS. Suspension. Front and rear: semi-elliptic locomotive type springs. Shock-absorbers: double type Hartford.
Wheels: disc. Tyres: 37.8 in. x 7.3 in., Dunlop. Brakes: hydraulic, also air brake. DIMENSIONS. Wheelbase. 15 ft. 5 in. Wheel track: 4 ft. 11 in.
Over-all length: 31 ft. 1 in. Width: 5 ft. 11¾ in. Height (top of body): 2 ft. 9¼ in. WEIGHT. 3 tons approx.

1931 NAPIER-CAMPBELL *BLUE BIRD* SPECIFICATION
COUNTRY OF MANUFACTURE. Britain.
ENGINE. Napier Lion aircraft. Cylinders: 12. Cubic capacity: 24 litres. Max. power: 1,350–1,450 b.h.p. at 3,600 r.p.m. Centrifugal supercharger.
TRANSMISSION. Gearbox: K.L.G. Ratios: 4.01, 2.27, 1.58. SUSPENSION. ½-elliptic. WHEELS. Type: Dunlop steel disc.
Tyres: Dunlop, 35 x 600 front, 37 x 600 rear, tyre r.p.m. at record speed—2,195 r.p.m. DIMENSIONS. Wheelbase: 12 ft. 2¾ in.
Track, front: 5 ft. 4 in. Track, rear: 5 ft. 2 in. Length: 25 ft. approx. WEIGHT. 71 cwt.

SELDOM has any automobile aroused so much interest as the new Napier-Campbell, the great racer with which Captain Malcolm Campbell is hoping early next month to break the world's land speed record.

Last week we were able to publish the first exclusive and authoritative description of the new car illustrated by Bryan de Grineau. This week we explain further its many ingenious features.

It should be realized in the first place that the Napier-Campbell car is the most powerful ever constructed, for the Napier racing aero engine which forms its power unit gives off some 1,450 h.p. at 3,600 r.p.m. and weighs only 1,140 lb. This works out at a weight of only .78 lb. per horse-power developed. In spite of its enormous power output, the engine is most compact, as may be realized from the fact that it is only about 64 ins. long, 37 ins. wide and 34 ins. high. The actual engine used by Captain Campbell is one of six built for the last Schneider Trophy race, and special permission had to be obtained from the Air Ministry before Captain Campbell could be supplied with it.

* * *

Each of the 12 cylinders is separate, and they are arranged in three banks of four each, one of which is vertical and the other two inclined on each side at an angle of 60 degrees. The bore and stroke are respectively 139.7 mm. and 130.17 mm., giving a capacity of 24,000 c.c. and a ratng of 145 h.p. The engine is supercharged by a cen-

trifugal type blower at its forward end, the three Claudel-Hobson carburetters with their Venturi-shaped air intakes being bolted to its casing. The two Watford magnetos are fitted at the rear end of the crankcase, one on each side, and dry-sump lubrication is, of course, employed, the oil reservoir, which contains five gallons, being mounted on the off side of the engine.

The history of the "Blue Bird," as Captain Campbell's car is named, dates from 1926, when it was designed and built around an unsupercharged 450 h.p. Napier engine. The car secured the world's speed record early in 1927, and established a record of 206.95 m.p.h. at Daytona in 1928. After undergoing considerable modification it was taken to South Africa in 1929. Here the world's five-mile and five-kilometre records were taken at 211.49 m.p.h. and 216.04 m.p.h. respectively.

It was realized, however, that much

higher speeds could be obtained by better streamlining of the body, apart from fitting a more powerful engine.

Mr. R. A. Railton, of Thomson and Taylor, the well-known Brooklands experts on racing cars, entirely redesigned the car, and in May of last year he prepared designs and a Plasticine model, with which exhaustive wind-tunnel tests were carried out. By modifying the contour here and there, it was found possible to reduce the frontal area to only 14.5 sq. ft., although this is greater than that of the "Golden Arrow," which established the present record of 231 m.p.h. in the hands of the late Sir Henry Segrave. In order to streamline the body more efficiently it was necessary to redesign the chassis, shifting the central casing of the rear axle and the torque tube 7 ins. sideways. All the designing and assembly of the chassis were carried out at Brooklands by Thomson and Taylor.

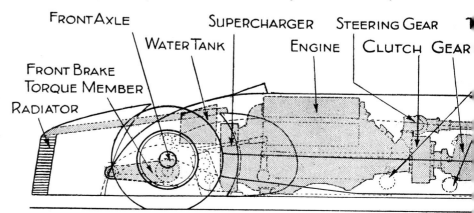

A phantom view of the supercharged Napier-Campbell "Blue Bird" which acts as a key to the very

...way drawing of the "Blue Bird," which, in conjunction with the sketch below, enables one thoroughly to grasp the salient features of the construction. ...e details are the separate cowling of the radiator, the adoption of the principle of the Handley-Page slotted wing in reducing wind resistance, the off-...e gearbox, propeller shaft and final drive, the seating of the driver low down alongside the propeller shaft and the strong tubular construction de-...tect the driver in case of accident. The engine is a 1,450 h.p. 12-cylinder supercharged Napier, similar to that built for last year's Schneider Trophy race.

An interesting point is that the two rear springs are provided with a different amount of camber, so that when the car is at rest the body is slightly tilted towards the off side. This has been done so that when the engine is developing its full power its torque is such as to bring the chassis back to an even keel. A bulkhead is fitted just behind the engine so as to minimize the risk of danger to the driver in the event of fire.

As was explained in the issue of *The Motor* dated January 6th, the wind resistance is greatly reduced by fitting the radiator in the front. By being separately cowled and carried in front of the body proper, wind resistance is still further reduced by adopting the principle of the Handley-Page slotted wing, by which the main air stream is lifted off the front and top of the body. The radiator and its cowling are carried on what would appear to be rather flimsy

supports, but we are assured that these have been calculated to withstand the wind pressure on the radiator besides any shocks to which it might be subjected due to the uneven surface of the beach at Daytona.

The ventilator for the cockpit performs the dual functions of blowing away any fumes from the engine and preventing any suction or back draught drawing the air into the cockpit. Were it not for the small ventilator the back draught would be so great as to be capable of blowing the driver out of the cockpit.

All four wheels have been fitted with special streamlined fairings. These have been built so close to the tyres that there is no room allowed for the greater space taken up by a deflated tyre or one on which the tread may have given trouble. Consequently, the last five inches or so of the fairings are of very thin aluminium, so that this section

would crumple up without harm to the remainder of the wheel fairing in the event of tyre trouble.

Many readers may have noticed the curious protuberance well forward on the bonnet of the car. This contains a small revolution counter which the driver will be able to see without taking his eye off the course. There is, of course, a very large revolution counter on the facia board. Owing to the manner in which it projects, the smaller revolution counter is used as a sight by which Captain Campbell should be able to steer a straight course.

The Frame 12 ins. Deep.

The chassis frame of the "Blue Bird" was built at Messrs. Vickers, River Don Works. Some 12 ins. deep at its widest part, the frame passes under the rear axle, but is upswept over the front axle. Tubular cross members are used throughout, some being machined from solid steel billets. Two of these cross members support at its forward end the sub-frame, which carries the engine, the unit being suspended at three points, one spherical socket being at the front and two at the rear. The petrol tank, which is made by the Gallay Radiator Co., contains 23 gallons and is mounted fairly high up behind the driver; the filling orifice is concealed by the upholstery behind the driver's head. The radiator is of the Serck honeycomb type; as previously explained, it is carried in front of the car, but the huge header tank is housed just in front of the engine. The cooling system contains 22 gallons of water.

Ace wheel discs are fitted and the steel wheels have been designed by the Dunlop Rubber Co., who have also produced the tyres, after a series of special tests to ensure their being able to with

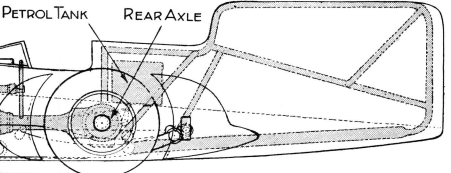

...way drawing at the head of the page, which is made from the most interesting side of the car.

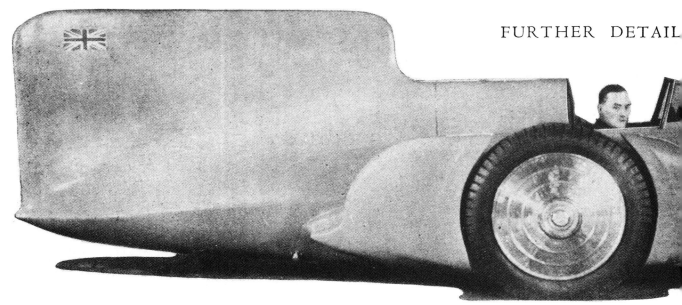

stand the stresses imposed upon them at high speeds. The clutch is of the multiplate type, Ferodo lined, Ferodo, Ltd., having assisted considerably in the design of this component. The gearbox is of the constant-mesh type, each gear being engaged by dog clutches, while the ratios are 1.58, 2.27 and 4.01 to 1. A reverse gear is, of course, also provided, and the box was built by K.L.G. Sparking Plugs, Ltd.

The front axle is made in two pieces joined in the middle by substantial flanges, while special provision has been

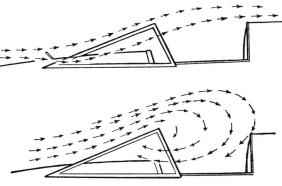

The radiator is separately cowled and carried in front of the body proper, thus reducing wind resistance. The air is guided by the slot to follow the body contour.

made for relieving the springs of torsional stresses. Two Marles steering gears are used, separate drag links in two sections conveying the motion from the steering gearbox to the front wheels on each side. A massive tie-rod is used in addition, and the Ackerman action of the steering is maintained by the lay-out.

Half-elliptic springs are used front and rear. They are of the Woodhead-type with weldless solid eyes and solid lug plates and rebound clips. The front springs measure 3 ft. 1 in. in length, and those at the rear 4 ft. 2½ ins. The springs are anchored to the axles by a double set of U-bolts, manganese bronze spring blocks being utilized. Hartford shock absorbers and Silentbloc bushes are employed, four shock absorbers being fitted to each axle.

The Alford and Alder type front-wheel brakes are provided with large logarithmic cams mounted on special carriers which form the universal joints of the operating shafts. The whole arrangement is set well within the centre line of the steering, and has been found so satisfactory that it has not been

necessary to alter it to any appreciable extent during the past four years.

All four wheels are equipped with 18-in. internal diameter drums with a width of 1⅝ ins. To avoid overheating of the brakes thin fins are machined on the outside of the drums. The shoes, made in Wilmil alloy and specially lined by Messrs. Ferodo, Ltd., are identical in the front and rear brakes. The reaction plates for the front brakes are formed by extension lugs integral with the stub axles, the rear reaction plates, which are of steel, being bolted to suitable flanges solid with the steel arms of the rear-axle casing. The brakes are applied by Clayton-Dewandre vacuum servo. Smith's instruments are installed throughout and include oil and air pressure gauges, revolution counter, water and oil thermometers.

The bodywork, by Gurney Nutting, Ltd., is built according to the designs of Mr. R. A. Railton. It was built in the astonishingly short time of 36 days and nights, the framework, of large-diameter steel tubes, being covered with aluminium panels. The tail portion is the only fixed part of the body. The three detachable sections respectively cover the engine, the cockpit and the space between the cockpit and engine. The body, consisting of over 600 sq. ft. of

Diagrams showing how the ventilator for the cockpit forms the dual functions of dispersing any fumes from the engine and preventing any suction or back draught drawing the air into the cockpit. (See text.)

This fine photograph gives a good impression of of which Capt. Malcolm Campbell is seen seated. the radiator forw

aluminium panelling, is spray painted with 5½ gallons of saxe-blue cellulose enamel. The driver's seat is fitted with Moseley Float-on-air cushions and a specially designed Triplex glass windscreen will be used.

The wheels are covered by polished aluminium discs with two annular ribs swaged in them so as to give them added rigidity. They are secured by rings screwed on to the hub shell.

Preparations for the Attempt.

Few people realize the magnitude of the organization connected with any attempt on the world's records. It may, therefore, be interesting to give a rough idea of the stores and spare parts which Captain Campbell is having to take with him to America.

The car itself, which was on view last Tuesday at Rootes, Ltd., Piccadilly showrooms, is leaving for New York to-morrow, January 14th, aboard the "Homeric." The mechanics will travel with the car, and so, probably, will Capt. Campbell, although he may possibly defer his journey until the 21st.

In order to make certain that his car will run on fuel of exactly the same quality as that on which it was tested, Capt. Campbell has had to send his fuel over to Daytona in advance. Only a few ships are allowed to carry petrol, so that the arrangements were made in

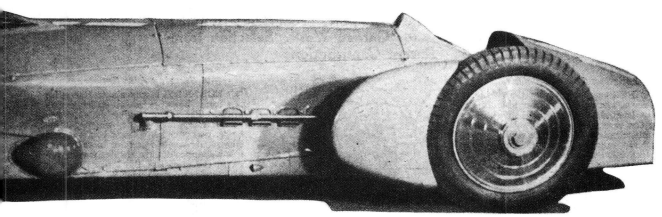

atic proportions of the "Bluebird," at the wheel streamlining of the wheels and the mounting of he body and axle.

good time. Some 300 to 400 gallons of fuel were dispatched, together with 100 gallons of oil, fully 300 sparking plugs and innumerable cases of tools and spare parts. The latter are of all descriptions and include shock absorbers, ball races and roller bearings, road springs, engine parts, instruments, windscreens, body parts, upholstery and alternative bevels for varying the rear axle ratio.

A Spare Engine.

On this occasion Campbell has actually sent a second engine over to the U.S.A.—not so much because he expects to use it, but because he will derive more confidence from the knowledge that he has left nothing to chance.

Three dozen spare tyres and tubes and nearly two dozen wheels have been sent over, besides a pair of the gas starters, with " booster " magnetos, necessary to start the engine.

When Campbell went to S. Africa in 1929 he had to take 56 cases of parts, but, even so, he had to purchase an aeroplane to maintain contact between his base on the dried-up lake of Verneuk Pan and Cape Town. He also had to take out the whole of the R.A.C.

electrical timing gear and two timekeepers to control the attempt.

It may not be generally realized that if Campbell succeeds in knocking one second off the late Sir Henry Segrave's time over the measured mile, the increase in speed obtained will amount to 17 m.p.h. He may thus beat the record by a handsome margin even if he covers the distance a few hundredths of a second faster. Hence the need for using special apparatus capable of measuring time to one hundredth of a second. Only a few sets of such

Duplicated steering is fitted and the sketch shows the ingenious lay-out of the system.

apparatus are to be found in the entire world.

Campbell is aiming at covering the mile in 15 secs., equivalent to the astonishing speed of 4 miles a minute! If fortune should smile upon him, however, and he succeeded in taking only 14 secs., his speed would work out at no less than 257.14 m.p.h.

In order to prevent a competitor from putting up a wonderful performance with the wind behind him, and then waiting for the wind to veer round and so help him again, the international body controlling record attempts has decreed that the course has to be covered both ways within a space of 30 minutes. The mean of the time taken in each direction is then calculated.

It is generally desirable to change the tyres between the "out" and "home" runs, for, including accelerating and slowing down, the car covers about 11 miles on each attempt, or 22 miles on the double run. Campbell does not consider that the 30 minutes allowed leaves enough time for changing the wheels and applied to the A.I.A.C.R. in November to extend the limit to one hour. His proposal was turned down.

Campbell Not Changing His Tyres.

So great is his confidence in the specially built Dunlop tyres he is using that he is not going to change them between his two runs over the course. This will save a great deal of time, as each wheel, complete with its tyre, weighs 2 cwt. and requires three men to change it. The aluminium disc, secured by a screwed ring, has first to be removed from each wheel, after which 10 large nuts have to be unscrewed, so to change all four wheels would take rather a long time.

Campbell, brave though he is, cannot be called foolhardy. So, although we feel that we should prefer him not to risk a second run at four miles a minute on the same tyres, however good they are, we can only assume that he has calculated it all beforehand and is taking no unwise chances.

One of the unique features of the giant racer is the manner in which the transmission system is offset. Note also the barrel-shaped gearbox and the cranked gear lever. Note sockets for jacks in the foreground.

THE AUSTRALIAN ATTEMPT
ON THE
WORLD'S SPEED RECORD

Details of the Car and the Course

Showing the location of Ninety-Mile Beach on the west side of the North Island of New Zealand.

PREPARATIONS are now well advanced for the forthcoming attempt on the world's land speed record by the Australian driver, Norman ("Wizard") Smith, who is expected to arrive in New Zealand at the end of January and to make his run by the middle of February on the Ninety-Mile Beach, at the far north of the Dominion. Details of the car, which is progressing well, have now been announced, while arrangements for the accommodation of Smith and his party at the beach are being put in hand.

The car is designed on similar lines to the "Golden Arrow," and the engine is a 1,450 h.p. 12-cylinder supercharged Schneider Trophy type Napier, similar in every respect to that installed in Capt. Malcolm Campbell's Napier Campbell "Blue Bird."

The frontal area of Smith's car is less than the "Golden Arrow," the overall height being only 3 ft. 2 ins., against 3 ft. 8 ins. Another difference between the two cars is in the streamlining at the sides. Smith's car is to have the fairing behind the rear wheels prolonged into two fins, one on each side, while the upper portion of the bonnet will be slightly different. Running back from a tri-pointed nose similar to the record-holder, the bonnet will be sloped slightly upward, the idea of the designer being to utilize the enormous wind-pressure to hold the car down.

There is only a very small clearance, and the driving seat is only 7½ ins. off the ground, the driver sitting between two propeller shafts. The steering gear is duplicated and coupled direct to both front wheels, with a track rod between, and both axles are held in position with radius rods. Each of the disc wheels is turned out of a solid ingot.

The task of designing the car has been a severe one for Mr. D. Harkness,

who is supervising its erection in the workshops of Harkness and Hillier, Ltd., Sydney. Work on the chassis was commenced long before the arrival of the engine, and to enable this to be achieved all designing was done with blue prints of the engine forwarded from England as soon as permission to use the engine had been obtained from the Air Ministry.

A further difficulty is that the engine remains the property of the British Government, and must be returned as soon as the record attempt has been made. In order to preserve secret the details of the engine, Smith has guaranteed that only himself, the designer and two mechanics are to be allowed to

touch it. No one else will even see it, and while it is in the car, both in Australia and New Zealand, it will be carefully guarded.

The tyres, which have been specially made and are declared to be safe up to a speed of 310 miles per hour, contain 12 layers of special cord, while the tread is but 1-64th of an inch thick.

The car will cost about £6,000 without the engine, which is said to entail a further £8,000, and the whole expense is being borne by a prominent resident of Sydney, Mr. Fred. H. Stewart, in whose honour the car will be named the "Fred. H. Stewart Special." Mr. Stewart will accompany Smith to New Zealand and witness the record attempt. It has been his aim and also that of Mr. Harkness to construct a car of entirely British components. Every part will be of Empire origin, the engine, tyres and wheels being English, while the rest of the vehicle will be Australian. The track used, of course, is in British territory.

Of the Ninety-Mile Beach a number of facts have already been published. The beach lies about 250 miles north of Auckland, on the rugged west coast. On arrival at Auckland it is probable that the car will be shipped to Whangarei, a distance of 90 miles, and from there transported by rail and road. The distance from the railhead to Kaitaia, the nearest township to the beach, is nearly 60 miles, the road running through hilly country clad in beautiful native bush. Kaitaia itself is 25 miles from the portion of the beach which will be used for the record attempt.

In order to take advantage of favourable conditions as soon as the tide permits, Smith and his party intend to

Continued on page 36

"Wizard" Smith (left) and Don Harkness, the designer of the car for the attempt on the world's speed record. The car in the picture is the "Anzac," a Cadillac chassis with a 12-cylinder Rolls-Royce engine, with which it is also hoped to obtain world's records.

CAMPBELL'S NEW DAYTONA CAR

The Latest "Blue Bird" Built to Defend Britain's Land Speed Record. Behaviour of Car an Unknown Quantity Until the Day of the Actual Attempt. How the Difficulties Have Been Met.

THE man whose job it is to supervise the design of one of the gigantic cars for the world's land speed record has no light task from any point of view. True, he has not the responsibility for the engine, and some of the parts that have to be used are already made, and do not have to be designed, but, as against that, it is extraordinarily difficult to fit the various components into place, and, what with one thing and another, the process reminds one not a little of the most interesting form of jigsaw puzzle. In fact, there are many ways in which the task would be made easier were it possible to design a racing machine of this type as one coherent whole from the very beginning, for as it is the designer is limited in hundreds of unexpected directions by the fact that the various parts can be fitted together only with difficulty.

Moreover—and this is the biggest difficulty of all—there is no chance whatever of discovering whether or not the machine is right, whether it will be tractable or unmanageable, until that tense moment when the car is taken out for the record. At that point many thousand pounds have been paid, and there is a possibility that the payment has been futile. If the machine should prove impossible to hold, or even insufficiently fast, there is no chance of rectifying mistakes at last made obvious by practical trial, and the failure is broadcast throughout the world by people only too anxious, it would seem, to interpret the car's troubles in the worst possible way.

On the other hand, though the car's useful life may not extend for more than five minutes' serious action on almost deserted sands, and though that may seem very little return for an immense expenditure, yet success is at least as widely broadcast as failure, and success appeals to the imagination of millions of people.

The car with which Campbell is now to attempt to beat the existing record of 231.446 m.p.h. over a flying kilometre is easily the most interesting of the long range of machines which have borne the pet name of "Blue Bird." The chassis commences with two gigantic tapering side-members braced very thoroughly by tubular cross-members and strengthened even more by a length of armoured under-pan just about the centre, precautions which are necessary because the whole handling of the car depends upon the frame remaining rigid. In front two more big girders form a sub-frame on which the engine rests.

The engine is a Napier designed for high-speed aeroplane work, developing slightly over 1,300 h.p. from three banks of four cylinders arranged in the shape of a broad arrow, and giving a total capacity of 23,942 c.c., with a bore of 139.7 mm. and a stroke of 130.17 mm. Actually,

Captain Malcolm Campbell with the plasticine model of his new car, and the finished chassis.

the engine faces the wrong way, as what in the aeroplane would be the transmission for the tractor screw points towards the gear box, while the end which would be immediately in front of the pilot is, in the car, just behind the radiator, a change necessary, of course, in adapting the power unit to the car's transmission.

The cylinders are very light, and round them are formed light steel water-jackets, in which water is circulated by a big centrifugal pump arranged to feed through pipes on each side of each block, with an additional pipe on the exhaust side as a precaution, and a return flow to the radiator from the back of each block. In this car the radiator is a separate unit right in front of the machine and carried on a special frame outside the streamline body, so that the air passing through the tubes does not go through the body itself.

This is a good example of one of the difficulties encountered, for the radiator must be in the full blast of the air stream, has to be small and light, but cannot form the front of the body, or the inside of the body would be filled with air which, emerging from the cockpit round the driver, would cause interference and increased wind resistance. As it is, only the radiator is in front, the water entering through one upper tube and returning through two other tubes, while what corresponds to the top tank of an ordinary radiator in this case is a separate large tank in the nose of the streamline body, fitted with a filler cap and a valve which opens only if steam develops, and otherwise prevents water escaping down the vent pipe as a result of violent acceleration.

On the head of each block of cylinders is compactly arranged a pair of camshafts, one for the inlet, one for the exhaust valves, with a single vertical drive from the crankshaft. The exhaust is discharged through long but narrow ports to short steel exhaust pipes which just project through the body, those of the port cylinders coming out of the left, those of the starboard block on the right, while the centre block pipes are longer than the others and emerge on the left also. Since the three blocks are in line, circumferentially round the crank case, there are a single master rod and two auxiliary rods with wrist pins on each crank pin, and the rods operate aluminium alloy pistons which are very short and comparatively thick.

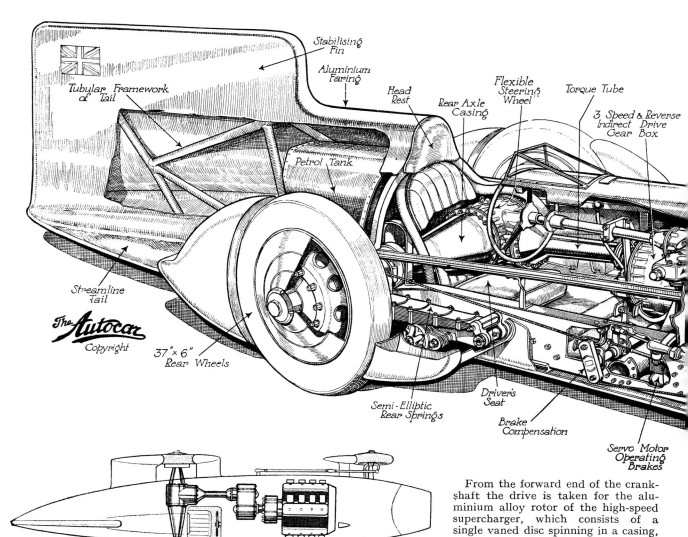

Showing how the drive and the rear fin of the new car are off-set in order to obtain a low seat for the driver.

From the forward end of the crankshaft the drive is taken for the aluminium alloy rotor of the high-speed supercharger, which consists of a single vaned disc spinning in a casing, with, around the casing, three big carburetters having air intake pipes that look like fishtails. The gas is sucked into the casing and forced by the rotor into three pipes for the intake ports of the three cylinder blocks.

Fuel has to be fed to the carburetters by a big mechanical pump which itself is supplied from a small fuel tank in the machine's tail, just behind the driver. Here there is another point, for the column of fuel in the big pipes leading to the pump is much affected by the acceleration of the car. As a stand-by there is a separate air-pressure system with a hand-operated pump. The cylinders of each block have a sparking plug on either side, making twenty-four plugs in all, which are fed by two twelve-cylinder magnetos arranged each to fire four plugs in each block, so that the engine can run with one magneto or the other, though, of course, it normally operates with both.

For starting there is a panel on the left-hand side of the frame with a small hand fuel pump, a nozzle connected to piping running to each cylinder, and a socket for a hand magneto attachment. The engine is first primed, and then gas from containers is passed through the nozzle and so to the engine combustion spaces, where it operates on the pistons and starts the crankshaft running. So great is the pressure of gas required that the pipes from the containers have to be armoured.

Curiously enough, it is one of the carburetters which limits the possible ground clearance of the car, because its air intake is so low ; and, further, the air intake has to be covered carefully by the undershield without baffling the orifice, and a hole in the nose of the body is cut to supply the air well away from the sand of the

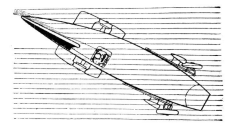

The purpose of the rear fin is to assist in rectifying any deviation from the straight by means of the air surrounding the car at speed.

The jacking system to facilitate wheel changing.

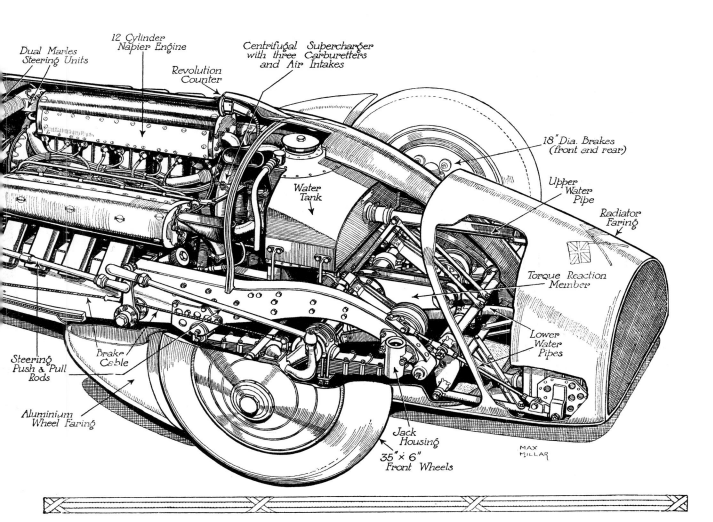

Dual Marles Steering Units

12 Cylinder Napier Engine

Revolution Counter

Centrifugal Supercharger with three Carburetters and Air Intakes

18" Dia. Brakes (front and rear)

Water Tank

Upper Water Pipe

Radiator Faring

Torque Reaction Member

Lower Water Pipes

Steering Push & Pull Rods

Brake Cable

Aluminium Wheel Faring

Jack Housing

35" x 6" Front Wheels

MAX MILLAR

beach. For aeroplane work there is no flywheel; for the car the reduction gearing provided for the tractor screw is removed, the crankshaft fitted with a flywheel, and, in the limited space available, a disc clutch has to be introduced to take the drive to the gear box, which clutch has to be operated by an ingenious compound lever movement from the pedal, because the spring pressure on the plates is naturally very high.

The gear box itself is something of a problem, since, if it were normal, the propeller-shaft should pass down the centre of the chassis, the driver's seat would have to be very high, and the driver higher still. Accordingly, the propeller-shaft has to be taken out of the way, which is arrived at by carrying the engine drive through the clutch to the lay-shaft of the three-speed box, the drive from the lay-shaft gears passing to gears on another parallel shaft considerably to one side, and the latter shaft driving the single universal joint and massive propeller-shaft encased within a ball-ended torque tube, which therefore runs close to the left-hand side-member, and, of course, pushes the car. With the propeller-shaft thus off centre the driver's seat can be dropped in between the torque tube and the right side-member, but at a much lower level than either and immediately above the armoured section of the underpan. In consequence, also, the casing of the massive bevel and pinion for the rear axle is well on the left side of the car, the driving shaft for the right-hand wheel being longer than that for the left, and both being inside immense steel sleeves. All the weight at the rear is carried on the axle casing, only the drive passing through the shafts.

Suspension Details.

The front axle is a massive oval beam flanged and bolted to a radius rod running forward to a bracket on a cross-tube and so arranged that the radius rod governs the amount of caster action for the steering pivots and that angle can be altered by using various lengths of anchorage bracket. On either side of the radius rod are two massive double-acting shock absorbers of friction type, and the spring pads can swivel slightly on the axle, a thing necessary because the springs are anchored in front of the frame and shackled at the rear. Each leaf is independently clipped to its fellow, the two uppermost leaves running from shackle to shackle. At the rear the same type of spring is shackled at both ends, but the shock absorbers are arranged one in front, the other behind, each axle sleeve.

Brakes are, naturally, a difficulty, for the mere application of the shoes to the drums at very high speed would generate immense heat, and the type of lining adopted for the shoes has to be effectively a bad conductor so that the heat passes to the drum—not to the shoes—and so is dissipated. As it is, the first decrease in speed is left to the wind resistance of the body, the brakes coming into action when the car has slowed appreciably. The driver's pressure on the brake pedal is increased by a big vacuum servo motor, while the shoes are operated by cables actuating in front short camshafts in brackets under the axle, the arrangement being that the brakes on each side of the car are compensated front to rear in relation to each other.

For steering, the horizontal column, held by brackets from the gear box, controls a bevel actuating a horizontal shaft in an aluminium casing, and at each end of this shaft are cam gears that normally are the steering gear of an ordinary car, each controlling a short, vertical shaft which moves a tube running from a horizontal lever to a steering arm on the axle pivot; thus one pivot is pushed, the other pulled by separate steering gears, and the two front wheels, in addition, are coupled by a tie-rod.

As to control, the driver, sitting with the spring-spoked steering wheel immediately in front of him, has a curious-looking throttle pedal on the right, and the clutch and brake pedals in the normal relative positions, while the steering wheel has only three spokes, since an extra spoke would interfere with his view of the instruments on the dashboard. On the left-hand side is a short gear lever, and near it an even shorter lever locked by a big hand wheel and used only if the reverse gears have to be engaged. Between the driver and the engine is a big aluminium bulkhead of the type that the Americans call, significantly, a firedash. Owing to the complicated nature of its movement, and the things that get in the way, the throttle pedal pushes and pulls what amounts to a cable in a brass tube.

Testing the Body.

Now as regards the body—always one of the most important items, since head resistance is of vital importance. First of all the body was modelled by R. A. Railton, who is responsible for the design of this car, in plasticine, and the plasticine model was put through wind tunnel tests and gradually altered until the results were satisfactory, one of the changes made being that the directional fin on the tail was greatly increased in size. Then the body itself was made with aluminium panels over a framework, the tail panels being secured to a very stiff, tubular, internal frame, rigidity being essential. The purpose of this fin is to prevent the car from turning sideways, pressure on the fin immediately increasing if the tail swings at all, and thereby bringing the car back to the straight. In the tail, just behind the driver, is the fuel tank, and the level of the driver's head is continued by a ridge on the body, which tapers

Continued on page 93

The chassis from the front, before the water-cooling unit was attached.

FOUR MILES A MINUTE

Campbell Obtains Record in Five Minutes Without Stopping Engine or Inspection of the Car. Amazing Speed Despite Haze and Bumpy Sands. Speed Raised by over 14 m.p.h.

ON Thursday last, February 5th, at Daytona Beach, Florida, Capt. Malcolm Campbell raised the world's land speed record from 231.362 m.p.h. to 245.736 m.p.h., an increase of 14.374 m.p.h.

Travelling first in a southward direction his speed was 246.575 m.p.h. On the return journey he averaged 244.897 m.p.h., the variation in time of the two runs being only .10 secs. The speed works out at approximately 360 ft. per second.

Immediately after, Campbell essayed the flying mile International Class H record (up to 750 c.c.) with a supercharged Austin Seven. He failed by 6 m.p.h., but on Friday was successful, the speed being raised from 87.76 m.p.h. to 94.031 m p.h.

WELL, he's done it! Capt. Malcolm Campbell has covered the measured mile at Daytona at the mean speed of 245.736 m.p.h., thus making still more unassailable the position of land speed supremacy held by Great Britain.

(From our American Correspondent.)

NEW YORK CITY.
Saturday, February 7th.

[BY CABLE.]

ON Thursday last England clinched her hold on the water, land and sky world's speed records. Overcoming the worst weather and beach conditions faced by any driver attempting the record, Campbell averaged 245.736 for two mile run on the rough, wet Daytona Beach under the electrical timing supervision of the American Automobile Association.

The whole job took less than five minutes. The first man to drive four miles a minute made his first run southwards at 246.575 m.p.h. and returned at 244.897 m.p.h. His time for the first run was 14.60 secs., and for the second run 14.70 secs., an average of 14.65 secs.

Campbell afterwards said he was dissatisfied and might try for a higher speed, of which the car is fully capable, despite advice to rest on his laurels.

An Exciting Incident.

During the attempt he encountered and conquered deadly difficulties. Heavy haze and water pools over the beach all day caused a postponement until four o'clock. The result of the first run was announced less than a minute after the completion, but Campbell was already on the return journey without a change of tyres or inspection of the car. The officials admire the way he goes at things resolutely, carefully but without hesitation. The record was

a great achievement for British motor design and Campbell's skill, courage and technical ability. Low visibility during the first run almost made him miss the red light at the

curve at the start of the measured mile, and he headed for the deadly sand dunes. Campbell, however, recovered his vision just in time and swerved the car correctly. He also dodged a man on the course on a motorcycle and went on for the world's greatest car record speed which, however, was reduced by wet sand.

From 1,450 h.p. to 7 h.p.

At the end of the second run he received congratulations from everybody, and after posing for the movies jumped into his Austin Seven and made two runs against record for cars less than 45 cu. ins., the speed of which stood at 87.76.

An impression by Bryan de Grineau of Capt. Campbell's outlook when travelling at over four miles a minute.

CAMPBELL'S AMAZING FEAT

With Next Tuesday's Issue
an Exceptionally Fine F

CAPT. MALCOLM CAMP
THE NAPIER-CAMPBEL.

Specially Dra

A MEMENTO OF

He averaged 81.09 m.p.h., thus failing by six miles.

In the "Blue Bird" Campbell shifted to second speed at 80 m.p.h. and to high at 125 m.p.h. He suffered from bad earache as the result of air pressure. During the runs he received radio congratulations from his family.

England Supreme.

With the amazing new English outboard motor boat mark made recently nothing important in speed records remains—England holds them all!

Campbell later decided to rest upon his laurels, and on Friday rounded off his magnificent achievement by beating at the second attempt the International Class H record, for cars up to 750 c.c., with his supercharged Austin Seven. His mean speed over the mile was 94.031 m.p.h. The first run was 94.069 m.p.h. and the second 93.994 m.p.h. He also broke the kilometre record at a mean speed of 93.968 m.p.h. The previous record for the mile was thus well beaten.

Campbell proposes to stay in Florida for a week before his return to England. He says that it is practically certain that the "Blue Bird" will be sent to Buenos Aires as an exhibit alongside the "Golden Arrow" in the forthcoming British Empire Exhibition.

From Our Special Representative.

DAYTONA BEACH, FLORIDA,
February 5th.
[BY CABLE.]

CAPT. MALCOLM CAMPBELL added to his speed laurels to-day and is the only man living who has travelled 200 miles an hour on land. Campbell broke the world's automobile speed record when he rolled over the mile course in two directions for an average speed of 245.736 m.p.h. to better by 14.37 m.p.h. the record set by his fellow countryman Sir Henry Segrave in 1929.

He drove south on the Beach speedway in his Napier "Blue Bird IV" in 14.60 secs. at a speed of 246.575 m.p.h. and came back in 14.70 secs. at 244.897 m.p.h., the mean time being 14.65 secs.

At the same time he broke the kilometre record, his average speed being 246.086 m.p.h. Afterwards he drove an Austin Seven which he brought from England at a speed of 81.090 m.p.h.

A Bit Disappointed.

Thousands saw the daring Englishman's sensational performance to-day under conditions that were not ideal. The Beach Speedway was bumpy in spots and visibility was poor. "At no time could I see more than 300 or 400 yards ahead," he said. "I am a bit disappointed because I know 'Blue Bird IV' will run faster. It was picking up all the time, but I had to slow down at rough places on the Beach. Under better conditions I should have gone much faster. The thing I am most proud of is that I am the first man to drive four miles a minute." Campbell calmly lighted a cigarette after accomplishing the feat and said he was not the least bit nervous. He smiled after the first run had been made, kissed his mechanic and said "Watch me!" Then he completed setting up the new record.

A Daring Performance.

"Blue Bird IV" performed beautifully throughout the runs and the tyres stood the test with hardly visible sign of use. Campbell used the same set for both dashes, refusing to change after the first run had been completed, and was on his way back immediately.

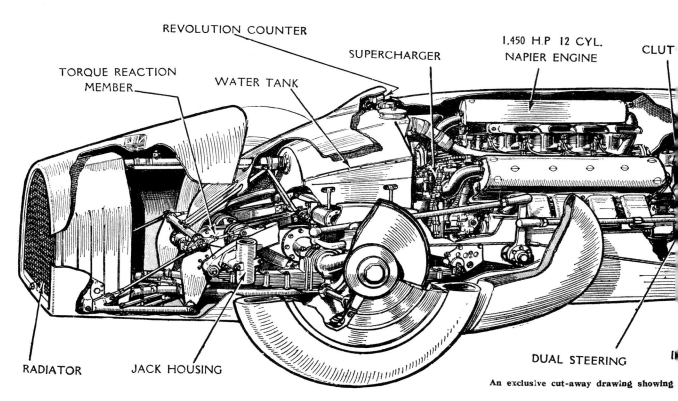

REVOLUTION COUNTER

SUPERCHARGER

1,450 H.P 12 CYL. NAPIER ENGINE

CLUT

TORQUE REACTION MEMBER

WATER TANK

RADIATOR

JACK HOUSING

DUAL STEERING

An exclusive cut-away drawing showing

A MILE AT 245.736 M.P.H.

To-day's daring performance was the third time that he had taken his 4-ton giant machine on the course, and each time he sped at two hundred or more miles an hour in tuning up. On Tuesday (February 3rd) he said he had attained a speed of 260 m.p.h. for a moment, according to his revolution counter, when his gear lever slipped into neutral and he coasted the mile at 194 m.p.h., officially timed.

To-day he regained the world record he set in February, 1928, and which was broken two months later by Ray Keech by one mile and bettered again in 1929 by Segrave. Campbell's previous record was 206.956 m.p.h., while Segrave's average speed was 231.362 m.p.h.

How the Record was Broken.

THE wind was blowing strongly and patches of water still lay on the hard sand when Campbell set out on the greatest adventure of his long and eventful career. The conditions were none too good—indeed, the officials pleaded with Campbell to hold the car back; not to go "all out" on a course that might well harbour hidden dangers.

So the great Napier Lion aero engine was started up and roared its challenge to the world. Campbell had already made a preliminary survey of the course in an ordinary car. Visibility was still none too good owing to the spray that was blowing across the course, but although the sands were wet they were as hard and firm as concrete.

A Quick Decision.

Campbell paused only for a moment's thought. It was a case of "Now or never." He was sufficiently confident of "Blue Bird's" speed to be able to beat Sir Henry Segrave's previous record of 231.36 m.p.h., but he feared that if he were to wait until conditions improved still further he might wait in vain. It was better, therefore, to put the existing record up by a few miles now rather than defer the attempt in the hope of doing a very much higher speed.

Realizing that in the existing conditions the handling of the car might prove somewhat different from when it was being driven on a dry surface, Campbell decided to take a longer run than he would normally have done before entering the measured mile. This would give him a few precious seconds to accustom himself to the new conditions, so instead of the four miles which he would normally have used in which to get up speed, he went right down the beach for a distance of nearly five miles before he turned the car and let in the clutch on the great attempt.

Well Over 100 m.p.h. in Second Gear.

With a whining roar, reminiscent of the Schneider Trophy seaplanes (for, indeed, the engine in the "Blue Bird" is of identical type to that used in the 'plane that did so well in the great air race in 1929), the long blue car gathered speed at an incredibly rapid rate. In a little over a mile it was doing 125 m.p.h., still only in second gear. Then Campbell had to change into top. The sands were wet, as we have already mentioned, and the pull on the steering when he took one hand off the wheel to change gear must have been terrific. Nevertheless, in went top gear and the car still continued to accelerate at an amazing rate.

Aiming, so to speak, with the cowling of the small rev. counter at the

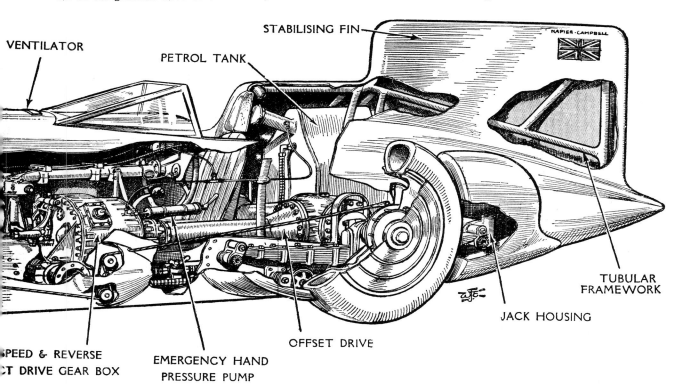

VENTILATOR

STABILISING FIN

PETROL TANK

NAPIER-CAMPBELL

TUBULAR FRAMEWORK

JACK HOUSING

OFFSET DRIVE

SPEED & REVERSE T DRIVE GEAR BOX

EMERGENCY HAND PRESSURE PUMP

hanical details of Capt. Malcolm Campbell's Napier-Campbell "Blue Bird," with which he broke the world's land speed record.

forward end of the bonnet fixed on a distant landmark, Campbell put his foot hard down and . . . . hoped for the best. Naturally, at a speed of 200 m.p.h. or more, if the car swerves at all, it merely does so to an imperceptible extent. Nevertheless, every untoward movement of the great car has to be instantly corrected by the driver, so that although to the onlookers Campbell appeared to be steering a perfectly straight course he was in reality handling the wheel as if the car were pointing first left and then right. When he struck some of the wet patches of sand there was an extraordinary effect of suction, which slowed the car down to such an extent that it was just as if Campbell had applied the brakes. Indeed, he

Decelerating after such an amazing speed requires even more care than accelerating, and it was three miles before Campbell could slow the car sufficiently to be able to turn it, in a wide sweep, and start back to cover the course in the reverse direction, which is necessary under the rules governing world's record attempts over short distances.

During those three miles Campbell put in some rapid thinking—very rapid, since those three miles were probably covered in considerably under two minutes !

He had to consider the wisdom of going back over the course in the reverse direction, using the same set of tyres. The tyres, it should be realized, are specially light, in order that their centrifugal force at high

Discussing his achievement afterwards, Capt. Campbell said that the car was nowhere near all out, but he realized that under the admittedly unfavourable beach conditions it would be sheer folly to use the full power of the engine; therefore, driving at a speed which he knew was sufficient to break the existing record, he played for safety.

Campbell's Practice Runs.

One of the most impressive features of Capt. Campbell's achievement is the fact that he succeeded in breaking the record on what was, to all intents and purposes, the first real official trial. True, he made a run on the previous day, and had been timed by the A.A.A. officials, but conditions were bad and Campbell was not really trying, and, running in one direction, top gear jumped out of mesh, with the result that he had to take his foot off the throttle and allow the car to coast over the measured mile. He was timed officially doing this, and it is interesting to see that he had gathered so much momentum that he actually averaged 194 m.p.h. over the distance. Campbell, it is alleged, claims to have reached approximately 260 m.p.h. before his gear slipped out. After reaching the end of the course Campbell turned round and ran northwards against the wind. This time top gear stayed in and he was timed at 201.707 m.p.h. over the kilometre.

The following contributed to Capt. Campbell's success :—

Engine, Chassis and Bodywork.

1,450 h.p. Napier supercharged racing aero engine ; car designed by Mr. R. A. Railton, of Thomson and Taylor, Ltd., Brooklands ; car erected by Thomson and Taylor, Ltd. ; chassis frame by Vickers ; Hoffman ball bearings ; petrol tank by the Gallay Radiator Co. ; Ferodo lined clutch ; gearbox built by K.L.G. Sparking Plugs, Ltd. ; Marles steering gear ; Woodhead road springs ; Alford and Alder brakes with Clayton-Dewandre vacuum servo ; brake shoes of Wilmil alloy by W. Mills, Ltd., Birmingham ; Serck honeycomb radiator ; Vickers steel throughout ; Silentbloc bushes by T. B. Andre and Co., Ltd. ; Claudel-Hobson carburetters by H. M. Hobson, Ltd. ; Watford magnetos by North and Sons, Ltd. ; bodywork by J. Gurney Nutting and Co., Ltd., London.

Captain Malcolm Campbell surrounded by admirers while waiting to make a trial run at Daytona.

told a friend afterwards that each time he struck one of the wet patches he was literally thrown forward in his seat.

One would think that in making the supreme effort of his career Campbell would only be able to fix his eye on the objective and go flat out. Nevertheless, this amazing man found time, when he was doing considerably over four miles a minute, to glance at his rev. counter and notice that the revolutions corresponded to a speed of some 252 miles an hour.

However, in far less time than it took to write the preceding paragraph, the measured mile was covered. Somehow Campbell had steered his projectile through what seemed to be an infinitesimal gap between the high posts marking the finishing line.

speed may not be too great; therefore, the tread, to all intents and purposes, is no thicker than a sheet of paper. However, the tyres were guaranteed by their makers, the Dunlop Rubber Co., to have a life of 30 secs., at the maximum speed of which the car was capable ; so, putting his full trust in the guarantee, Campbell, without even stopping to examine the engine, went straight off back over the course. Swiftly the posts marking the start and finish of the measured mile flashed into view. Once again, with immense caution, Campbell brought the car to rest.

Officials rushed up to him and clapped him on the shoulders until they were bruised, dragged him from the tiny cockpit of the great racer and told him that he had broken the record by over 14 m.p.h.

Accessories, Fuel and Equipment.

K.L.G. sparking plugs ; Moseley Float-on-Air pneumatic upholstery ; Triplex glass windscreen ; Castrol oil by C. C. Wakefield and Co., Ltd. ; tyres and wheels by the Dunlop Rubber Co., Ltd. ; instruments by S. Smith and Sons (M.A.), Ltd. ; Andre shock absorbers ; Pratt's ethyl petrol ; Petroflex petrol tubing by Hobdell, Way and Co., Ltd. ; Ace wheel discs by Cornercroft and Co., Ltd.

CONGRATULATIONS, CAMPBELL!

WE are certain that all readers will join with us in offering our heartiest congratulations to Captain Malcolm Campbell on his marvellous achievement in setting up new figures for the flying mile record—the fastest speed ever reached by man travelling on land. It is a splendid thing he has done, and it shows what manner of man he is, for no mere pretence is the training to which he has submitted. His self-control must be perfect, his mind and body in the most balanced condition, for at such a speed the movements of the limbs must be under perfect control, perfectly timed, as clearly any delay in action may all too easily spell disaster.

Captain Campbell would be the first to agree that in his success he is not alone to be congratulated. Behind this remarkable effort lies the work of many people, designer, draughtsmen, manufacturers, mechanics, and so on, and the success of the venture is a splendid tribute to the excellence of their efforts. Great Britain can still, despite the pessimists, produce men who are capable of work of the very highest order, and of producing articles which will beat those of their rivals. We may justifiably pride ourselves on the fact that the records in the air, on land, and on the water are all held by Englishmen, driving or piloting British machines, and the value of that fact on British prestige abroad is by no means to be ignored. It proves the supremacy of British materials and workmanship, and is surely a fitting answer to those who affirm that the old country has passed its zenith, and is now on the down grade.

Capt. Campbell, who, of course, has played a great part in raising the land record to its present height, and who, incidentally, is the only man living who has driven a car at over 200 miles an hour, set out to raise the record to over four miles a minute, so as to place it as far as possible out of the reach of other aspirants, and his ambition has been realised. We congratulate him, and also we commend his wisdom in not being tempted to " have another go," for the purpose of setting up a still higher speed. Instead, he went out and put up a magnificent performance in an Austin Seven, covering the flying mile at an average speed of 94.31 m.p.h. To the ordinary motorist, this is far more easily comprehended than the other record, and one marvels that so small a car could be tuned up to travel at such a speed.

We repeat, it is a remarkable tribute to British materials, British workmen, and a British driver, and we are proud of them all !

The Editor

A.D. 1971—" THE CAMPBELL STILL COMING !"

The "Blue Bird" in its large crate being unshipped in New York on arrival from England.

The men behind the scenes who have played so great a part in the production of the "Blue Bird." Captain Campbell is seen in the centre.

F OR the past few weeks all eyes have been turned toward Daytona Beach, in anxious expectation of great deeds by that intrepid and genial " speed merchant," Captain Malcolm Campbell, who had taken over a reconstructed " Blue Bird " Napier-engined car in the hope of retaining for Britain the world's speed record on land, and it was soon seen that the car was capable of beating the existing figures. Then, yesterday week, Thursday, February 5th, those who were listening to the wireless news heard that Captain Campbell had set up new figures.

On his first run, in a southward direction, his average over the measured mile was 246.575 miles an hour, and on the return journey northward it was 244.897 m.p.h., giving a mean average speed for the two runs of 246.736 miles an hour, or more than fifteen miles an hour faster than the 231.36 m.p.h. set up by the late Sir Henry Segrave.

What a speed! Just think what it is—more than four miles a minute! At such a speed it would be possible to travel from London to Yeovil in half an hour, to Brighton in 13 minutes, or to Holyhead in a little more than an hour! Well may Campbell be known as " The fastest man on land."

Captain Campbell had had some very satisfactory trial runs in the " Blue Bird," on the last of which his gear slipped out, with damaging results to the engine, which had to be changed before the record-breaking attempt.

On the day itself, conditions were bad, visibility was poor and the beach itself was not as hard and smooth as it had been during the trials. Campbell, however, was anxious not to disappoint the large crowd which had gathered, and in face of the advice

of the officials not to attempt too large a margin over the existing figures, he went for it and put the figures up considerably.

He took 5½ miles for his flying start, which is a mile and a half longer than usual, and flashed up the course at terrific speed. The rules allow half an hour between the runs, for the purpose of tyre changing, but Campbell took the risk of not delaying for that purpose, and after a very short rest started on his return journey, after which the mean speed for the two runs was announced, and Campbell got out of his car amid thunderous applause from the great audience.

The car itself was described in our issue of January 16th. It is virtually the " Blue Bird " built in 1926, which secured the record early in 1927, and other records in South Africa at Verneuk Pan, in 1929. It has, however; been entirely re-designed and rebuilt, and extensive tests in the wind-tunnel with plasticine models were carried out to ensure the greatest possible reduction of wind-resistance. In fact, everything possible was done to

An artist's impression of the "Blue Bird" at speed typified by "The Spirit of Speed" trophy presented by Lord Wakefield.

All that is visible of Captain Campbell when in the driving seat. His face is protected by a small Triplex windscreen.

CAMPBELL'S NEW RECORD

ensure that while the car would be capable of putting up new figures, it would be as safe as human endeavour and ingenuity could make it.

All those concerned with the great attempt must be congratulated on their part. Mr. R. A. Railton, the designer, Napier Motors for their wonderful engine—the same as that used in the Schneider Trophy seaplanes—Messrs. J. Gurney Nutting for their bodywork, Dunlops for their tyres, a most important part of the car's equipment, and one which has to stand almost unbelievable strain, and all those others who have worked so hard.

But in the glory and wonder of this remarkable achievement, while heaping our congratulations upon driver, manufacturers, designers, mechanics and so on, let us not forget the many anxious hours, hours of worry and apprehension, passed by those who waited at home. Mrs. Campbell, and the little son and daughter—the last two perhaps happily too young to realise the terrible danger. To Mrs. Campbell we must raise our hats in token of admiration of her self-sacrifice. She did not stand in his way, but encouraged him in his great adventure, and stayed at home to await .... Who knows? Only a woman can appreciate what she must have experienced during the anxious hours of waiting !

Here is the intrepid driver telling the " talkie " man all about his ambitions.

Those who remained behind. Mrs. Campbell with her two children and their dog at their home in Surrey.

A photograph just received from Daytona showing Captain Campbell taking a picture of the beach where his record run was made.

An Australian in N.Z.

Norman ("Wizard") Smith, one of the most famous Australian racing drivers of his day, had broken most of the big motor racing records in Australia—but he was motivated by a restless desire to keep on going one better. One hot Sunday in 1929 Smith and his friend Jack H. Mostyn were talking about breaking records as they were repairing a puncture near Lonsdown Bridge, in Sydney. Out of this conversation grew the idea of Smith's tackling something really big next time—and this idea later culminated in his resolution to beat Sir Malcolm Campbell's land speed record.

Norman Smith had every reason to feel confident of his ability to break records—for, by the time he was ready to try to beat Campbell, he held no fewer than 51 speed records. He first became famous in Australia in 1921 when he beat 55 other contestants in the Victorian Alpine Contest. In his most gruelling run, when he drove 3,811 miles from Fremantle to Brisbane in six days three hours, he never slept more than 10 minutes a day for more than six days, and he generally drove for 24 hours at a stretch. In the year he had his conversation with Jack Mostyn, he became the top racing driver in Australia by easily winning Lord Wakefield's trophy for amassing more points than any other driver in Royal Automobile Club of Australia races—which helped him to decide to go beyond his brilliant successes in Australia by tackling the most famous record in the world, the land speed record.

Smith decided, though, to move up to the land speed record in stages. The first step was to tackle the Australian and New Zealand 1 mile record, and also the world's 10 miles record. Don J. Harkness, a Sydney engineer, was selected to design a car capable of achieving a speed of about 150 m.p.h. Smith had heard good reports of Ninety Mile Beach, New Zealand, and he had also heard that Muriwai Beach in New Zealand was a good venue. He made up his mind to carry out his attempts on the records at one beach or the other in New Zealand.

His first car, built in Sydney, was called the *Anzac*. This comprised a Cadillac chassis powered by a 500 h.p. Rolls-Royce engine. This car reached a speed of 142 m.p.h. in tests in Australia. On the last day of 1929 Smith arrived in Auckland from Sydney on board the *Maunganui*. The speed he had to beat, to win the world's 10 miles record, held by the Frenchman Marchand in a Voisin, was 133.54 m.p.h. He felt quite confident he could also set a new mark for the Australian and New Zealand 1 mile record. After inspecting the two alternative sites available in New Zealand, he selected Ninety Mile Beach, North Auckland, for his attempts.

The danger to the tyres from the sharp toheroa shells was what Smith feared when he let the Rolls-Royce engine of the gold-painted *Anzac* fully out for the first time, on Ninety Mile Beach on Saturday 11 January 1930. The tyres had already had to be changed, because they were ripped by the white shells, after the *Anzac* was towed to the start of the course, and Smith noticed more sharp shells on the wet sand when he made his first run, from north to south, after the tide had gone

out, shortly after 11 a.m. However, his rev.-counter indicated 2,100 r.p.m. by the end of the measured strip, and he completed his run south without mishap.

Rain on his goggles made vision ahead poor on his run back, so that he did not use his telescopic sight but steered by the line of flags. The decrease in visibility towards the end of the return run caused him to raise his foot somewhat from the throttle pedal. After the run he discovered a cut in the left rear tyre caused by the shells. Nevertheless, he had successfully broken the Australian and New Zealand 1 mile record by setting up a speed of 146.341 m.p.h. He was astonished to find how little wheelspin had been experienced, and, despite the danger from the toheroa shells, he had had his faith in Ninety Mile Beach as a venue for future record attempts confirmed.

About 4 p.m. on 17 January 1930 he made his attempt on the world's 10 miles record. Don Harkness sat beside him, as mechanic, when he made his two runs over the 16 miles course, steering by the line of flags. Afterwards the four timekeepers at the start compared their stop-watches with those of the four timekeepers at the finish. Smith's average speed of 148.637 m.p.h. easily beat Marchand's speed for the existing 10 miles record (although this was subsequently not recognised by the international body because the method of timing was not approved). What pleased Smith, though, was that his speed for the 10 miles was faster than his speed for the 1 mile that he had achieved six days earlier.

The speeds Smith had set up were faster than both the records he had gone to New Zealand to break, and, encouraged by his successes, he went back to Australia to make his preparations to return to Ninety Mile Beach for an attack on the land speed record.

The *Fred H. Stewart Enterprise*, the car in which Smith planned to tackle the record, was powered by a 12-cylinder Napier *Lion* aircraft engine. This supercharged engine was similar to that used in the British aircraft participating in the 1929 Schneider Trophy race, and was obtained following a request to the British government by the Australian Prime Minister. The *Enterprise*, like the *Anzac*, was designed by Don J. Harkness. The appearance of the car was not dissimilar from that of the *Golden Arrow*, and it was also painted gold. Two stabilising fins were mounted at the tail. The height of the car was low, and the centre of gravity was also low, and the wind resistance was claimed to be much lower than that of the Blue Bird in which Campbell had set up the existing record.

Smith arrived with the *Fred H. Stewart Enterprise* at Auckland, New Zealand, from Sydney on board the *Ulimaroa* on 8 December 1931. His objective was to beat the existing land speed record of 246.09 m.p.h. set up by Sir Malcolm Campbell at Daytona. Shortly after Smith arrived in New Zealand he received a cable of best wishes for his success from Campbell. However, a race was to develop between Smith and Campbell as to which of them was to make his attempt on the record first.

Smith planned to attempt the flying mile, 5 miles, and 10

miles world's records. However, week after week he was compelled to postpone his attempts because the surface of the beach was not suitable. The condition of the beach was so poor that the timing officials went home. As a result, when, on 18 January 1932, the surface of the beach was the best it had been for some time, there was no point in his making an attempt because no one was present to time him officially. His anxiety to tackle the flying mile record grew as news continued to reach him of the preparations of Sir Malcolm Campbell to make a fresh attempt at Daytona.

The first record he attempted to break, though, was the world's 10 miles record. On Tuesday 26 January 1932 a lorry towed the *Enterprise* to the start. Smith, wearing white overalls, climbed in, and drove down the beach. The wetness of the surface was a serious hazard, and spray thrown up on to the windscreen obscured his vision throughout the run, causing him to slow up several times.

Now he was moving towards the red board marking the start of the measured course. He glanced at the white needle of the rev.-counter moving around its black dial as the speed built up. Then he was moving towards the red board at the finish of the measured strip. After the rear tyres were changed, because toheroa shells had ripped them, he made his run back down the beach. The amount of water on the surface was so great that he was completely drenched, and covered with sand, by the time he reached the end of his run.

His last exceeding of the existing 10 miles record was not recognised as a new record because it was timed by stop watches. This time he wanted to make sure he received official recognition, and his breaking of the light beams of the timing track switches at the beginning and end of the measured strips was carefully recorded in violet ink by the traces of three pens on strips of paper. These traces indicated an average time of three minutes 39.401 seconds, an average speed of 164.084 m.p.h. He had broken the world's 10 miles record.

Sir Malcolm Campbell's record for the flying mile was still what he was really trying to beat, though. Week after week, however, he had to postpone his attempt because the beach was too wet. He sent a cable to Campbell wishing him luck. Then he received news that Campbell had set up a new land speed record of 253.97 m.p.h. at Daytona Beach. Smith still hoped to do better.

The danger resulting from spray on his windscreen, which slowed him up during the attempt on the 10 miles record by obscuring his vision, was what was holding back his attempt on the record. The only part of the beach suitable for use was that close to the water—but he was afraid to use its smooth surface because it was wet, causing the dangerous spray. To give him good visibility, R. Dalley and H. Nattrass fitted a circular revolving section to the windscreen. This device finally enabled him to end the repeated postponements by permitting him to use the smooth surface near the sea despite the spray thrown up off the wet sand.

The flying mile record was still not the record he tackled, though. The record he attempted to break was the world's 5 miles record. He made his bid on 1 May 1932. His biggest fear was overcome: the revolving section of the windscreen gave him good visibility despite the spray. But now a mechanical difficulty held him back: after he had gone about 2 miles, reaching a speed of about 170 m.p.h., water on the magnetos caused a short circuit. The engine started to misfire, then stopped altogether, and finally flames came out of the engine after the sparks caused the bottom carburettor to catch fire.

This further set-back, following months of postponements owing to the wetness of the surface of the sands, finally caused Smith to give up his attempts on the records at Ninety Mile Beach, New Zealand, and he went home to Sydney.

The outcome of this challenge by Norman ("Wizard") Smith, the Australian in New Zealand, was that Sir Malcolm Campbell remained the holder of the world's land speed record.

CAMPBELL'S "BLUE BIRD."

Details of 1,450 h.p. Challenger Now Awaiting Trials.

The unknown quantity. An impressive view of Capt. Campbell's monster which is now ready for the World's Land Speed Record.

IN any attempt on the record for the highest speed in any element, experience can only be a guide up to the point reached in previous attempts. Such experience is, however, of vital importance in anticipating the difficulties likely to occur at an increased speed, and it is Capt. Campbell's unique experience of this particular work which must give everyone connected with the present attempt the greatest possible confidence.

The actual car, although virtually an entirely new vehicle as a whole, incorporates a large amount of the chassis of the previous cars used by him. Many people might consider this made the construction an easier matter, but anyone who has had any experience of re-designing or modifying the simplest contrivance, will realise that it is often far easier to start with a clean sheet than to adapt something which is already in existence.

To Mr. Railton, of Thomson and Taylors, fell the task of re-creating the present car, and whatever the result of the attempt, anyone who has had an opportunity of inspecting the Napier-Campbell, will agree that the greatest praise is due to him and to his firm for the ingenious and efficient manner in which the job has been done.

The chassis has been designed to enable the driver to sit as low as possible, and this has meant that both the seat and the transmission, have been offset. One of the difficulties of a vehicle of this type, is that the mechanical details are so much governed by the shape of the body. This was decided on after exhaustive wind tunnel experiments with a Plasticine model, and possesses many unusual features, the chief of which is the fact that the body is not symmetrical. Owing to necessity of including the driver's compartment in the streamlining scheme, it has made it impossible to have the car the same on each side, which gives it a peculiar appearance when viewed from above.

The body was built by J. Gurney Nutting, of Chelsea in the remarkable time of only six weeks, and is one of the finest examples of panel beating we have ever seen. The framework consists of steel tubes, and it is so constructed that the tail is the only fixed section. The rest is made in three sections, one covering the Napier engine, one the cockpit, and the third, the intermediate space. The top of the scuttle is less than 45 inches from the ground, while the clearance under the chassis is only 5 inches.

Campbell's Own Views.

In discussing the prospects of the attempt with Capt. Campbell, prior to his departure for the States, we found him very modest in his statements, and while evidently confident, he adopted the very wise tone of refusing to make any rash statements as to possible speed, and pointed out that after the event was the only time for going into this !

Commenting on the increased power of the latest Napier engine he said, " This engine gives 1,450 h.p., as against 850 h.p. from the engine I used previously. There is no doubt that the power is sufficient to improve on the present speed, but the greatest factor is the stability of the car, which at the speed of a new record is bound to be somewhat of an unknown quantity.

" From my previous experience of such attempts I know some of the difficulties encountered, and though we have done all the experimenting we can, theory and practice are not always in agreement. However, we will hope for the best ! "

With this we wished him luck in his adventure and departed, feeling that if any man could drive that car at a speed in the region of 250 m.p.h., Malcolm Campbell would do so.

* * *

The specification of the car is as follows :—

Chassis.—The chassis frame has been built at Messrs. Vickers' River Don Works. The frame is underslung under the rear axle to provide a very low layout, the centre of gravity being considerably under the centre line of transmission.

Tubular cross members are used throughout, some of which are made out of solid forgings and machined.

The engine is supported on a sub-frame, made under a similar principle as the chassis, and providing a three-point suspension by one spherical socket in the front and two at the rear.

The petrol tank is mounted at the rear end of the chassis and has a capacity of 23 gallons, and was made by the Gallay Radiator Co.

The oil tank is mounted inside the frame members alongside the engine and contains five gallons.

The wheelbase is 12ft. 2¾ins., the front track 5ft. 4ins. and the rear track 5ft. 2ins.

Wheels and Tyres.—Special wheels of the steel disc type have been designed and built by the Dunlop Rubber Co., with tyres by the Dunlop Company designed after a series of special tests to ensure their being capable of standing up to the high speeds anticipated.

Fairings to streamline the wheels and tyres leave only 1½ins. clearance between the tyre and the fairing, so a section 5ins. deep of the fairing near the tyre is made of very light sheet, so that in the event of a tyre deflating, this will be torn to pieces without locking the wheel.

Engine.—The engine is one of the latest type Napier racing engines, as fitted to the Gloster-Napier seaplane which set up a speed of 336 m.p.h. Special permission has had to be obtained from the Air Ministry for the use of the engine by Capt. Malcolm Campbell.

Only certain information is allowed to be divulged, as it is still on the Air Ministry Part Publication List, and the following is the brief information available :—

Number of cylinders	12
Arrangement	Three blocks of four each, one vertical, two at 60°.
Bore	5½ins.
Stroke	5⅛ins.
Horsepower	Approx. 1,450 h.p. at 3,600 r.p.m.
Weight of engine	1,140lbs.
Weight per h.p.	0.78lbs.
Length overall to centre of airscrew	64–13/16 ins.
Width overall	37⅜ins.
Height overall	34⅛ins.

Clutch.—The clutch is of the dry multiplate type, Ferodo lined. Messrs. Ferodo having greatly assisted in the design of the clutch.

Gearbox.—Three speed constant mesh, all dog clutches. The gear ratios are 1.58, 2.27, 4.01 and re-reverse. Built by K.L.G. Sparking Plugs Ltd.

Rear Axle.—The central casing of the rear axle is offset 7ins., so as to enable the driver's seat to be brought within 10ins. of the ground.

The final drive, which for the higher speed has a ratio of 1.58 to 1, is of the bevel gear type. Full floating axle shafts are provided, and the driving dogs at the hub end are formed solid with the axle shafts.

Front Axle.—The front axle is made in two pieces joined in the middle by substantial flanges and provision has been made for relieving the springs of torsional stresses.

Steering.—Both front wheels are directly controlled by the steering gear, while the track rod is retained. Two Marles steering gears are used in connection with the device, and although the lock of each wheel is directly controlled, the Ackerman action is maintained by the layout.

Suspension.—Half elliptic springs are provided in front and rear, the springs being of the Woodhead type with weldless solid eyes and solid lug plates and rebound clips. The dimensions of the springs are, at the front 3ft. 1in., and 4ft. 2½ins. at the rear. The spring blocks, which are made of manganese bronze, anchor the springs to the axles by a double set of clamping " U " bolts.

A feature of the springing is the fact that each rear spring has a different camber, so that when the car is at rest there is a slight list, but when engine torque comes into play it brings the car on an even keel.

Hartford shock absorbers and Silentbloc bushes are utilised and fitted

Brakes.—Four wheel brakes are provided, controlled by foot pedal, with an auxiliary control by vacuum servo of the Clayton Dewandre type.

The front wheel brake mechanism of the Alford & Alder system provides large logarithmic cams, mounted on special carriers which form the universal joint, and the whole of the arrangement is set well within the centre line of steering, a difficult thing to obtain in the ordinary way owing to the small width of the drums.

The brakes on the four wheels are all of the same size. The brake drums are made from solid forgings of special high carbon steel, and having an internal braking surface of 18ins. diameter and 1⅝ins. width. Thin fins for cooling purposes are machined on the outside. The shoes, made in " Wilmil " alloy, specially lined by Messrs. Ferodo, Ltd., are also identical, both for front and rear, and are operated by the same logarithmic type of cam as described above. The rotation plates for the front are formed by extension lugs made integral with the stub axle, and the rear reaction plates which are made also in steel are bolted to suitable flanges solid with the steel arms of the rear axle casing.

Radiator.—A special Serk honeycomb radiator has been designed, and the system has a specially large water capacity. The radiator is situated in the front of the car.

There is a gap between the radiator and the front of the actual body, the casing of the radiator being streamlined with that of the rest of the body.

This arrangement was decided on after considerable experiment, as providing the minimum of wind resistance, and also relieving the pressure inside the body, which is bound to occur with a normal radiator arrangement.

Instruments.—Smith's instruments are installed throughout, including a rev. counter mounted on the front of the body, offset to the same extent as the driver, which can be used as a sight when driving.

246·08 M.P.H./

OF all the names connected with motor racing since the beginning, that of Malcolm Campbell stands out as representing the triumph gained by perseverance. Although having longer motor racing experience than any other Englishman now taking part in the sport, his career has not been one of unbroken good fortune. On the contrary, the record of his steady climb to fame as our foremost all-round driver, has been a story of continual difficulties and repeated misfortune. The fact that in spite of every setback his skill and perseverance have established an unrivalled reputation, makes this achievement even more remarkable. His crowning success, the breaking of the land speed record at Daytona by the very handsome margin of 15 m.p.h. and the raising of this record to the amazing speed of 246 m.p.h. is a fitting end to his endeavours for many years.

A Long Career.

Twenty-five years ago Campbell started racing, being at the same time interested in aviation, on which he did a lot of work in the very early days. Then came the war, and it is only natural that he continued his flying in the R.F.C., and the experience of engines in those days gave him valuable knowledge. After the war he returned to motor racing and in 1920 handled Talbots, as well as Schneider and Peugeot. These were the days of hill climbs and sprint events and he was a prominent figure at these functions. In 1921 and 1922 he broke various hill-climb records but then his ideas turned to larger game, and when K. Lee Guinness, on the 12-cylinder Sunbeam had reached 129 m.p.h., Campbell bought the car and proceeded to raise the record to some 136 m.p.h.

His next attempt on the land speed record was at the meeting in Denmark at the Fanoe Islands, but owing to the electrical tuning apparatus not being passed officially the speeds achieved could not be claimed, and it was not until 1924 that he reached new figures. Still driving the Sunbeam, this time at Pendine, he raised the mean speed to 146.16 m.p.h.

for the kilometre, but did not gain the mile record until 1925 when he exceeded 150 m.p.h. for the first time.

It was evident that the limit of the old Sunbeam had been reached, so in 1927, he started to build the first "Bluebird" with a Napier engine, which was the basis from which the present record breaker was evolved. In this car 174.2 m.p.h. was reached at Pendine. He was still working against disappointments, however, and his record fell to the big Sunbeam in the hands of the late Sir Henry Segrave. Spurred on rather than discouraged, he reconstructed Bluebird, and raised Segrave's speed of 203.79 m.p.h. to 206.956 m.p.h. only to have his record again beaten by Ray Keech by half a mile an hour.

Once more he set about the reconstruction of his car and went to Verneuk Pan, in South Africa, where he was not only faced with terrible difficulties due to the country and climate, but further knew that Segrave, with the Golden Arrow was at Daytona. Before he could get conditions suitable for his attack on the record he was to learn that the Golden Arrow had put up the astounding speed of 231.36 m.p.h.

The Verneuk Victory.

Such a series of discouragements would have daunted most men, but Campbell was determined not to leave Africa without some records, and he performed the remarkable feat of averaging 211 m.p.h. for 5 miles, and 216 m.p.h. for 5 kilometres, records which are likely to remain unbroken for a very long time to come.

Still determined to gain the coveted record for the highest speed on land, he started the greatest reconstruction in "Bluebird's" career. This was carried out by Thompson and Taylor of Brooklands and the design was carried out by Mr. Railton. Campbell's troubles were not over when he left for America, as there were still financial arguments in connection with the Daytonaa uthorities. However, these were eventually smoothed over, and at last the car was ready for her trial runs.

The actual breaking of the record was carried out just as it should have been. There was no undue waiting about, no violent last minute alterations. Everyone connected with the design, building, and equipment of the car had carried out their work with such accuracy and thoroughness that after the trial runs Campbell went out for his actual attempt.

Those few seconds during which the shapely blue car flashed down the sands of Daytona at a speed never before reached on land, may have seemed all too short to the watching thousands. To the driver they were the crowning effort of a career of dogged persistence in the face of difficulties, a fitting reward to the many who had helped directly and indirectly in the attempt, and a fine vindication of the efficiency and enterprise of British engineering.

Accessories Before the Fact.

The following contributed to Campbell's great achievement :—

1,450 h.p. Napier supercharged racing aero engine ; car designed by Mr. R. A. Railton, of Thomson and Taylor, Ltd., Brooklands ; car erected by Thomson and Taylor, Ltd. ; chassis frame by Vickers ; Hoffman ball bearings ; petrol tank by the Gallay Radiator Co. ; Ferodo lined clutch ; gearbox built by K.L.G. Sparking Plugs, Ltd. ; Marles steering gear ; Woodhead road springs ; Alford and Alder brakes with Clayton-Dewandre vacuum servo ; Serck honeycomb radiator ; Silentbloc bushes by T. B. Andre and Co., Ltd. ; Claudel-Hobson carburetters by H. M. Hobson, Ltd. ; Watford magnetos by North and Sons, Ltd. ; bodywork by J. Gurney Nutting and Co., Ltd., London.

K.L.G. plugs ; Moseley Float-on-Air pneumatic upholstery ; Triplex glass screen ; Castrol oil by C. C. Wakefield and Co., Ltd. ; tyres and wheels by the Dunlop Rubber Co., Ltd. ; instruments by S. Smith and Sons (M.A.), Ltd. ; Andre shock absorbers ; Pratt's ethyl petrol ; Petroflex petrol tubing ; **Ace wheel discs.**

THE "WIZARD" SMITH WRANGLE

What the Row is About. Description and First Photographs
Explaining the Impasse between Driver and Designer

(From Our New Zealand Correspondent)

The cause of all the trouble between driver and designer of the " Fred H. Stewart Enterprise " is the addition by the driver, "Wizard" Smith, of a somewhat crude front radiator which would appear to nullify the body streamlining. The fairings behind the front wheels contain water. The photograph was taken at Ninety Mile Beach.

AUCKLAND, *January 6th*.

AN unfortunate feature of Norman "Wizard" Smith's attempt on the world's land-speed record has been the difference which has arisen between the driver and the designer of the " Fred H. Stewart Enterprise," resulting in the departure for Sydney of Don Harkness a few days after the remainder of the party left Auckland for the Ninety Mile Beach.

The difference, which first became felt before Smith and Harkness left Sydney, arose over the cooling system to be employed on the car.

From the outset, Harkness paid the greatest attention to streamlining, and it was his endeavour to reduce the frontal area of the car as much as possible. He succeeded to a marked extent, the car being lower than the " Golden Arrow " and offering a lesser wind resistance, the difference being estimated at 30 per cent. Harkness's design included radiators in fairings forward of the front wheels, with water tanks in the fairings behind the wheels, these, he contended, being sufficient to cool the engine. On the other hand, Smith was not entirely satisfied with this arrangement, and when the car arrived in Auckland it carried the

The car as originally designed, but without the wheel fairings, which were intended to include radiators in front and water tanks at the rear of the front wheels.

fairings behind the wheels, but the radiators had not been fitted.

While the party was in Auckland during the Christmas and New Year holidays the dissension between the two men became greater, only terminating when Harkness remained in Auckland after the rest of the party left for the Beach. He refused to make any comment, and returned to Sydney on January 8th, his only remark being that he hoped to come to New Zealand again in time to see the record broken. He also wished Smith luck in his venture.

Smith was accompanied to the beach by two mechanics, a tyre expert, an ignition expert, a Sydney chemist, representatives of C. C. Wakefield and Co., and a local radiator manufacturer. A radiator of rather crude design and mounted in a similar manner to that on the "Blue Bird" was fitted shortly after the car arrived at the Beach. The radiator, consisting of three blocks of honeycombing behind each other, was made in Auckland to Smith's design.

Car Never Tried Out as Designed

The car was tested with this radiator, the engine being started and run for a period and the car later being driven varying distances along the Beach. The car was never tried out with Harkness's radiators.

Apart from the difference between Smith and Harkness, everything went well after the party's arrival in Auckland. Smith was tendered a civic reception the day after his arrival, while the car was placed on display for more than a week. The party left for the Beach by car on

A close-up of "Wizard" Smith in the cockpit of the "Fred H. Stewart Enterprise."

January 2nd, while the "Enterprise" was shipped by coastal vessel to Awanui and taken from there to the Beach on a six-wheeled British truck. It was immediately housed in the garage constructed by the Automobile Racing Club, a special structure which was made sandproof and in which mechanics were on guard in shifts day and night.

Very stringent regulations were made for controlling the public on the beach. Jurisdiction over the sands during the preparations and the attempt was vested in the club by the Minister of Marine, with the result that only official cars were allowed to travel on it. Although the action of the Club in closing the Beach frequently when Smith was likely to make a run was criticised, precautions were necessary, as only a very small police force was available to guard the long stretch and keep the public within bounds. Flying was also prohibited over the por-

tion of the Beach used in the attempt whenever Smith had his car out, in case he was distracted by shadows or a forced landing became necessary.

Since the foregoing story was written by our New Zealand correspondent, Smith has been out on two occasions. The first time he broke the 10-mile flying start world's record, which stood to the credit of Mrs. Stewart at 137.21 m.p.h. His mean speed of two runs was 164.084 m.p.h., which is a very medium performance when it is realized that Mrs. Stewart's car is only a 2-litre job, and especially when compared with Sir Malcolm Campbell's figure of 211.49 m.p.h. for five miles and 216.04 m.p.h. for five kilometres.

Later Smith made an attack on the land speed record, but failed by approximately 33 m.p.h. On his outward run he averaged 224.945 m.p.h. and on the return journey his speed dropped to 199.285 m.p.h.

AUSTRALIAN ATTEMPT ON THE WORLD'S SPEED RECORD

Continued from page 18

camp on the beach itself, while sheds to house the car and also Smith's other car, the "Anzac," are being constructed at the edge of the track. At present the beach presents a scene of solitude, there being only a few scattered houses set back among the sandhills. One advantage of the locality lies in its inaccessibility, in that, although numbers of spectators will gather from all parts of the North Island, there will not be massed crowds.

Accommodation has been booked for some time past at the nearest hotels and boarding-houses. In addition to Smith's party there will be a large number of officials of the Auckland Automobile Association housed. Provision for these has already been made at one end of the beach. The timing,

which will be carried out by special apparatus brought out from England at a cost of £500, will be in the hands of Mr. H. Butcher, who has secured the permission of the Royal Automobile Club to do so. He will have a large number of assistants, while the flagging of the course, a distance of probably five miles, with flags as close as 50 yds. apart on the mile itself, will be another task which must be speedily carried out as soon as the tide has receded.

It is understood that Smith will drive the "Anzac," the Rolls-Royce-Cadillac in which he made an unofficial 10-mile record of 148 miles an hour last year, in an attempt to set a new mark for 50 kilometres if a sufficiently long stretch of beach is suitable. Whether he will finally decide to try for this dis-

tance or not, he will make some record attempt in this car.

Of Smith himself, it only remains to be said that he is the most prominent driver in Australia and New Zealand. During his career he has held 55 track and road records, one of his most notable achievements being when he set a new record between Perth and Brisbane, at the same time establishing new times for each section of the long run, from Perth to Adelaide, Adelaide to Melbourne, Melbourne to Sydney, Sydney to Newcastle and Newcastle to Brisbane. He also held the Auckland-Wellington road record in New Zealand, and in this connection it is interesting to note that when he visited New Zealand last year he was served with a summons for speeding issued by the Huntly Town Board for an offence committed on his record run four years previously. Smith may be said to occupy the same position in Australia as the more famous "Cannonball" Baker does in the United States.

—AND NOW 253 M.P.H.!

CAMPBELL WITH "BLUE BIRD" LOWERS LAND SPEED RECORD ONCE AGAIN.

THE most remarkable feature of the recent history of the World's Records for the mile and kilometre has been Sir Malcolm Campbell's consistent progress in steadily increasing the speeds with his veteran car.

From the time that he finally decided that the old Sunbeam had reached its practical limit, he concentrated on building a special car to capture the coveted land speed record, and although the car which has just recorded a further triumph, has been redesigned and modified in detail, shape, and layout since its first successful effort at Pendine in 1927, it is basically the same vehicle. Which speaks volumes for the quality of the materials in the transmission and chassis generally.

Soon after the first edition (with a body closely resembling the normal racing car of that time), had succeeded in raising the record to 174.88 m.p.h. Campbell had to suffer the disappointment of seeing his speed eclipsed by Segrave's wonderful achievement on the big twin-engined Sunbeam, which by putting up a mean speed of 203.79 m.p.h. for the mile, set him a formidable task.

First Daytona visit.

Campbell's racing career has contained a host of disappointments, and he was far too set on this record to be deterred by anything. The "Blue Bird" was accordingly modified, one of the successful Napier engines of the type which had won the Schneider Trophy in 1927 was installed, the streamlining was completely redesigned, and Campbell went to Daytona and increased the record speed to 206.95 m.p.h. only to see Ray Keech on the 3-engined White "Triplex" beat his record by less than one mile an hour.

Again his car was modified and this time he went to South Africa, where his difficulties at Verneuk Pan gave him a further chance to demonstrate his amazing tenacity of purpose. Space forbids any recounting of this great adventure, but while he was there the wonderful "Golden Arrow," designed by Captain Irving and driven by the late Sir Henry Segrave, put up the terrific speed of 231.44 m.p.h. at Daytona.

In reply Campbell, although knowing his car could not reach this speed, attacked and secured other records, notably the

5 miles and 5 kilometres, at over 211 m.p.h., and returned to England to prepare for yet another attempt to secure his ambition of being the fastest man on earth.

More modifications.

It was evident that more than detail modifications were required if the record was to be secured, and the car was placed with Messrs. Thompson and Taylors, and under the genius of Mr. Railton, began to take on the form we know to-day.

In this form, criticised by many, with another Napier engine of the best this famous firm could provide, Campbell once more left for Daytona.

It was now four years since the record had been his, but those years had not been wasted, and the result of the work that had been put in was the new speed of 246.09 m.p.h. which was recorded last year, as a result of which His Majesty was pleased to confer the honour of knighthood upon Campbell, and many of us began to hope that Sir Malcolm would rest content with his achievements.

Such, however, was not his idea, and to those who suggested that a further attack was foolhardy, there was presented a very strong argument in favour of another attempt. Hitherto every attempt had been a great and hazardous step into the unknown, and all who essayed it took their lives in their hands, more completely than any driver in any other attempt on record.

Thanks to the untiring and successful research of the engineers at Fort Dunlop, the all-important question of tyres had been faithfully attended to until they had become one of the most reliable factors of the whole adventure.

Now, therefore, a new stage had been reached. For the first time in the recent history of the record, a proved and fully tried car was available, which was known to be capable, with only detail improvements, of a comparatively small but very

definite improvement over its previous best.

Once more Mr. Railton took a hand, but this time it was to overhaul and not to redesign. Practically the only visible sign of difference was the slightly smaller radiator, which the experience gained in the previous attempt had shown to be permissible.

Just before the car left for America for the recent successful attack on the record, we asked Mr. Railton what increase he expected, and he replied, "About 8 m.p.h. most probably." All of which, when the new record mean speed of 253.97 m.p.h. was achieved on February 24th of this year, shows that the unknown is steadily becoming known, and that the science of ultimate speed on land is, thanks to the pioneers, becoming much more exact.

The actual occasion of the lowering of the record was really intended for a trial run, but was so successful that the record was taken, and as favourable conditions did not recur, still remains. The highest speed one way was 267.45 m.p.h. with the wind, and two days later attempts were made on the five miles, five kilometres, and ten kilometres, with the result that these records now stand at the wonderful figures of 242.75 m.p.h., 247.94 m.p.h. and 238.66 m.p.h. Surely, proof indeed that there is at least one aspect of fast motoring in which this country has no rival.

Accessories before the fact.

The following are some of the products which helped to make this record possible.

Pratts' Ethyl, special, Dunlop wheels and tyres, Napier engine, K.L.G. plugs, Castrol oil, Petroflex piping, Claudel-Hobson carburettors, Woodhead road springs, Terry valve springs, Ferodo clutch linings, Smith's instruments, Duron Brake Linings, Watford magnetos, Serck radiator, Gallay tanks, Alford and Alder front brakes, David Brown gears, E.N.V. axle bevels, Triplex windscreen, Moseley air cushions, André shock absorbers, Bluemel steering wheel, Hoffman bearings, and Gurney Nutting body. The car was built and prepared by Thompson and Taylors of Brooklands.

CAMPBELL'S WONDERFUI

Land Speed Record Raised to 253.968 m.p.h., an Increase of 8 m.p.h.— over the Mile—Kilometre, Five Kilometre, Five Miles and 10-Kilometre the Latter by 86 m.p.h.—Car to be at Brooklands on Ea

FOR the third time in succession Sir Malcolm Campbell's visit to Daytona Beach has been crowned with glory. This brilliant and daring driver, who is now in his 48th year, last week set up five new wonderful records, including the raising of the land speed record to 253.968 m.p.h., an increase of close upon eight miles an hour, this being the mean average speed for one mile. His fastest run in one direction with the wind was made at 267.458 m.p.h., which is equivalent to travelling at the rate of 392 feet per second, or going from London to Brighton in 11½ minutes.

He shattered his figures for five miles and five kilometres made at Verneuk Pan, South Africa, and beat the previous 10-kilometre record by 86 m.p.h.!

Sir Malcolm now holds the coveted land speed record for the sixth time. He was the first to average four miles a minute and has travelled farther at high speeds on land than anyone in history. Sir Malcolm has definitely finished his attempts for this year, but is already thinking of a further attack next year. He will appear with the record-breaking car at Brooklands on Easter Monday.

The new figures are as follow :—

FIVE NEW WORLD'S RECORDS
THE FLYING MILE

South, 267.458 m.p.h., 13.46 secs.; north, 241.773 m.p.h., 14.89 secs.; average, 253.968 m.p.h., 14.17 secs. Previous record by Campbell at Daytona, 245.733 m.p.h.

THE FLYING KILOMETRE

South, 262.242 m.p.h.; north, 241.303 m.p.h.; average, 251.340 m.p.h. Previous record by Campbell at Daytona, 246.086 m.p.h.

FLYING FIVE KILOMETRES

Average speed, 247.941 m.p.h. Previous record by Campbell at Verneuk Pan, 216.04 m.p.h.

FLYING FIVE MILES

Average speed, 242.751 m.p.h. Pre-

vious record by Campbell at Verneuk Pan, 211.49 m.p.h.

FLYING TEN KILOMETRES

Average speed, 238.669 m.p.h. Previous record by B. Borzacchini (Maserati) at Cremona, 152.90 m.p.h.

(From our Special Representative.)
DAYTONA BEACH, *February 24th.*

SIR MALCOLM CAMPBELL set up three new world's records here on Wednesday, but said he was very disappointed and would try again on

Sir Malcolm (dark coat with dark flannel trousers) watches his mechanics push "Blue B
It will be noted that many of the spectators are clad only in bathing costumes, the w

The arch of the pier through which Sir Malcolm Campbell passed at 100 m.p.h. It is 40 ft. in width and situated one mile from the North end of the course. This was what prevented the attack on the 10-mile record.

Thursday to better his figure made today. The British "Daredevil," as the American newspapers term him, announced he would make a test run today, but actually established new records and a new maximum speed, the fastest of two runs made as he sped south before a strong wind being 267.458 m.p.h. over the measured mile. He then turned quickly at the end of the 12-mile course without changing tyres and came north at 241.773 m.p.h. for an average of 253.968 m.p.h., breaking his own record by more than 8 miles an hour. The first mile run took 13.46 secs., and the second dash 14.89 secs., the average time for the mile being 14.175 secs. The record he set up last year was 245.733 m.p.h.

RECORDS

st Run, 267.458 m.p.h.
rld's Figures Shattered,
Monday

Two other records went at the same time, his average for 1 kilom. being 251.340 m.p.h., or 8.90 secs., and his 5-kilom. record being 241.569 m.p.h., in average time of 46.30 secs. The timing equipment was set up for the 5-mile record also, but the tapes broke.

a special roped-off enclosure near the Pier.
this time of the year being very warm.

All the records broken to-day were previously held by Sir Malcolm. He was very disappointed in failing to make a better speed and was determined to try to set the mile record at 265 m.p.h. on Thursday.

DAYTONA BEACH, *February 26th.*

ALTHOUGH he was disappointed in his failure to drive "Blue Bird" at an average speed of at least 260 m.p.h. in setting a new mile record, Sir Malcolm Campbell established a new record for the mile and four other distances that probably will stand until he again breaks them himself. After breaking three records on February 24th, the first day he went out to boost speed marks higher, he came back two days later to break one of these records

A characteristic study of Capt. Sir Malcolm Campbell, who has for the sixth time broken the world's land speed record.

all over again and add two new ones to his list.

His assault on the speed records this year was one of the most amazing in the history of Daytona Beach, where speed records have been set for a quarter of a century. Prospects indicate that next year may bring still more interesting speed trials with Sir Malcolm having tentatively accepted an invitation to return and with Norman "Wizard" Smith, the Australian, and Barney Oldfield, veteran American, having been extended invitations to compete.

Sir Malcolm made only three visits to the Beach this year. The first was to test his "Blue Bird," and his best speed was just over 130 m.p.h. His next visit was his first record-breaking day—February 24th. With a 20-mile wind blowing, visibility fair, and the Beach none too good, he announced he would make a test run south before the wind and then two record-breaking attempts.

Upon starting what was to be the test run, he found the Beach to his liking, opened the throttle and roared away over the 12-mile course to run a measured mile in 13.46 secs. at 267.459 m.p.h., taking officials, Press and spec-

tators by surprise. His run back was made at 241.773 m.p.h. for a new world's record mile at 253.968 m.p.h.

The one-kilometre and five-kilometre record fell at the same time, his new mark for one kilometre was 251.340 m.p.h., and he hung up a new five kilometre mark at 241.569 m.p.h. He had previously set the mile record here in 1931 at 245.733 m.p.h. and the kilometre record at 246.086 m.p.h. His previous five-kilometre record was 216.045 m.p.h., made at Verneuk Pan, South Africa, in 1929.

On February 25th there was no wind, the Beach was excellent and visibility extremely good, despite rain which he would have disregarded if Mayor E. H. Armstrong, of Daytona Beach, had not stepped in and refused to allow Sir Malcolm to take the great risk of driving through it.

February 26th dawned clear, but the wind again was strong and the Beach was beginning to crack up, presenting a rugged surface of tiny ripples in spots that caused wheelspin and prevented Sir Malcolm setting a new mile record at 260 m.p.h.—his average speed for the mile was 251.748 m.p.h.—but failing to hinder him in a mad dash for new marks over 5 kilometres, 5 miles and 10 kilometres.

The new 5-kilometre record went up to 247.941 m.p.h., the 5 miles was made at 242.751 m.p.h. and the 10 kilometres at 238.669 m.p.h.

In breaking his own 5-mile record set in 1929 at Verneuk Pan, Sir Malcolm added more than 31 m.p.h., and the 10-kilometre mark was shattered even more thoroughly. It had been set by B. Borzacchini at Cremona, Italy, in 1929 at 152.9 m.p.h., and thus was boosted nearly 86 m.p.h. when Sir Malcolm sped over the distance at an average two-way speed of 238.669 m.p.h.

Sir Malcolm Campbell did not go out after the 10-mile record, although he was confident he could have broken the present unofficial standing one of 164.084 m.p.h. set recently by "Wizard" Smith. The old official record is 137.21 m.p.h. set in 1930 by Mrs. G. M. Stewart in France, and probably would have been extremely easy to shatter.

Sir Malcolm's decision to forgo the 10-mile record was prompted by the fact that the beach here is only 12 miles long with a pier adding a hazard to high speed one mile from the north end of the course. As it was Campbell ran under this pier between pilings 40 ft. apart at 100 m.p.h.

With his record-smashing runs this year Sir Malcolm captured the imagination of American fans as few others have done before him. Nearly 20,000 persons stood for hours along the sand dunes to watch him on the three days he ran. It was his third visit here, and townspeople have accepted him almost as one of their own.

In recognition of his accomplishments he was presented with a plaque by the Mayor on behalf of the city.

The Amazing Tyres

NOT long ago the tyre designers were very dubious as to whether they could successfully equip a car for speeds around 200 m.p.h. Now Campbell has achieved a maximum of over 265 m.p.h. on pneumatics, and so confident was he of the reliability of his Dunlops that he did not even take the trouble to change them for the return run.

Most people imagine that a stout cover and thick tread are used for this job; in actual fact, centrifugal force would tear such a tyre to pieces long before 200 m.p.h. was reached. To prevent disruption from this cause the covers are made extremely thin; yet these slender envelopes of rubber and cotton are sufficient to retain the compressed air, which sustains a load of several tons and transmit an immense tractive effort. The life of these tyres at 250 m.p.h. or so is estimated to be not longer than a couple of minutes.

It is a real thrill to see one of these tyres tested in the experimental department at Fort Dunlop. A stout bulkhead of steel separates the observer (with his various controls and instruments) from the testing apparatus which is viewed through slits. A wheel carrying the inflated tyre is supported on a beam above a drum. The wheel and drum are brought up to the required revolution speed independently, by electric motors, and while this is being done one can see the tyre growing in diameter owing to centrifugal force. Then comes the supreme test; tyre and drum are gently brought together and the load is applied.

For what seems a very long minute we watch the fragile tyre, loaded in a way which seems almost fantastic, spinning like a giant top. Then controls are operated, the wheel lifts and commences to slow down, and with quite

a sigh of relief we realize that the test is over. By such experiments, repeated time after time, the design has been brought to its present high pitch of efficiency.

"Blue Bird's" Equipment, Accessories and Fuel

The following items contributed to Sir Malcolm Campbell's success:— 1,450 h.p. Napier supercharged racing aero engine; car designed by Mr. R. A. Railton, of Thomson and Taylor, Ltd.; car erected by Thomson and Taylor, Ltd.; chassis frame by Vickers, Ltd.; Hoffmann ball bearings; petrol tank by the Gallay Radiator Co.; clutch linings by Ferodo, Ltd.; E.N.V. gears; gearbox built by K.L.G Sparking Plugs, Ltd., with gearwheels made and cut by David Brown and Sons, Ltd.; Marles steering gear; Woodhead road springs; Alford and Alder brakes with Clayton Dewandre vacuum servo; brake shoes of Wilmil alloy by W. Mills, Ltd.; brake cables by British Wire Products; Serck honeycomb radiator; Vickers steel throughout; Silentbloc bushes and André shock absorbers by T. B. André and Co., Ltd.; Claudel-Hobson carburetters by H. M. Hobson, Ltd.; Watford magnetos by North and Sons, Ltd.; Duron brake linings by Brake Linings, Ltd.; Petroflex petrol tubing by Hobdell Way and Co., Ltd.; Ace wheel discs by Cornercroft, Ltd.; Pyrene fire-extinguisher; instruments by S. Smith and Son (M.A.), Ltd.; Triplex glass windscreen; Dover spring steering wheel; engine valve springs by Herbert Terry and Sons, Ltd.; Moseley Float-on-Air upholstery; and the sheet-aluminium panelled Belco-finished body was built by J. Gurney Nutting and Co., Ltd.

For his record attempt Sir Malcolm Campbell used K.L.G. sparking plugs, Wakefield Castrol oil, Dunlop tyres and wheels, and Pratts Ethyl spirit.

Receiver Appointed to the Star Co.

WE are informed that a receiver has been appointed to the Star Motor Co., Ltd., one of the oldest concerns in the industry, but that the situation will not affect Guy Motors, Ltd., as the capital invested by that company in the Star business was written off Guy Motors accounts, published some nine months ago.

Seven New World's Records

AN attempt on the world's 24-hour and 48-hour records was commenced on Sunday last by G. E. T. Eyston, Kaye Don, E. A. D. Eldridge and A. Denly driving a Delage. At the time of going to press they had secured the following world's figures:—500 kiloms. at 189.577 k.p.h.; three hours at 189.630 k.p.h.; 1,000 kiloms. at 188.309 k.p.h.; six hours at 188.484 k.p.h.; 1,000 miles at 187.264 k.p.h.; 2,000 kiloms. at 186.816 k.p.h.; and 12 hours at 180.29 k.p.h. Two International Class records were also beaten, these being 200 miles at 189.052 k.p.h. and 500 miles at 187.866 k.p.h.

The mechanics who share in Campbell's success: (Left to right) L. Villa, S. McDonald, J. Coe, W. W. Baguley and H. Leech, a survivor of R101.

SIR MALCOLM CAMPE

F EW cars are as fascinating as the huge machines which are built at very great expense for a few seconds' run in order to register the highest speed at which a man and machine have travelled on land, and few cars are more difficult to design or prepare.

For one thing, preliminary trials are practically impossible, and so no one can say exactly how the great car will behave until it is actually taken far away to the place where the record is to be attacked. Every time, therefore, the unknown has to be faced, and the difficulties of the work are increased by the fact that the responsibility of the machine is greater than usual in that it must either possess the requisite stability at the speed it is to attain or there is no possibility of forcing it to attain that speed.

Moreover, as time goes on, the number of places where it is possible for the cars to attack the record is reduced, and, since there are quite enough unknowns to face without having to choose a course on which no car has previously attained approximately the same speed, it follows that the only reasonable thing is to go to Daytona. Now Daytona is limited for length, and consequently for each attack the acceleration of the car becomes more important which means more power, first of all, and then special efforts to make it possible to transmit that power through the tyres without violent slip, which would ruin the special type of tread necessary to resist the disruptive effect of centrifugal force.

Famous Record Breaker Reconstruct. Trophy-ty

Sir Malcolm Campbell's latest machine is practically an entirely new car. The engine is that famous Rolls-Royce power unit of $36\frac{1}{2}$ litres, 152.4 mm. bore, and 167.64 mm. stroke, which was originally intended for the Schneider Trophy 'plane, and which has had to be adapted to drive a clutch through a flywheel, and so the gear box and the transmission. The awkward part of this is, of course, that the enormous high-speed centrifugal blower has to be at the front end of the chassis, where its diameter makes it none too easy to arrange the power unit in the frame while allowing the body to be of a shape that is supposed to offer the least resistance to the wind; and, of course, the carburetters below the blower come dangerously near to the ground if special provision is not made to safeguard them. It is probable that this power unit develops something like 2,300-2,500 h.p., according to the fuel which can be used; and the

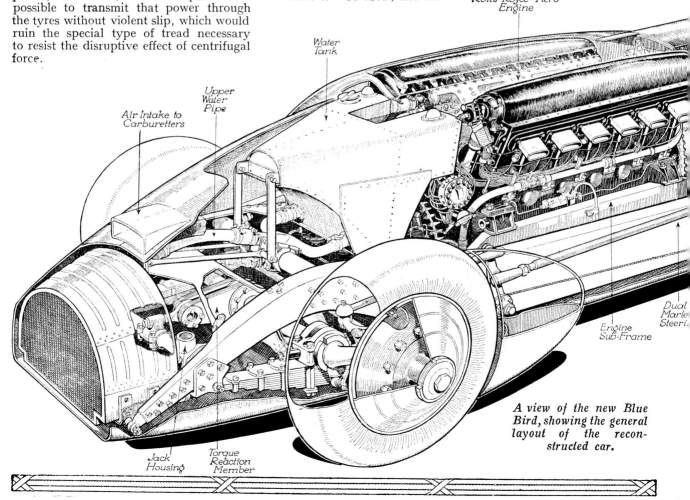

12 Cylinder, 36,582cc. supercharged Rolls-Royce Aero Engine

Water Tank

Upper Water Pipe

Air Intake to Carburetters

Dual Marle Steeri.

Engine Sub-Frame

Jack Housing

Torque Reaction Member

A view of the new Blue Bird, showing the general layout of the reconstructed car.

ELL'S NEW "BLUE BIRD"

d Fitted With Rolls-Royce Schneider
ngine

fuel, of course, has to be very special, one kind being satisfactory for comparatively long runs, another for sprints.

In the actual aeroplane engine the speed at which the machine was passing through the air was allowed to assist the air into the carburetters and so into the superchargers, and, to a moderate extent, the same is true when the engine is installed in a car. Cooling, difficult enough in the racing aeroplane, is difficult also in the car, and the radiator has had to be replaced in the nose of the

a reasonably clear view ahead without impairing the shape of the body. Behind the driving seat is a massive, bevel-driven axle and a small tank, which is really a large tank if you consider it in terms of the time for which the car is running, and the fuel consumption can be as high as is necessary for power.

With most racing cars it is essential to cut down weight, even for the smallest item. In these cars there is, as it were, power to play with, and, since the machine can be made more stable if its weight is increased, not only are the side-members now gigantic, but what look like armour-plate cross-members have

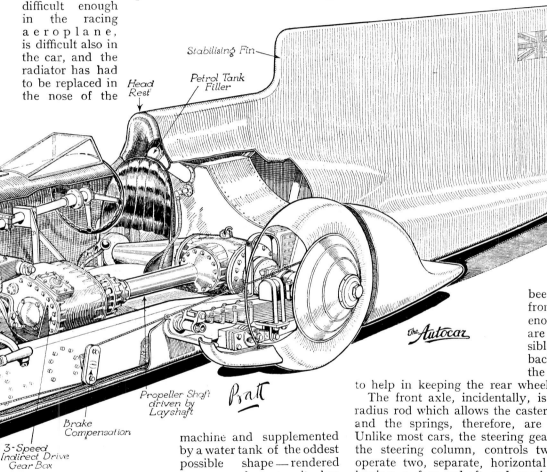

Stabilising Fin

Petrol Tank Filler

Head Rest

Propeller Shaft driven by Layshaft

Pratt

The Autocar

Brake Compensation

3-Speed Indirect Drive Gear Box

been added to stiffen the front of the frame, while enormous blocks of lead are placed wherever possible round about the back axle and in between the flanges of the frame to help in keeping the rear wheels down.

The front axle, incidentally, is located by a special radius rod which allows the caster angle to be adjusted, and the springs, therefore, are free at either end. Unlike most cars, the steering gear, that is, the gear on the steering column, controls two other gears which operate two, separate, horizontal "drop" arms, each having a fore-and-aft rod carried forward to a stub axle, in addition to which there is a tie-rod.

machine and supplemented by a water tank of the oddest possible shape — rendered necessary because it has had to fit into the only space available.

Behind the engine is a flywheel which is practically a ring to carry the big clutch, and the next problem was to bring the driving seat down between one side-member and the propeller-shaft, which is done in this case by transmitting the drive to the main shaft of the gear box, but taking it to the propeller-shaft from the lay-shaft, which is well away on the left side of the gear box, and so bringing the propeller-shaft and its torque tube close to the left side-member. Even so, it has been no easy task to place the controls, steering wheel, and driver's seat so that the driver can have

Finally, the whole record depends on the tyres, for, quite apart from the terrific speed as a destructive element, the centrifugal force is so great on the spinning tyres as to be capable of ripping away at once any ordinary tread, and consequently these tyres have practically no tread at all, and the testing of them is a matter of some anxiety. The wheels are immense steel discs held on by a ring of nuts and studs, each wheel needing two men to lift it off or on, for which reason special jacks are installed on the car, one at each corner of the frame.

BLUE BIRD IN ITS LATEST FORM

ONCE more Sir Malcolm Campbell is setting out to do battle with the World's Land Speed Record, and with the additional power provided by the new Rolls-Royce engine, which is of the same type as was fitted to the Supermarine seaplanes which won the 1931 Schneider Trophy, he should be able to make a substantial improvement on his present record of 253.9 m.p.h.

The "R" type Rolls-Royce engine, which was developed from the normal H or Buzzard series, is a twelve-cylinder V engine with bore and stroke of 6 and 6.6. inches (152 mm. and 168 mm.) with a total capacity of 36,582 c.c. The blocks are aluminium castings set at 60°, and have integral heads with aluminium bronze valve seats. High carbon-steel liners are used for the bores, and water leakage is prevented at the points where the liners bear on the blocks by an aluminium ring at the top end and a rubber ring at the bottom end. Hiduminium, a light and strong alloy developed by Messrs. Rolls Royce, was used in the racing engines in place of aluminium.

Each cylinder has two inlet and two exhaust valves and each cylinder block has a single overhead camshaft driven from the supercharger end of the engine by shaft and bevel gears. The valve rockers are pivoted at their outer ends and their inner ends bear on the valve stems. They pass under the camshafts, and have "humps" near their inner ends on which the cams operate. This form of construction is used in order to reduce the overall height and so the frontal area of the engine. The camshaft drive is taken from a shaft mounted in line with the crankshaft and flexibly driven from it.

Two plugs per cylinder are used, and the two twelve-terminal magnetos are driven by a cross shaft at the supercharger end of the engine.

The aluminium pistons have concave heads and very short skirts, their depth being only about half that of their diameter. The hollow gudgeon pins are fixed in the pistons and oil is supplied to the little ends through drilled connect-

ing rods. These are made of steel and those on one side of the engine have forked ends carrying steel blocks, which are lined with white metal and bear on the crankshaft. The blocks are also faced with white metal and the other big-ends of the rods pass through the forks and fit round the blocks.

The crankshaft is of course hollow and lubricated by pressure. It runs in seven main bearings.

The supercharger is of the centrifugal type and air is drawn into it from both sides. It is driven by sun and planet gears from the flexibly driven auxiliary shaft in line with the crankshaft. The gear-ratio is not given, but is probably about 12 to 1, while the diameter of the supercharger is very much bigger than that on the Buzzard.

The two carburettors on the Schneider Trophy engine were at the supercharger end of the engine, at the bottom of the casing and mixture was drawn through them to each side of the rotor. A specially

Continued on page 93

Power ! The " R " type Rolls-Royce aero engine which has been installed in Sir Malcolm Campbell's " Bluebird."

SIR MALCOLM CAMPBELL'S
New Record Breaker

Full Details and Exclusive Illustrations of the New 2,500 h.p. "Blue Bird," Together with an Interview with the Designer

WHEN Sir Malcolm Campbell, in February last, raised the world's land speed record from 246.09 m.p.h. to 253.97 m.p.h. at Daytona the "Blue Bird" was equipped with a 1,450 h.p. supercharged aero engine. The engine to be used in the forthcoming record attempt is a 2,500 b.h.p. supercharged Rolls-Royce of identical design to that which secured the Schneider Trophy for Great Britain in 1931.

The power unit has 12 cylinders arranged in two banks of six, with the supercharger located at the forward end. The bore and stroke respectively are 6 ins. (152.4 mm.) and 6.6 ins. (167.64 mm.), giving a capacity of 36,582 c.c., or approximately five times that of the 40-50 h.p. Rolls-Royce "New Phantom" car engine. The horse-power rating by R.A.C. formula is 173.28, and 2,350 b.h.p. is developed at 3,200 r.p.m. The weight of the engine is 1,630 lb., which is equivalent to 11 oz. per b.h.p. Two B.T.H. magnetos supply h.t. current to the K.L.G. sparking plugs. The engine is lubricated with Castor oil supplied by C. C. Wakefield and Co., Ltd. Considering the terrific horse-power developed, the unit is wonderfully compact. The overall length is 91.45 ins., the height 40 ins., and the width 30 ins.

The engine is carried in a subframe and on account of the greatly increased horse-power available this year an even more massive frame—

A frontal view showing the squat appearance, the two protruding banks of cylinders and the air intake for the supercharger.

produced by John Thompson Motor Pressings—has been installed. From the engine rearwards the design has only undergone minor modifications. The drive is transmitted through a Duron faced clutch which has been enlarged to cope with the increase in power.

The three-forward-speed and reverse gearbox is of the constant mesh type. By using an indirect drive the propeller shaft is offset in relation to the crankshaft, thus allowing the driver to be seated alongside instead of above it. This

has also enabled the overall height of the car to be reduced. The gearbox, incidentally, is entirely new and the gears were cut by the E.N.V. Engineering Co., from Firth-Brown special alloy steel.

The part played by the steel manufacturers is one of the most important in construction, and for most of the vital parts in the engine and transmission Firth - Brown B.N.C. and B.N.D. special alloy steels are used.

Externally, the redesigned "Blue Bird" is considerably different from

SUPPLIERS TO THE 'BLUE BIRD.''

ENGINE, CHASSIS AND BODYWORK.

2,500 h.p. Rolls-Royce Schneider Trophy supercharged aero engine; car designed by Mr. Reid A. Railton, of Thomson and Taylor, Ltd.; car erected by Thomson and Taylor, Ltd.; main chassis frame by John Thompson Motor Pressings, Ltd.; B.N.C. and B.N.D. steel in engine and transmission by Firth-Brown; Hoffman ball bearings; petrol tank by the Gallay Radiator Co.; E.N.V. rear axle bevel; Marles steering gear; Woodhead road springs; Alford and Alder brakes with Clayton Dewandre vacuum servo; clutch plates by W. A. Tyzack and Co.; Duron clutch and brake linings by Brake Linings, Ltd.; brake shoes of Wilmil alloy by W. Mills, Ltd.; Serck honeycomb radiator; Silentbloc bushes by T. B. Andre and Co., Ltd.; B.T.H. magnetos; Rolls-Royce carburetter; nuts and bolts by A. P. Newall; body designed by Thomson and Taylor, Ltd., and constructed by J. Gurney Nutting and Co., Ltd.

ACCESSORIES, FUEL AND EQUIPMENT.

K.L.G. sparking plugs; Castrol oil; Dunlop tyres and wheels; Andre shock absorbers; instruments by S. Smith and Sons (Motor Accessories), Ltd.; B.T.H. and Smith batteries; Pratts Ethyl petrol; Petro-Flex petrol tubing by Hobdell, Way and Co., Ltd.; Ace wheel discs by Cornercroft and Co., Ltd.; windscreen by Cox and Co., fitted with Triplex glass; Moseley Float-on-Air upholstery.

A close-up of the cockpit, the windscreen and the facia. The driver obtains his view of the numerous instruments through the steering wheel.

CAMPBELL'S NEW "BLUE BIRD"

what it was in February last. The radiator, instead of being carried on outriggers, is now supported upon extensions to the front dumbirons, which are an integral part of the chassis side members. An entirely new header tank of unusual contour has had to be designed so as to blend into the outline of the 12-cylinder V-type engine. A detached snout, which was a feature of the car 12 months ago, no longer characterizes the car, for the radiator cowl joins the engine cowling at the top and the air, after passing through the radiator, escapes through two very large louvres located one on each side of the engine cowling, the latter actually being recessed between the banks of cylinders.

A centrifugal blower takes in its supply of air from a special louvre mounted well forward on the nose of the car and takes the air in with an added force due to the speed. This alone will probably be worth about 2 lb. supercharging.

The front axle, which is mounted in large diameter phosphor bronze trunnion bearings carried on massive springs, is arranged much as before with the already familiar radius member to ensure that, whether at full speed, or when braking, the axle shall move only in a predetermined arc. Huge Andre shock absorbers are mounted fore and aft.

Alford and Alder brakes are used and these are assisted in their action by a Clayton-Dewandre servo, the braking cylinder being coupled directly to the pedal. In this con-

nection a Bowden cable is used to open or close the suction valve.

The Rolls-Royce engine, being appreciably longer than the power unit previously installed, has necessitated lengthening the entire chassis. The overall length of the car is approximately 27 ft. and the wheelbase is 13 ft. 8 ins. The rear track is 5 ft. and the front track is

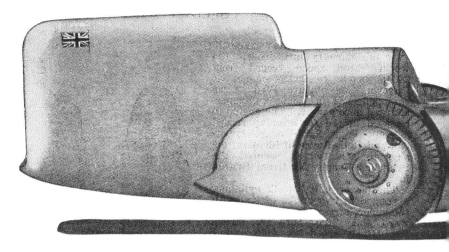

A photograph which gives some conception of the tremendous length of the new "
the driver is able to obtain quite a good view, for the body is recessed bet

5 ft. 3 ins., while the weight is approximately 4½ tons.

Another interesting feature is that the two rear springs are provided with a different amount of camber, so that when the car is stationary the body is slightly tilted towards the off side. The idea of this is that when the engine is developing its full power the torque is such as to bring the chassis back to an even keel. The springs are of the Woodhead type with weldless

solid eyes, solid lug plates and rebound clips.

The driver is provided with an array of instruments, all of which have been manufactured by S. Smith and Sons (M.A.), Ltd. In the centre of the facia is a large dial revolution indicator, reading from 1,000 r.p.m. to 3,500 r.p.m., and with a subsidiary scale indicating that at 3,200 r.p.m. the speed of the car will be 300 m.p.h. This instrument is fitted with a maximum hand so that the highest speed of the engine can be ascertained after the run. On the left of the facia are two electric petrol gauges, one of which is fitted to the rear tank and the other to the bottom tank. These tanks are interconnected and the gauges have been calibrated so that the contents of either or both tanks can be read at a glance. The instruments are connected to a Smith six-volt battery. The other instruments include a blower gauge, reading up to a pressure of 20 lb. per sq. in., a fuel pressure gauge with a reading up to

A three-quarter rear view showing the contours of the huge stabilizing fin and how the overhead covers of the cylinder blocks form a part of the external surface.

10 lb. per sq. in., water temperature and engine oil temperature gauges reading up to 100 degrees C., and oil pressure gauge reading up to 125 lb. per sq. in., and a gauge reading up to 150 degrees C. which informs the driver as to the temperature of the rear axle. All these instruments are fitted with parti-coloured dials, so that the position of the pointer can be seen over an appropriate colour division, thereby indicating the normal functioning of the

wheels will be fitted with Ace discs; these were not in place when our photographs were taken.

The Cox windscreen framing is of trapezoidal shape, giving strong support to three panes of Triplex glass. The driver's seat is fitted with Moseley Float-on-Air upholstery and immediately behind it a very strong arched cross-tube is fitted, bolted to the frame, which constitutes the main support for the tail.

The seat is fitted with a strong

safety strap and the driver sits close to a spring-spoke steering wheel which is practically vertical. This operates a duplicated steering system through a Marles mechanism. The facia panel is shaped to fit the contour of the body and the dials are viewed through the steering wheel.

The great car, viewed complete, is extremely impressive, the increase in length making it more graceful than last year's "Blue Bird."

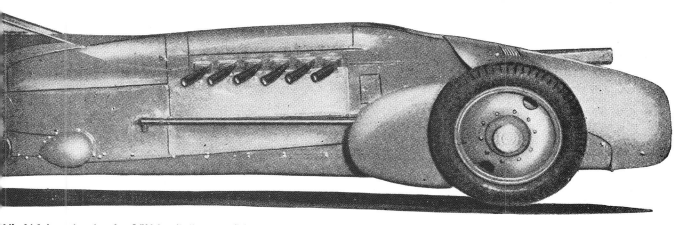

...," which is equipped with a 2,500 h.p. Rolls-Royce Schneider Trophy type supercharged engine. Despite the length forward of the cockpit two banks of cylinders. Note also the opening behind the nose through which the air escapes after rushing through the radiator.

medium operating the gauge. Other items on the facia include a St. Christopher mascot and a clock.

The body was designed by Mr. Reid A. Railton and was built in remarkably short time by J. Gurney Nutting and Co., Ltd., of Lacland Place, Chelsea, London, S.W.3. It is a magnificent example of panelled aluminium work.

The body really "grows" forwards and rearwards from the engine, as this unit naturally fixed the cross-sectional area of the whole whale-shaped structure. In order that no space should be wasted the overhead covers of the cylinder blocks form a part of the external surface, the panelling being arranged to merge flush with the forward and rear edges of these covers. Another concave panel fills in the space between the blocks, forming a shallow valley down which the driver obtains his line of sight forwards.

The aluminium panelling is secured to a skeleton structure of tubes and angle-irons by bolts throughout; no wooden members are employed. Consequently, any portion of the panelling can fairly readily be removed. Easier access to vital parts, filling orifices, etc., is provided by special trap-doors. The petrol tank is mounted behind the driver's seat and a supply of special Pratts' Eythl fuel has been sent out for the car. The panelling is finished in blue cellulose, specially treated in order to secure a very smooth surface, which should reduce skin friction to a minimum. The

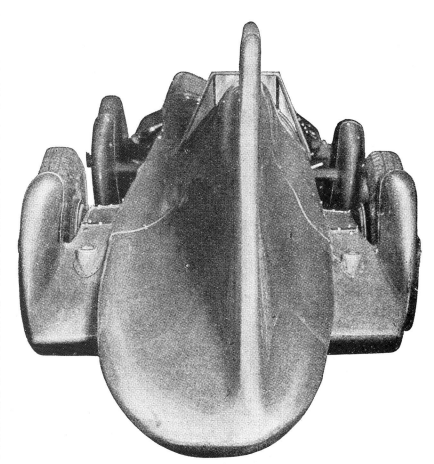

This aspect shows how the body and stabilizing fin are offset to enable the driver to sit low down alongside the torque tube.

THE "Blue Bird," Sir Malcolm Campbell's giant Rolls-Royce-engined record-breaker, which is being taken over to Florida this month for an attempt on the world's land speed record has, our readers know, been considerably altered since Sir Malcolm Campbell's wonderful achievement last year.

The chief novelty lies in the use of a Schneider Trophy-type Rolls-Royce aviation engine, developing something like 2,500 h.p. The change in power unit (a 12-cylinder Napier was fitted previously) has necessitated lengthening the chassis, while owing to the unique form of air intake used on the Schneider-type Rolls-Royce engines, the front cowling has also been altered. A large "nostril," if such a term may be used, on each side of the snout takes the place of the annular aperture through which, last year, the hot air escaped from behind the radiator.

Weighty Questions Involved

Being anxious to know something of the weighty questions involved in the design of a 300 m.p.h. racer, a representative of *The Motor* sought out Mr. Reid A. Railton, the talented engineer responsible for the alterations to the "Blue Bird." He was in his bungalow at Brooklands next to the workshops of Thomson and Taylor, who specialize in the design and construction of racing cars, and who were responsible for rebuilding Sir Malcolm Campbell's car.

So modest is Mr. Railton that he

told us quite frankly that, in regard to most of its features, the "Blue Bird" was simply a "scaled-up" model of an ordinary modern racing car. That is to say, the nature of the springing, the steering, etc., were exactly like those which would be found on a smaller racing car, but were, of course, made correspondingly larger and heavier to suit the immense size and power of the "Blue Bird."

The Problem of Wheel Adhesion

One of the most serious problems to be faced is that of wheel adhesion. Had money been no object, it is not improbable that the car would have been entirely redesigned, and four-wheel drive incorporated, as only by driving on all four wheels would it be possible to keep down the weight of the car without sacrificing wheel adhesion. As it is, however, the old car has had to be converted in the best way possible with the resources available.

Already there is 1½ times as much

weight on the back wheels as on the front, while a considerable amount of lead ballast is further used to keep the driving wheels on the ground. Indeed, the "Blue Bird" has been built on locomotive lines, dead weight being added whenever the weight of the components of the car was insufficient to secure adhesion. For instance, there is approximately three-quarters of a ton of lead over the rear axle. The tubular cross-members at the rear of the chassis, together with other parts of the frame, are filled with lead, and the driver sits on quite a large ingot of the same metal. Much more ballast is, of course, required when running on sand than on hard concrete, as wheel spin is more likely to develop.

Nothing can be done in the way of tyre tread design to ensure a better driving grip, because the tyre treads have to be as light as possible, owing to the effect of centrifugal force, which would fling off a heavier tread. The actual

Designer Reveals '

An Interview with Mr. Reid A. Rai
and Difficulties Entailed in Re-desi
Special for the New Attempt on the V

2,500 H.P 12 CYL ROLLS-ROYCE ENGINE

WATER TANK

TORQUE REACTION MEMBER

AIR SCOOP TO SUPERCHARGER

RADIATOR

JACK HOUSING

SUPERCHARGER

SUB-FRAME

CLU

A part cutaway drawing of Sir Malcolm Campbell's 2,500 h.p. Rolls-Royce-engined car with which he is
equipment are used exclusively. The sketch also shows the salient features in cou

lue Bird" Secrets

who Relates Some of the Problems
Sir Malcolm Campbell's Campbell
d's Land Speed Record Next February

treads on the Dunlop tyres are only about 1-32 of an inch thick, and the tyres are inflated to 120 lb. per square inch.

Mr. Railton went on to tell us the pros and cons of the "fin" which is such a characteristic feature of the stern of the "Blue Bird." There are two points of view regarding such a fitment. In theory, a fin ensures directional stability, the idea being that should the car get into a skid the pressure of the air on one side of the fin, at speeds of 250 m.p.h. or more, would be so great that it would pull the tail of the car straight again.

The fin was fitted largely as a result of tests of streamline forms made in a wind tunnel. Obviously, any aircraft suspended in such a device must have a fin in order to make certain that it is kept in its proper location. The position is altered somewhat, however, in the case of a car which sits on the ground, and wheel adhesion can largely be depended upon to prevent the tail of the car swinging one way or the other.

Those who are not in favour of fins for ensuing directional stability actually argue that with a side wind of only, say, 15 m.p.h. blowing, this would be quite enough to keep on forcing the tail of the car to one side, with the result that the vehicle would tend to proceed more or less crabwise.

Gyroscopic Effect

Indeed, the gyroscopic effect on the front wheels has far more influence than is generally believed in keeping the car straight. Imagine the two big front wheels rotating at some 2,500 r.p.m., and think of the tremendous force which would be required to turn them to right or left. So great are these gyroscopic forces, in fact, that should the car get into a skid and the tail swing round, thus deflecting the front of the car, the front wheels would insist on rotating in the same direction as they were doing before the skid occurred, and would automatically straighten the car out, the steering wheel spinning harmlessly through the driver's hands.

The springing problems are not so serious as the ordinary motorist would imagine. As Mr. Railton pointed out, in order to make certain of breaking the record, Sir Malcolm Campbell would have to wait for a perfect day when there were no bumps on the varying Daytona Beach, so that as near perfect adhesion as possible could be ensured. If then there were no bumps, there would be no necessity for the springing to be anything out of the ordinary.

It comes down to this, that if the beach is sufficiently smooth to guarantee reasonably good adhesion of the rear wheels, then it is sufficiently good for a normal type of springing system to prove effective.

Guarding Against Wheel Tramp

"What do you do to guard against the dangers of wheel tramp or wobble?" we asked Mr. Railton.

"Of course," he replied, "we have to balance the wheels very accurately indeed, and the oversize shock absorbers are fitted in such a way as to damp out any tramping tendency that might develop. The front of the chassis also has been

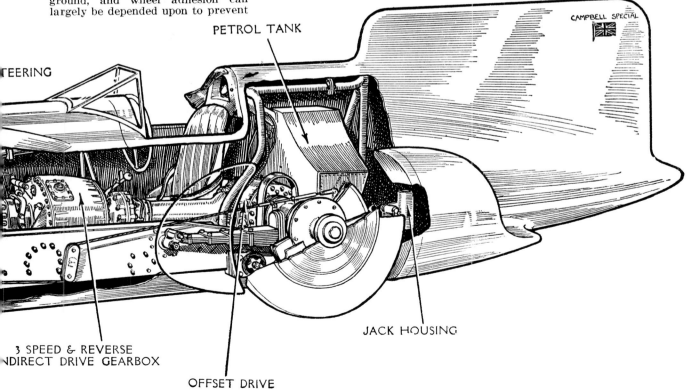

PETROL TANK

CAMPBELL SPECIAL

TEERING

JACK HOUSING

3 SPEED & REVERSE
NDIRECT DRIVE GEARBOX

OFFSET DRIVE

t to beat the world's land speed record at Daytona Beach, Florida, next February. British components and while additional details of the engine and chassis will be found on the preceding pages.

Mr. Reid A. Railton, the designer of the "Blue Bird."

made so stiff that any tendency towards wheel wobble is quelled before it has a chance to assume measurable proportions."

Considering the size of the engine, the radiator of the "Blue Bird" does not seem very large. Commenting upon this, we asked Mr. Railton how far the "Blue Bird" could be expected to run at full speed without boiling. He told us that the cooling system was worked out in such a way that no harm would result if the water were allowed to boil for a few seconds. The cooling system contains 30 gallons of water and two 1-in. pipes are provided to carry away the steam which would be generated in the event of boiling.

Small Fuel Capacity

The petrol tank also seems small compared with the size of the car, but it must be borne in mind that the world's land speed record is run over a mile at the outside, although, of course, a considerable distance is required to get up speed

so, it would be possible to run up to 100 m.p.h. on bottom gear and 200 m.p.h. on second gear without harming the engine in the least. Given an absolutely flat surface for about 15 miles, and perfect weather conditions, the car is theoretically capable of reaching 300 m.p.h. in still air. The gear ratio on top is 1.2 to 1.

Of course, the whole car is designed for the sole purpose of attaining high speeds for comparatively short periods. For instance, it is only possible to make the back axle and gearbox as small as they are owing to the short time during which they have to work on maximum load. Indeed, they are not called upon to carry the maximum load for more than 90 seconds at a time. The masses of metal incorporated in the gearing both in the gearbox and the rear axle heat up gradually during the attempt on the record, while the run is concluded and the car slows down again before the temperature of the gears gets

100 m.p.h., for any brake small enough to get inside the wheel without adding to the head resistance of the car would be too small to be of any value at really high speeds. If brakes were designed to slow down the car from over 200 m.p.h. they would have to act on the transmission and be water-cooled."

Owing to its size (7½ ft. in length) and the high gear ratio employed the Rolls-Royce Schneider Trophy-type engine, even at 300 m.p.h., is work-

The Rolls-Royce supercharged 2,500 h.p. aero engine which has a capacity of 36½ litres. It is identical to the type that secured the Schneider Trophy for Great Britain in 1931, and is approximately five times the capacity of the 40-50 h.p. "New Phantom" engine.

and slow down subsequently, so that each run is of about 7 miles.

Actually, the 28 gallons of petrol that are carried are just about enough for 10 minutes running all out or, say, about two runs over the course.

As a matter of interest, we asked what sort of speeds the "Blue Bird" could be expected to reach on its intermediate gears without exceeding the safe revolutions of the engine. Although it is not expected that Sir Malcolm Campbell would do

dangerously high. The load on the teeth in the rear axle can perhaps be imagined when it is stated that it amounts to 6,000 lb. per inch width.

"Presumably," we remarked, "the brakes are only used when manœuvring the car, such as running it down to the beach prior to making an attempt on a record, or going for a practice run?"

"Of course," said Mr. Railton, "Sir Malcolm would not think of using his brakes at speeds of over

ing no harder than the power unit of an ordinary touring car at normal road speeds. The engine revolutions would reach 3,200 r.p.m. approximately at 300 m.p.h.

Mr. Railton was inclined to agree with us when we told him that our purely personal opinion was that the record would be raised to just over 280 m.p.h. We can only wait now until Sir Malcolm Campbell has achieved his great task, an undertaking in which we wish him all possible success.

MORE PHOTOGRAPHS OF "BLUE BIRD"

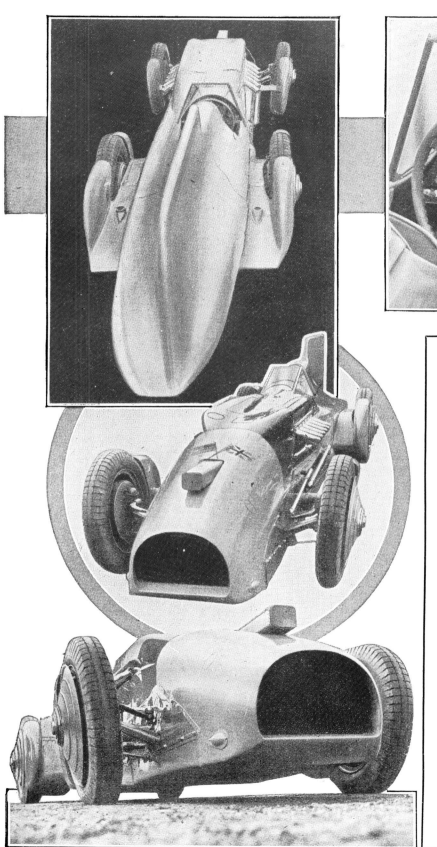

Interesting Facts About the Forthcoming Record Attempt

In order to attain 280 m.p.h. the new Blue Bird will have to cover the mile in 12.81 secs. The 1932 record figure was 14.17 secs. (253.968 m.p.h.).

280 m.p.h. represents a speed of $4\frac{2}{3}$ miles per minute, or $388\frac{2}{3}$ feet per second.

At this speed (280 m.p.h.) a car would travel from London to Brighton in 10 minutes 41 secs.

At a rough calculation Blue Bird will consume nearly a gallon of petrol in covering the measured mile. It will not have time to use more!

At 280 m.p.h. the wheels, carrying tyres of some 3 ft. diameter, will turn at about 2,500 r.p.m.

At such high revolution speeds the enormous centrifugal force causes the tyres to grow, lifting the whole car to the extent of about an inch.

The engine has a capacity of $36\frac{1}{2}$ litres and develops 2,350 b.h.p., representing an output of nearly 65 h.p. per litre. It weighs only 11 oz. per b.h.p. developed.

The cylinders are arranged V-fashion in two rows of six each, two connecting rods working upon each of the six crankpins.

The kinetic energy of the car at full speed will amount to something in the neighbourhood of 23 *million* foot-pounds.

This energy must be dissipated by wind resistance and braking to bring the car to a standstill. It is an amount sufficient to propel a medium-sized private car some 20 miles at 40 m.p.h.

SIR MALCOLM CAMPBELL'S GREAT ACHIEVEMENT.

" BLUEBIRD " BEATS HER PREVIOUS SPEED BY 18 M.P.H. AND RAISES THE WORLD'S LAND SPEED RECORD TO THE COLOSSAL FIGURE OF 272 M.P.H.

272 MILES per hour! As the B.B.C. announcer calmly broadcast the news that Sir Malcolm Campbell had once again broken the world's record for the flying mile with a speed of 272.108 m.p.h., it required an almost impossible amount of imagination to appreciate fully the nature of his great achievement. Probably the fastest land speed ever witnessed by the majority of British motor-racing enthusiasts is the 137 m.p.h. lap speed of Sir Henry Birkin at Brooklands. Seen at close quarters from the Byfleet Bridge this speed looks terrific, as indeed it is. Now try (we say "try" purposely, for the most elastic imagination will be hopelessly inadequate), to picture "Bluebird" travelling at approximately double the velocity of Sir Henry Birkin's Bentley's lap speed.

So fast does the great car go that, if it were possible to race at such a speed on a track circuit, after starting level "Bluebird" would cover two laps to the Bentley's one. Again, supposing the cars were being timed over a beach-run like Daytona, with a flying start at their maximum speeds, "Bluebird" could give the Bentley a half-mile start in one mile and the cars would cross the finishing line together.

It was on Wednesday, February 22nd, that the record attempt was finally made; after a trying period of waiting for the conditions of the beach to improve. In many ways, however, this delay was a good thing, for it allowed Sir Malcolm's return to health after a severe bout of influenza to be fully accomplished, and sundry last-minute adjustments of the car to be made. The morning dawned misty and unpromising, but later the visibility improved as the mist lifted, and a decision was made to go out for the record there and then.

Through the length of beach available having been reduced from 11 miles to 9, the speed of "Bluebird's" first run was awaited with great interest. 50,000 people were lining the sand hills down the length of the course as the car set off to gather speed. The mist was still heavy enough to make everyone anxious for the welfare of the driver, but with superb judgment Campbell held the car under perfect control, as it hurtled into sight like a projectile. Then came the news "273.566 m.p.h." and a cheer went up from the excited spectators.

At the far end of the beach Sir Malcolm

pulled up, and the car was immediately worked upon by mechanics, who changed all the tyres and checked over the machine. All this took about half-an-hour, and then the driver climbed back once more into the narrow cockpit.

On the second run the car seemed to bump a good deal, and at one moment gave a sudden lurch, but with his customary skill Sir Malcolm held the car to its course and recorded the terrific speed of 270.676 m.p.h. Quickly the mean average was worked out, and the spectators went wild with excitement when it was announced that "Bluebird" had set up a new world's record for the flying mile with a speed of 272.108 m.p.h.

One hardly knows how to start praising all those connected with this marvellous achievement. The driver, Sir Malcolm Campbell, who has broken the land's speed record no fewer than four times during the last few years at a speed of over 200 m.p.h. The designer, Mr. Reid Railton, whose genius has enabled the great car to be controllable at hitherto untried speeds. The erectors, Messrs. Thomson & Taylor, Ltd., and the manufacturers of the component parts. The Rolls-Royce engine, which has repeated the Schneider Trophy and World's Air-Speed record in such a convincing manner, developing 2,350 h.p. at 3,200 r.p.m. and weighing only 11 oz. per h.p. The manufacturers of the tyres, the Dunlop people, on whose efforts the success of the record and the life of the driver depend to a fundamental degree, having to combine resistance to the cutting effect of small shells with the thinnest possible tread. The accessory suppliers, notably Messrs. C. C. Wakefield & Co., Ltd., whose Castrol oil has been used on every occasion when 200 m.p.h. has been exceeded. The Smith instruments, vital to the necessary co-ordination between driver and car; the Bluemel flexible steering wheel, relieving the driver of excessive fatigue; and Pratt's, whose Ethyl was used once more, together with K.L.G. plugs. Finally, the mechanics who travelled with the car to Daytona, under the direction of the ever cheerful Villar.

Altogether a marvellous show, of which every Britisher has every reason to be extremely proud.

Here are the official figures :

Mile	Speed m.p.h.	Time secs.	Old Record m.p.h.
Southward Run	273.556	13.16	267.459
Northward Run	270.676	13.60	241.77
Average ...	272.108	13.23	253.968
Kilometre.			
Southward Run	271.802	8.187	262.24
Northward Run	271.472	8.24	241.30
Average ...	271.636	8.235	251.340
5 Kilometres.			
Average ...	257.295	—	247.941

"Bluebird" in the grounds of Sir Malcolm Campbell's house at Povey Cross, prior to being shipped to Daytona.

CAMPBELL'S 6th VICTORY

The Land Speed Record. A Comparison Between the First Record in 1898 and Sir Malcolm Campbell's Magnificent Run at 272·108 m.p.h. From One Mile to Nearly Five Miles a Minute

Sir Malcolm Campbell.
From a pastel by R. E. Poulton of "The Autocar."

DECEMBER 18th, 1898. A long, straight, French, macadam road, bordered by stone kerbs, flanked by young trees, each with its supporting post, cut clean across the park of Achères. It was a rather drizzly winter day, and the road, usually deserted, was now unwontedly awake, for the first land speed record in history was about to be timed. Six timekeepers fussed portentously over certain marks indicating the start and finish of a two-kilometre stretch with a one-kilometre line in its centre, then, ignoring the fire of questions, synchronised their watches in a manner suggesting a religious rite confined only to the high of caste.

Down the road a little knot of serious men worked hard on four machines, a De Dion tricycle, two Bollées, and a most fearsome affair—Count Chasseloup-Laubat's electric Jeantaud—carrying a low, boat-shaped body on top of which the driver was perched with only his legs under cover. The idea was to time the cars over one standing, followed by one flying, kilometre, and rash people had talked of forty miles an hour.

One by one the cars went down the road. Anxious consultations followed each run, and then, with an indescribably ringing hum, the electric car went away, accelerated at a marvellous pace, and, rocking on its narrow pneumatic tyres, with its driver bending grimly over the wheel, dashed past the lines, using all the power its batteries could give for just that one short run. And when it stopped the first recorded land speed record was 39.24 m.p.h. over the flying kilometre. The weight of the Jeantaud was given as 3,204.5lb., its power—for a brief minute or so—a problematic 40 h.p.

Promptly a rival appeared, Jenatzy, with another electric car, also streamlined after the ideas of the period. A match was arranged, and this time, before many interested spectators in the fine, cold sunlight of January 17th, 1899, the challenger achieved 41.42 m.p.h., only to be beaten a minute or two later by Chasseloup-Laubat, whose Jeantaud, with an extra battery or so, put up 43.69 m.p.h., a brilliant display of blue flame and a strong smell of burning rubber enthralling the spectators just before the car reached the finish of the kilometre.

On January 27th, Jenatzy, with new and more powerful motors, just reached 49.42 m.p.h.; on March 4th Chasseloup-Laubat's car put up 58.25, and at that Jenatzy produced the famous *Jamais Contente*, a terrible-looking cigar-shaped machine on four tiny little wheels, which was promptly regarded as a dangerous freak that only a man tired of life would attempt to drive. It was argued by sombre scientists that at the speed this car might travel no man could breathe; they said the steering was dangerous—as we now know it was—they said the car would turn over, that the tyres could not stand up to the work.

But all was ready by April 1st, 1899. Once more the timekeepers performed rites proper to the occasion with due ceremony, and were about to re-mark the finish when there was a shout, high officials leapt for life, and down among them

An impression of the new Blue Bird at speed on Daytona Beach. By F. Gordon-Crosby.

sped *Jamais Contente*, going well in a cloud of dust, with big blue sparks all over the place. Then there was trouble. Jenatzy, ever impatient, his lean, expressive face white with rage, red beard bristling, shook both fists at an inoffensive sky, calling gods and devils to witness the incapacity, the gross incapacity of near relatives of mules, misappointed timekeepers. He raged, he danced, but nothing could get over the fact that the officials stated definitely that he had refused to wait. And the car could only do that one run. Moreover, it was rumoured that one of the sacred watches had been dropped by a timekeeper.

However, on April 29th the scene was reset. Jenatzy was restrained with difficulty by many pacificatory friends, and then, in one short terrific rush, the record was put up to 65.82 m.p.h. The mile-a-minute mark had been passed at last, the man lived who had achieved it! In the due course of time the news filtered round to arouse great enthusiasm among the few votaries of the new cult, but such of the world as heard of it were either annoyed or anxious to point out the foolish uselessness of the proceedings.

* * *

Note the change to-day. Sir Malcolm Campbell's—and the knighthood is significant—2,300 h.p. supercharged Rolls-Royce-engined monster, weighing some four tons or so, has for many months

been the centre of much interest. The cost of the car has been discussed, and that alone must be twenty times the cost of *Jamais Contente*. Now the car has to journey almost across half the world to find a place where its speed can be realised, and there it is greeted by gorgeously dressed bands, by publicity on every hand, and it is, indeed, the centre of attraction, the chief lure, of a very pleasant sunlit American resort, Daytona.

Almost every movement the car makes, and practically every word its driver can be persuaded to utter, are transmitted forthwith by telegraph, telephone, by cable or by wireless, to an expectant world, and newspaper after newspaper gives the latest news as to whether the attempt is possible or not within the next few hours.

Electrical timing has replaced the watches, the advantage of a following wind is allowed no longer, for the machine has to make runs once in each direction over the course, and only the average counts. Instead of two kilometres, twelve miles of course are needed, though only one kilometre and one mile of that count for the record.

Crowds line the beach to see the machine, while fast aeroplanes keep track of the monster, microphones record its sound, cinematograph cameras its movement, special police keeping the course absolutely clear the while. And only

when wind, beach and tide serve can the record be attempted at all. Thus, in one great tornado of sound, in two short rushes at tremendous speed, was the record broken again on Wednesday last, the speed in one direction being 273.556 m.p.h., in the other 270.676 m.p.h., the average—or mean—of the two times, which counts for the record, being 272.108 m.p.h., and at the terrific speed thus registered Sir Malcolm Campbell brings us one step farther forward to the magical milestone of 300 miles an hour, five miles, instead of one mile, in the minute.

There will follow feastings and rejoicing, dinners lunches and speeches for the next month, while writer after writer tries to convey speed in words. Did Chasseloup-Laubat or Jenatzy have more than one small dinner with friends, and perhaps an official? And Sir Malcolm has five times previously beaten the record, first at a speed of 150.86 m.p.h. with the twelve-cylinder Sunbeam at Pendine, then with the Napier-Campbell at Daytona, at 174.88 m.p.h., then at 206.95 with the modified Napier-Campbell, and once again at 246.09, in 1931, with a yet more modified version of the same car, and, last year, with a new Napier engine, he recorded a speed of 253.97 m.p.h., a remarkable performance for one man.

And there is a similarity between the first record and this, for people still said the car would turn over. Only two years

"Jamais Contente," the first car constructed solely to beat the world's land speed record. This machine was electrically propelled, and, handled by Jenatzy, attained 65.82 m.p.h. over one kilometre.

ago it was murmured that a man might not be able to breathe; the stability of the car has been questioned, though proved beyond doubt, and always there is the question of the tyres.

In these days the machine, aye, and all its individual parts, count for far more than it or they did all those years ago, and R. A. Railton, the designer of the machine, must be congratulated most heartily on the results, together with the many mechanics by whose work alone the record was made possible. And an equal share of praise is due to Dunlop's, in that the solution of the tyre problem is one of the most difficult of all the things which must combine correctly to bring the car safely through.

HISTORY OF THE WORLD'S LAND SPEED RECORD

Date.	Driver.	Car.	Speed. m.p.h.
1898	Chasseloup-Laubat	Jeantaud	39.24
1899	Jenatzy	Jenatzy	41.42
1899	Chasseloup-Laubat	Jeantaud	43.69
1899	Jenatzy	Jenatzy	49.42
1899	Chasseloup-Laubat	Jeantaud	58.25
1899	Jenatzy	Jenatzy	65.82
1902	Serpollet	Serpollet	75.06
1902	Vanderbilt	Mors	76.08
1902	Fournier	Mors	76.60
1902	Augières	Mors	77.13
1903	Duray	Gobr'n-Brillié	84.21
1903	Ford	Ford	91.37*
1904	Vanderbilt	Mercédès	92.30*
1904	Rigolly	Gobr'n-Brillié	93.20
1904	de Caters	Mercédès	97.26
1904	Rigolly	Gobr'n-Brillié	103.56
1904	Barras	Darracq	104.53
1905	Hemery	Darracq	109.65
1905	Bowden	Mercédès	109.75*
1906	Marriott	Stanley	121.57*

Date.	Driver.	Car.	Speed. m.p.h.
1909	Hemery	Benz	125.9
1910	Oldfield	Benz	131.72*
1911	Burman	Benz	141.73*
1919	de Palma	Packard	149.87*
1920	Milton	Duesenberg	156.04*
1922	Guinness	Sunbeam	129.17†
1924	Thomas	Leyland-Thomas	129.73†
1924	R. Thomas	Delage	143.31†
1924	Eldridge	Fiat	145.90†
1925	Campbell	Sunbeam	150.86†
1926	Segrave	Sunbeam	152.33†
1926	Thomas	Higham	169.23†
1926	Thomas	Higham	171.09†
1927	Campbell	Napier-Campbell	174.88†

Date.	Driver.	Car.	Speed. m.p.h.
1927	Segrave	Sunbeam	203.79*†
1928	Campbell	Napier-Campbell	206.95*†
1928	Keech	White Triplex	207.55*†
1929	Segrave	Irving Special	231.44†
1931	Campbell	Napier-Campbell	246.09†
1932	Campbell	Napier-Campbell	253.968†
1933	Campbell	Rolls-Royce-Campbell	272.108*†

* Over 1 mile.

† Average of runs in two directions.

MATERIALS AND COMPONENT PARTS USED IN CAMPBELL'S BIG CAR

No.	Part	Supplier
1	Car built by	Thomson and Taylor (Brooklands), Ltd.
2	Fuel	Pratts Ethyl (Anglo-American).
3	Wheels	Dunlop.
4	Tubes	Tubes, Ltd.
5	Engine	Rolls-Royce, Ltd.
6	Plugs	K.L.G.
7	Fuel Pipes	Petroflex.
8	Lubricating Oil	Castrol.
9	Steering Gear	Marles (Adamant Eng. Co.).
10	Carburetters	Rolls-Royce, Ltd.
11	Brake Servo	Dewandre (Clayton Dewandre).
12	Steering Wheel	Bluemel.
13	Springs	Woodhead.
14	Shock Absorbers	Andre (T. B. Andre).
15	Tyres	Dunlop.
16	Magnetos	B.T.H.
17	Radiator	Serck.
18	Body	Gurney Nutting.
19	Axle Bevels	E.N.V. Engineering Co.
20	Gear Wheels	David Brown and Sons.
21	Windscreen	Triplex.
22	Instruments	S. Smith and Son (M.A.), Ltd.
23	Fuel and Oil Tanks	Gallay Radiator Co., Ltd.
24	Clutch Plates	Tyzack and Son, Ltd.
25	Clutch Linings	Duron Brake Linings, Ltd.
26	Brake Linings	Duron Brake Linings, Ltd.
27	Frame	John Thompsons Motor Pressings, Ltd.
28	Pneumatic Cushions	D. Moseley and Sons, Ltd.
29	Wheel Discs	Ace (Cornercroft, Ltd.).
30	Front Wheel Brakes	Alford and Alder.
31	Aluminium Panelling	Gurney Nutting.
32	Ball Bearings	Hoffmann.
33	Finish	Belco.
34	Cables	Tru-lay Cables (British Wire).
35	Fittings	Tru-loc Fittings (Products).

Three New World's Records

Sir Malcolm Campbell Raises Land Speed Record by Over 18 m.p.h. to 272.463 m.p.h. for the Kilometre — Special Detailed Accounts of the Most Thrilling Drive in History

MANY INTERESTING FACTS AND FIGURES

Sir Malcolm Campbell starting off on a trial run at Daytona Beach. Note the post indicating the second mile.

(From Our Special Correspondent.)
DAYTONA BEACH, FLORIDA,
February 22.

IN the wildest ride he has ever taken, Sir Malcolm Campbell covered the mile to-day at 272.108 m.p.h. to set the land speed mark 18.140 m.p.h. above the record of 253.968 m.p.h. he made last year.

Zigzagging over the 11-mile course, and at least four times coming definitely near to crashing into the surf or sand-dunes, the British driver skimmed over the course, only 40 yds. wide, under the worst imaginable conditions, making the second of two runs with his left arm hanging limp at his side.

The tyres of "Blue Bird" were ripped to shreds in several spots. Tiny, but hard, sea shells cut through the first layer of fabric after cutting off the outer covering of rubber, and the amazing fact is that the tyres were not blown.

For the first time since his first run here in 1928 Campbell changed tyres after one run, with certain disaster staring him in the face had he sought to make both of the two runs required on the same set.

With visibility none too good, owing to the mist which gathered on the windscreen and over a course very bumpy in spots, the British driver ran south over the mile in 13.16 secs. for a speed of 273.556 m.p.h. In less than half an hour he was roaring back over the mile in 13.30 secs. at a speed of 270.676 m.p.h., for a two-way average time of 13.23 secs. and a speed of 272.108 m.p.h.

At the same time, the daring British driver set up a new kilo-

Campbell's New World's Records.

ONE MILE (FLYING START).

			Secs.	M.P.H.
South	..	..	13.16	273.556
North	..	..	13.30	270.676
Mean	..	..	13.23	272.108

Old Record: 253.968 m.p.h. (14.17 secs.).

ONE KILOMETRE (FLYING START).

			Secs.	M.P.H.
South	..	..	8.18	273.463
North	..	..	8.24	271.472
Mean	..	..	8.21	272.463

Old Record: 251.340 m.p.h. (8 90 secs.).

FIVE KILOMETRES (FLYING START).

			Secs.	M.P.H.
South	..	..	42.44	263.540
North	..	..	44.50	251.340
Mean	..	..	43.47	257.295

Old Record: 247.941 m.p.h. (45.11 secs.).

metre record of 272.463 m.p.h. in traversing the distance in 8.21 secs., and also broke the five-kilometre record in 43.47 secs. at an average speed of 257.295 m.p.h. He did not attempt the five-mile or ten-kilometre records.

Campbell's left arm was hurt last week in changing gear when he ran "Blue Bird" at 231 m.p.h. in a test run. With the injured limb tightly bandaged he started his runs to-day, but the strained ligaments caused trouble, and on the second of two runs he was forced to steer with only his right hand.

Campbell was definitely disappointed over the speed attained, believing that the "Blue Bird" is capable of doing much better. The tachometer showed 3,650 revolutions, but terrific side-sway and slippage in rough spots cost priceless fractions of seconds, and deprived him of 300 m.p.h.—his aim. His disappointment centres on the fact that his Rolls-Royce engine turned over sufficiently high for 330 m.p.h. at 3,650 revolutions, but no such forward speed was obtainable under conditions that caused wheels to spin and the car to sway.

"It was a ride to be remembered as terrible; thought at least once I was for it," Campbell said. "On the second run at the fourth mile, after crossing the measured mile, I ran

"BLUE BIRD" AT DAYTONA BEACH

An impression by Bryan de Grineau of Sir Malcolm Campbell setting up his new world's records.

within 10 ft. of the flags parallel to the shore line and breakers, and a moment later was in soft sand near the dunes. Only the beautiful performance of 'Blue Bird' enabled me to straighten out on to the course and continue without disaster.

"Fumes from the exhaust and sand came into the cockpit, to add hazard to many others with which I had to contend. I am not easily frightened, but only my extreme confidence in the car enabled me to make a second run under the most trying conditions ever encountered. I hope never to make another such run."

Inspection of the tyres after the run showed that the back tyres especially had hardly a spot as big as the end of a finger not cut. Otherwise the machine was in perfect condition, and stood up marvellously under the severe strain of going faster than any car before.

Appalling Hazards

With sea shells ripping the tyres, mist clouding the windscreen and the wind, at such a terrific speed, nearly tearing the goggles from the driver's forehead, a beach bumpy and irregular in spots, and the sun shining down to add glare to the many hazards, Campbell's record stands as the most amazing ever made, not only in point of miles per hour attained, but likewise because of the conditions under which he piloted "Blue Bird."

A doctor bandaged his arm after the run against further pain from strained ligaments, and found Campbell nearly exhausted from his battle with the giant machine.

The British driver said, "I know what 'Blue Bird' can do, and you may say I am very disappointed over the record, but feel fortunate in escaping with life under treacherous conditions that made the ride terrible. It gave me the feeling that I was 'for it' more than once, especially when, suddenly, I found myself off the narrow course with visibility less than 2 secs. ahead."

A solid wall of humanity, numbering many thousands, lined the 11-mile speedway to see the record runs, and gasped, then cheered, at the maddest dash ever made on land.

Campbell Returning Home

DAYTONA BEACH,
February 23.

CAMPBELL called off plans to-day for record trials from a standing start 1 mile and 1 kilometre on doctor's orders, due to sprained ligaments in left forearm previously mentioned. He said: "I am bringing my trials to an end before I should have chosen, but I hope to return next year and try again."

Speed Over the Kilometre

DESPITE considerable variations in the figures given for the speed (in m.p.h.) over the kilometre, the following figures for the times set up by Sir Malcolm appear to be unquestioned, viz. :—

South, 8.18 secs.; north, 8.24 secs.; mean, 8.21 secs.

The mean time over the mile was

Not a dance of victory—but simply donning overalls.

13.23 secs. If this be multiplied by the usual conversion factor of .6214 (representing the ratio between one kilometre and one mile), it will be found that *for the same speed,* Sir Malcolm's mean time for the kilometre would have been 8.22 secs. It therefore appears to be definite that his actual mean speed was higher for the kilometre than for the mile.

Using the same conversion factor our own calculations for the speed attained over the kilometre yield the following results, which agree closely with the figures cabled by our correspondent from Daytona :—

KILOMETRE RESULTS.

	Time secs.	Our Calculation k.p.h.	m.p.h.	Cabled Results m.p.h.
South	8.18	440.09	273.47	273.463
North	8.24	436.89	271.48	271.472
Mean	8.21	438.48	272.47	272.463

Very slight differences in the conversion factor employed naturally make quite a material difference to the speed calculated in m.p.h. However, the American Bureau of Standards accepts a definition of the yard in terms of the international metre, as being represented by 1 metre = 39.370000 ins., and this corresponds to the factor (.6214) which we have employed.

The Land Speed Record Explained

IT is not generally known that the expression " land speed record " is a general term for describing the fastest time ever accomplished over an approved distance, and that irrespective of whether it is, for example, a kilometre or a mile the fastest speed attained is the " land speed record." Thus the new figure over the kilometre is 272.463 m.p.h., which is higher than the speed for

Sir Malcolm Campbell watches his mechanics change wheels before he made a trial run some days before his successful record attempt.

CAMPBELL SECURES THE LAND

the mile—272.108 m.p.h. In reality, the speeds obtained rank merely as world's records for the distances in question.

The History of Campbell's Six Attempts

FOR the sixth time in eight years Sir Malcolm Campbell has broken the world's land speed record. At Saltburn Sands, in 1925, with a 350 h.p. 12-cylinder Sunbeam, his speed over a kilometre was 150.869 m.p.h. Two years later, at Pendine, with the original "Blue Bird," powered with a 450 h.p. 12-cylinder Napier-Lion engine, he raised the figure to 174.224 m.p.h. The late Sir Henry Segrave increased this figure the same year to 203.790 m.p.h. at Daytona, but in 1928 Campbell regained the record at 206.956 m.p.h. A few weeks later, however, the late Ray Keech secured the record for America at 207.552 m.p.h. In 1929 Segrave went to Daytona with the "Golden Arrow," beating the American by a margin of over 23 m.p.h.—231.44 m.p.h.—while at the same time Campbell journeyed to Verneuk Pan, South Africa, where he was unsuccessful in surpassing Segrave's figures. After a lapse of two years Campbell, in 1931, again went to Daytona with the "Blue Bird," once more redesigned, and beat the record easily—246.086 m.p.h. for the kilometre.

Although there was no other contender for the title he renewed his attack in 1932 and eclipsed his previous effort by raising the speed to 253.968 m.p.h.

Another Account of the Record Run
(From Reuters' Special Correspondent.)
DAYTONA BEACH, FLORIDA.
February 23.

"IT was the worst ride I ever had in my life," said Sir Malcolm Campbell, when interviewed by Reuters after his record-breaking effort here yesterday, when he sent his "Blue Bird" car over the measured mile at a new world record speed of 272.108 m.p.h.

Sir Malcolm actually set up three new world records, for in addition to putting up new figures for the mile, he broke the record for the kilometre with a mean speed of 271.636 m.p.h. and also for the five kilometres an average mean speed of 257.295 m.p.h.

"The beach was so rough that on several occasions I thought I was done for," he said. "If the car had not responded so magnificently to my touch I should have landed either among the sand dunes or in the ocean."

It was revealed that Sir Malcolm drove the car with one hand only. He had sprained his wrist last week while making some repairs to the car and he was forced to drive yesterday with only one hand.

In these circumstances, Sir Malcolm took terrific risks, for the beach was also in poor condition.

Mechanics at Daytona Beach getting ready to motion by compressed air

"At no time was 'Blue Bird' running with throttle fully opened," he said. "I was not able to let her all out. There is no doubt that the car would have done much better under favourable conditions.

"The car swayed so much from side to side that I dared not put my foot down on the accelerator until I had almost reached the measured mile. As it was, I hit two guide

AIR SCOOP TO SUPERCHARGER

TORQUE REACTION MEMBER

WATER TANK

2,500 H.P. 12 CYL. ROLLS-ROYCE ENGINE

RADIATOR

JACK HOUSING

SUPERCHARGER

SUB-FRAME

CLUTCH

engine for a trial run. The engine is put in
by a 5 h.p. Petter engine.

posts, which were smashed, to
smithereens."

"Blue Bird" was timed at 13.16
secs. for a speed of 273.556 m.p.h.,
beating last year's figures of 267.459
m.p.h. for this run by over 6 m.p.h.

After stopping and turning the car
Sir Malcolm made an inspection of
his engine and tyres. Finding them
quite in order he jumped into the
cockpit and flashed off again on the

northward run. There were no head
winds to hinder him on the return
run.

His speed for the run north was
270.676 m.p.h., nearly 30 m.p.h.
faster than last year's figures of
241.77 m.p.h. Sir Malcolm was
timed at 13.60 seconds on the second
run.

[It will be noted that the figures given
by Reuters differ from those previously given. There are also variations in the speeds published in
various papers. See page 141.—ED.]

Future Record Attempts—Why Four-wheel Drive Will Be Necessary

SPEEDS in the neighbourhood of
300 m.p.h. involve the expenditure of such prodigious power that
the problem of providing adequate
wheel adhesion becomes extremely
difficult. Sir Malcolm Campbell and
Mr. Reid A. Railton have, indeed,
said that had funds permitted they
would have put in hand an entirely
new chassis with four-wheel drive
instead of merely rebuilding "Blue
Bird" to suit the Rolls-Royce engine.

The ascertained facts regarding
Sir Malcolm's two runs, supplemented by a rough calculation of
the forces involved, show clearly
that the margin of safety in respect
of rear-wheel adhesion was ex-

tremely narrow. Foreseeing this, the
designer had concentrated as much
of the weight upon these wheels as
was consistent with the necessity of
adequate adhesion for steering purposes. Even so, the bumpy condition of the sands resulted in excessive wheelspin which might well
have had serious consequences. It
is really remarkable that the
Dunlop tyres withstood this strain,
together with the cutting action of
the shells with which the beach was
strewn. Extra adhesion could not
be provided by any tricks with tyre
treads; the speed is so great that
unless the tyres were made extremely thin they would tear themselves to pieces by centrifugal force.

An interesting point is that no
differential is employed in the
"Blue Bird" back axle. Consequently,
when one wheel momentarily loses
adhesion—and there must have been
many occasions upon which this
happened—the whole power of the
engine is transmitted through the
opposite wheel and tyre.

If and when another record-
breaking car is projected, there is
no doubt that four-wheel driving will
be adopted. This principle, in addition to providing the extra adhesion
which is so badly needed, would undoubtedly enhance the stability of
the car, making it much safer to
drive.

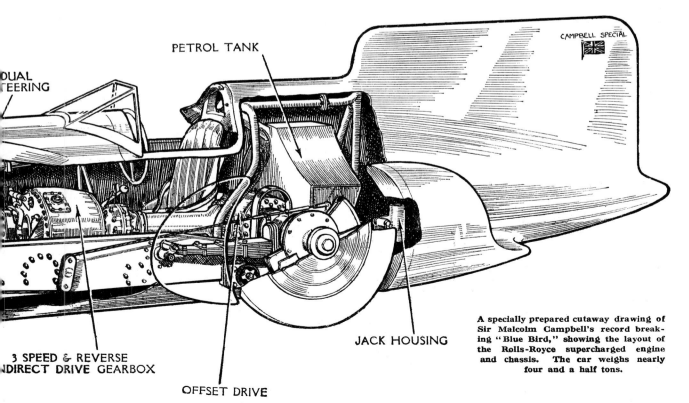

PETROL TANK

DUAL
STEERING

CAMPBELL SPECIAL

JACK HOUSING

3 SPEED & REVERSE
INDIRECT DRIVE GEARBOX

OFFSET DRIVE

A specially prepared cutaway drawing of
Sir Malcolm Campbell's record breaking "Blue Bird," showing the layout of
the Rolls-Royce supercharged engine
and chassis. The car weighs nearly
four and a half tons.

A side view of "Blue Bird" which conveys some idea of the length—27 feet.

Consequently, although rear-wheel driving has sufficed up to now, it is quite clear that much greater adhesion will have to be provided for future attempts; the only way in which this can be done is to convey the drive through a greater number of wheels.

To devise a four-wheel transmission without increasing the frontal area or departing from a trim, streamlined form, will tax the ingenuity of the designer to the utmost.

Some Facts and Figures

The mean speed of Campbell's mile figure is only .94 secs. faster than last year, although the increase in speed is 18.140 m.p.h. Had he improved upon his new mean time of 13.23 secs. by less than 1½ sec. he would have averaged 300 m.p.h.

272 m.p.h. = 4.53 miles per minute = 377 ft. per second.

London to Brighton in 10 mins. 24 secs.

Round the world, at the equator, in 92 hours.

Engine turning at 3,000 r.p.m.; rear wheels at 2,500 r.p.m.

Top gear ratio, 1.2 to 1; three-speed gearbox; final drive by spiral bevels; no differential.

Specially made Dunlop tyres running at 125 lb. per sq. in. inflation, tested at the factory up to 310 m.p.h.

A 4½-ton car with stored-up energy amounting to over 20 million foot-pounds at maximum speed.

Wheelbase, 13 ft. 8 ins.; track, 5 ft. rear, 5 ft. 3 ins. front; overall length, 27 ft.; length of engine, 7 ft. 7½ ins.

Features of "Blue Bird"

"BLUE BIRD"—the world's fastest car—was built for Captain Sir Malcolm Campbell in the precincts of Brooklands track by Thomson and Taylor, Ltd. to the designs of Mr. Reid A. Railton, of that concern. Its success represents an outstanding triumph, not only for the designer and the mechanics who painstakingly assembled the chassis, but also for the suppliers of the many vital accessories upon which the safety of the car depended.

Tribute must also be paid at the outset to the Rolls-Royce Schneider Trophy aero engine, the exceptional power-weight ratio and reliability of which are the envy of engine designers the world over.

Considering the power output—some 2,350 b.h.p.—this engine is decidedly compact, but nevertheless its length made considerable alterations to the chassis as compared with the Napier-engined car used in the 1932 attempt. The shape of the present car is really based upon the frontal area of the engine and the accommodation required by the driver. The beautiful aluminium-panelled body, or fairing, which presents a smooth, uninterrupted surface to the flow of air, was built by Messrs. Gurney Nutting on the basis of a model which had been subjected to wind tunnel experiments.

In general design the chassis follows the lines of an orthodox car with the engine in front and a transmission comprising a plate clutch, three-speed gearbox, enclosed propeller shaft and bevel-driven back axle. The transmission is, however, offset so as to permit the driver to sit low down alongside the torque tube.

A vital link in the system which converts engine power into propulsive effort is found in the rear tyres, which not only withstood the literally enormous disrupting effect of centrifugal force, but had also to convey over 2,000 h.p. from the wheels to the sand. These tyres were specially built at Fort Dunlop from Egyptian cotton and selected rubber, while the bead wires which retain the covers on the rims are of high-tensile steel, with a strength of 150 tons per sq. in. In the course of tests at the factory it was found that the tyre temperature increased at a rate of 40 degrees Centigrade per minute at maximum speed. In the actual record run, however, the heating effect may have been minimized by the cooling action of the damp sands and by the rush of air.

Figures like these emphasize the fact that the car is designed throughout for a sprint over a relatively short distance and, indeed, very many of the parts would not stand up to maximum power for more than

a brief interval of time. Thus, parts such as bearings and gear teeth, when heavily loaded, increase rapidly in temperature, as does also the oil with which they are lubricated, so that had the run been prolonged a bigger factor of safety would have been necessary, which would naturally have added considerably to the weight of the car.

A close resemblance to a chassis of orthodox design is found also in the suspension system, which consists of four Woodhead semi-elliptic springs fitted with Silentbloc bushes and damped by Andre shock absorbers. Then, again, the brakes are of Alford and Alder design, with Wilmil alloy shoes, and are lined with Duron fabric (as are also the Tyzack clutch plates); they are applied by a Clayton-Dewandre vacuum servo motor.

The steering gear is duplicated, with a direct connection to each of the front wheels, and is operated by a Marles reduction mechanism; other interesting chassis features are found in the frame, by John Thompson Motor Pressings, Ltd., the E.N.V. final drive, the David Brown gearbox, Gallay petrol tank, Serck radiator and Ace wheel discs. B.N.C. and B.N.D. alloy steels by Firth Brown, Ltd., are used for many parts of the engine and transmission, the numerous ball bearings are of Hoffmann manufacture, Tecalemit chassis lubrication is employed, and Newall bolts and nuts are used throughout.

Other important accessories which contributed to the success of the venture are K.L.G. sparking plugs, Castrol oil, Smith instruments and batteries, B.T.H. magnetos, Petro-Flex petrol tubing, a Cox windscreen, Triplex glass and Moseley Float-on-Air upholstery. The engine ran on a special grade of Pratts Ethyl fuel. The wood for the body was supplied by L. Bamberger and Sons.

"Blue Bird" on View

IMMEDIATELY "Blue Bird" arrives back in England it will be on view to the public at the premises of A. W. Gamage, Ltd., Holborn, E.C.1. The date will be announced later.

TESTED AT 310 M.P.H.

How they made Sir Malcolm Campbell's Tyres

THE tyres on which Sir Malcolm Campbell will attempt to break his own speed record, run at a temperature twenty per cent. cooler than any tyres hitherto made for him at Fort Dunlop.

"Very rapid heat generation is one of the main factors tending to destroy tyres like these," we were informed by a Dunlop official last month. "At 280 miles an hour the Blue Bird's wheels revolve about 2,500 times a minute, or 42 times a second and continuous hammering of the sand at that rate naturally generates heat very rapidly.

driven steel flywheel upon which they run. This machine is controlled from a room containing the switch gear, separated from the machine itself by a steel plate shield and the progress of tests is watched through peepholes in this shield.

"It was found in this test house that the tyre temperature rose about forty degrees centigrade per minute. That shows the very rapid heating at speed, although during an actual record attempt on sand there are other considerations to be taken into account. On the one hand, as sand is a deformable flat surface, the

materials and construction of this year's tyres which make them better than any yet made is the manufacture of the cord twist, made from specially selected Sakellarides Egyptian cotton fibre and specially woven, which now during flexing absorbs less power than before and is therefore cooler running. Relatively hard spots which would overheat the tyre locally at high speed have also been avoided by having the inner tubes specially made so as to be absolutely uniform in thickness round the circumference.

"In addition to rapid heat generation the other main problem with such tyres is how to cope with the effects of the high centrifugal force created during a speed bid. The tension in the wire coil of each bead due to centrifugal force is approximately seven tons and the tension in the side wall, tending to tear it from the bead wires is approximately 1,250 lbs. per inch width. Special high tensile bead wire, with a strength of 150 tons per square inch, has been used for this year's tyres, and the tread, which is made from raw rubber taken from a special blend reserved for racing tyres, is very thin, partly to avoid the tendency of high centrifugal force to throw the tread off the casing. A further improvement this year is the use of a special compound for the outer covering, the better to resist cutting and reduce the rasping action of the sand.

"Another effect of centrifugal force is to cause the tyre to increase approximately one inch in diameter at 250 miles an hour, even with the very high inflation pressure of 125 lbs. to the square inch. Manufacturing processes for the present covers have been improved in the direction of reducing the tolerance allowed on size to produce greater accuracy in shape, and so truer running, and the whole tyre shape has been modified to give a larger contact area during running and therefore distribute the stresses more evenly in the tyre."

All materials used for the tyres have been put through a laboratory test at each stage before being passed on to the next stage. Five factory departments have been concerned in making the tyres, and fifty operatives have handled the material for them.

Taking the temperature of one of the tyres after a test equivalent to a speed of 310 m.p.h. The massive steel driving flywheel can be clearly seen.

"The tyres about to be used on Daytona beach have each been tested on a special machine on which tyres can be run on load at speeds up to 310 miles an hour. Here tyre and wheel, the latter made at Coventry in the Dunlop rim and wheel works, and dynamically balanced at speeds of over 200 miles an hour, are mounted on a loaded arm which allows them to rest on a massive electrically

area of contact is much greater than on our testing machine. On the other hand, Daytona beach sand is usually damp and helps to cool the tyres; moreover, while on the testing machine a tyre carries a vortex of air round with it, whereas during a speed bid the air rushing past the tyre at over 250 m.p.h. causes very considerable cooling.

"Among the improvements in the

THE MOTORISTS' "PERMANENT WAY"

THE recent article in our columns on "Roads," has elicited many queries and comments of appreciation from our readers, who will shortly be able to see for themselves a very informative talkie film on the history of the motorists "permanent way." At the British Industries Fair at Birmingham the British Road Tar Associations stand will contain a comfortable little cinema theatre with tip-up seats, capable of accommodating 50 people at a time. Six times daily, lasting for 35 minutes, two films "The Highway" and "From Coal Mine to Road" will be shown.

"The Highway" traces the history of the roads from the rough sandy track of prehistoric times to the broad arterial road of to-day. It opens with some attractive "shots" of early transport—ancient British huntsmen returning with their "kill" on a sledge; pillion riding in the days when roads were impassable to wheeled traffic; and coaching scenes on the road to Bath.

The introduction of the wheel by the Romans was the start of the "Great War" between wheel and road. With the advent of the motorcar the wheel launched its heaviest attack, and the film gives

glimpses of motoring as it used to be, over roads thick with dust or deep in mud, with potholes every few yards.

But when things are at their worst, the roads are saved by British tar. Dust and mud are banished, and for the first time British roads are built strong enough to resist the "onslaught" of the wheel.

The film ends with excellent "shots" of arterial roads and by-passes, giving a vivid picture of the speed and weight of the traffic—cars, buses and heavy goods vehicles—which flows along them day and night in an unending stream.

NEWS FROM THE U.S.A.

THREE AMERICANS TO CHALLENGE ENGLAND'S SPEED SUPREMACY?

AFTER having been absent from competition for the world's one mile speed record for five years, it now appears that the United States will make a determined effort to wrest the record from Great Britain in 1934. Three famed figures in the American motor-racing world intend constructing machines for this purpose. They are Gar Wood, International speedboat champion, J. M. White, builder of the ill fated Triplex that set a 207 m.p.h. in 1928, and Harry Miller, well known race-car designer and builder. America's failure to stage an attempt to regain the record has not been due to lack of courage in its drivers, or initiative among its designers. The greatest cause for this failure is the present economic depression.

In addition, the deaths of Frank Lockhart in 1928, and Lee Bible in 1929, cast a pall of gloom over American lovers of speed, and the belief spread that high speed trials were impractical and did not contribute to the progress of the automotive industry. Now, the ease with which Sir Malcolm Campbell has catapulted down the beach has revived interest.

Gar Wood has offered to loan his giant Packard super-charged motors to young Billy Arnold for the purpose of building a challenger for the land record. Arnold and Wood have not yet announced plans for the car, but it is expected to be one of the largest speed mammoths ever to skim Daytona sands, if built.

J. M. White brought a crude-appearing machine, known as the 36 cyl. Triplex, to Daytona in 1928, and in March 1928, Ray Keech flashed down the beach to a new record of 207 m.p.h., astounding critics and fans alike.

The next spring, the late Sir Henry Segrave set a record of 231 m.p.h. in his " Golden Arrow," and White announced his Triplex would shoot for the record in a few days. Bob McDonogh had been offered the car, but turned it down on the advice of his manager, Tommy Milton. Wilbur Shaw, a new comer to racing, was offered the mount, but was under suspension of the A.A.A. at the time, and

By our American correspondent
T. MERIWETHER-SMITH.

could not drive. Finally, White turned the car over to Lee Bible, a garage owner in Daytona Beach, with little racing experience. The test ended in tragedy, when Bible lost control of his car at over 200 m.p.h., being killed instantly.

Three or four years ago, White said he was drawing up plans for a racing machine to regain the speed title. It would be a four-wheel-drive giant, capable of 500 m.p.h. (?). Then the Philadelphia truck designer disappeared from the public eye. This year, as Sir Malcolm set his new record at Daytona, White announced that he would have his car ready for the 1934 trials. No details were given.

Barney Oldfield announced his intention of trying for the record over a year ago, in a machine to be built by Harry Miller. Oldfield has indicated recently that he has far from dropped his plans, and it seems that 1934 will find the veteran at Daytona with a 24-cylinder, 6,500 pound car.

Original plans for the machine called for a super-streamlined car, with glass enclosed cock-pit, of 24-cylinders, developing 3,000 h.p. at 4,000 r.p.m. It would be

---

Announcement

In response to many requests from our readers for a regular bulletin of motor racing news from the United States, we have pleasure in announcing that we have secured the services of Mr. Taylor Meriwether-Smith as our American Correspondent. Mr. Meriwether-Smith has been intimately connected with motor racing for some years, and his notes will form a regular feature in " Motor Sport " in the future.

---

a four-wheel-drive car, with three super-chargers and six magnetos on its three banks of eight cylinders each. The car would be approximately twenty-six feet long, five feet less than Kaye Don's " Silver Bullet."

Oldfield announced his intention of driving this car himself, but it is believed that some young driver will get the car if it is ever built. " Stubby " Stubblefield, husky California star, seems to be the logical choice, as he has had world's of experience in all types of driving. Oldfield completed models of his car, and subjected them to exhaustive wind-tunnel tests last year.

The announcement of Hubert Scott-Payne's challenge for the Harmsworth motorboat trophy this year has caused widespread interest throughout the United States. It has been feared that no challenge would be made this year. Gar Wood is expected to use exactly the same Miss America that defeated Kaye Don at Detroit last summer. There is much speculation here as to the mechanical features of the new English boat.

Egbert " Babe " Stapp is busy completing a car in which he hopes to shatter Stubblefield's 148 m.p.h. record for 4-cylinder, non-supercharged cars. The machine is powered with a Miller motor, and has a unique, streamline body. Stapp is expected to drive the car in the Indianapolis classic in May, also.

Prominent racing drivers are very busy these days, preparing cars for the opening of the A.A.A. Championship season. The first race, which takes place on April 23rd, will be held over the Oakland Speedway in California. Bob Carey, National Champion of 1932, will be defending his honours for the first time, and is undecided whether to use his new 4-cylinder motor, or his old " 8," which carried him to last season's victories.

There are no indications thus far, that foreign competition will be seen at the Indianapolis race. It is possible, however, that three American drivers will compete abroad this year, one at the Nurburg Ring in Germany, the remaining pair at Monza, Italy.

BLUE BIRD

A CAR like the Blue Bird does not differ so fundamentally from the ordinary touring car as some people imagine. Its main features are really much the same, although their relative positions are rather different. Generally speaking, in an ordinary car the problem is to keep the machinery out of the way of the body and the passengers, while in Blue Bird the aim was to keep the machinery and the one passenger out of the way of the body. These two divergent claims naturally result in rather different-looking vehicles, although the general principles of construction are exactly the same.

It is pretty generally known that, in the case of a motor car going at a high speed, nearly all the power of the engine is being used to overcome the resistance of the air. The resistance offered by the friction of the tyres on the ground and by the internal working of the tyres themselves is comparatively small.

Some idea of the actual pressure of the air on the body may be gained by picturing the force required to push a two-ton lorry up Porlock Hill. Going a step farther, one gets a startling impression of the enormous power of the Rolls-Royce engine when one realises that it can overcome this enormous pressure and, given ideal circumstances, maintain a speed of 300 m.p.h. against it. This all means roughly that the fastest car will be the one with the most powerful engine in the smallest body.

Now, while it is comparatively cheap to build a special body to suit a given engine, it is very expensive indeed to build a special engine to suit a given body; and it is for this reason that these world's record cars have usually been designed round the best existing engine obtainable. The

Difficulties in Design of Daytona Cars. Some Notes on Sir Malcolm Campbell's Record-Breaker

R. A. RAILTON
Designer of Blue Bird

Mr. R. A. Railton.

Blue Bird in its latest form was designed round both a new engine and an existing chassis. The necessity for using the old chassis placed certain restrictions on the design and performance, but it was decided that the resulting economy of time and money justified these limitations.

The method of arriving **at the** actual shape of the body will perhaps seem disappointingly unscientific. We made an outline model of the chassis, including in it a solid lump of wood representing the *space required* for the driver. The whole model was then liberally plastered with plasticine until nothing could be seen except the wheels.

Next, the plasticine was gradually rubbed down by hand until the corners and knobs on the model could be felt near the surface, all the time keeping the contours as smooth and "streamlined" as possible. Finally, a plasticine nose and tail were stuck on, of such a shape that they merged naturally into the main body, and the whole was faired off to form what appeared to be the most promising shape.

The model was then placed in a wind tunnel to test its resistance, and further minor modifications were made until the shape of least resistance was found. The full-size drawings were made by the body-builders direct from the model.

I hope this makes clear the reason for the peculiar shape of these very fast cars, and it is really in this particular only that they differ fundamentally from the ordinary touring car. There is, however, one important point which does not trouble the touring car designer at all, but which is an ever-increasing difficulty with these big cars as speeds get higher, and that is wheel slip. Most drivers will remember occasions when on icy or very greasy roads they have felt the rear wheels begin to spin while accelerating on the lower gears.

Although Blue Bird is geared very high, is very heavy, and operates on a very hard sand surface, the power of the engine is so great that it only has quite a small margin of adhesion *even in top gear*. In both the lower gears the wheels would definitely spin if the throttle were opened fully. If the surface of the beach were sufficiently uneven to jolt the axle at all excessively there would be immediate wheel slip, and the driver would have to ease the throttle back. This is the chief reason why a successful record attempt can only be made on a nearly perfect surface.

In order to get even this narrow margin of adhesion on Blue Bird, it is necessary to have a certain minimum weight on the driving wheels, and to get this load it has been necessary to use nearly ¾ ton of lead ballast, in addition to lavishing weight in the construction of the chassis and body. An obvious way out of the difficulty is to use the weight on the front wheels by employing four-wheel drive, and it is probable that all world's record cars made in the future will be constructed on these lines.

It is probable that it will never be possible to discover it or to construct a surface so smooth as to prevent occasional wheel spin. Further, it is probable that even a small amount of spin on a tarmac or concrete surface would seriously damage the tyres, thus ruling out the use of such a surface for record attempts. On the other hand, a moderate amount of slip on a sand surface does not seem to damage them. This leads us to appreciate the benevolence of Providence, which equips the only known areas where the records can be made with what is probably the only surface upon which the tyres will stand up!

Too much praise cannot be given to the tyre manufacturers, without whose untiring research and unselfish enterprise these record attempts could not even be attempted. The tyres used are constructed on exactly the same principles as the ordinary commercial article, although the treatment of the materials and the shape of the section are varied to suit the special conditions. At very high speeds the heat generated inside the wall of the tyre so affects the strength of the rubber tread that it is liable to become detached by centrifugal force.

This difficulty is overcome by making the tread very thin indeed, so that its weight is a minimum, and so that it would do no harm if it did fly off. As the heat generated is roughly proportional to the amount the tyre deflects under the weight of the car, this deflection is kept at a minimum by using very high pressures. The actual pressure used in Blue Bird's tyres is well over 100 lb. per sq. in.

One feature of Blue Bird, and of other record-breaking cars, which seems to provoke a lot of interest, is the fin, or vertical plane at the rear of the body. This fin is intended to act like the feathers on an arrow, in the hope of giving it some directional stability independent of the steering gear. The model is sometimes tested

in a wind tunnel, exactly like an aeroplane model, and the fin adjusted until the model automatically keeps its nose pointed into the wind. The analogy with an aeroplane, however, is not a very sound one for several reasons, the most obvious (though not the most important) being that a car nearly always has to encounter a certain amount of side wind, under which condition the theory of the tail fin immediately comes unstuck. Actually, I am doubtful whether this fin does any good at all, and in my view the most important consideration is that it should not be large enough to do any harm. If a fin were *essential* at 250 m.p.h., it seems to me that it would be at least *desirable* at 150 m.p.h., and many cars without fins have been made and driven which show no signs of instability at the latter speed.

One interesting little point which hardly concerns the ordinary car, but which had to be carefully considered in the case of Blue Bird, arises in connection with the enormous torque of the Rolls-Royce engine. With the normal transmission layout, to which we were already committed in Blue

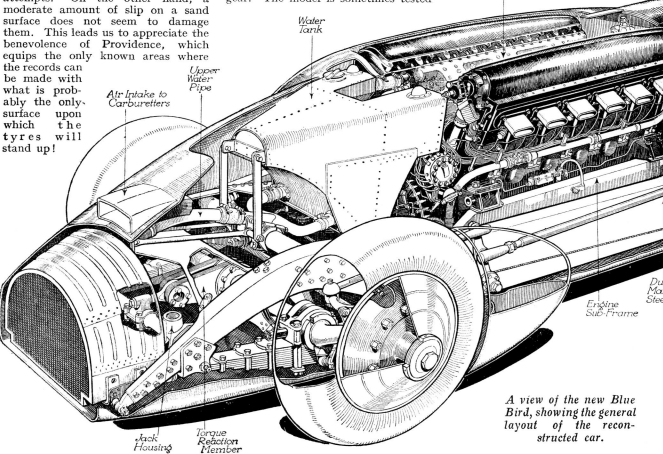

12 Cylinder, 36,582cc.
supercharged
Rolls-Royce Aero
Engine

Water
Tank

Upper
Water
Pipe

Air Intake to
Carburetters

Dual
Marle
Steer.

Engine
Sub-Frame

Jack
Housing

Torque
Reaction
Member

A view of the new Blue Bird, showing the general layout of the reconstructed car.

Bird, the torque-reaction is all the time tending to make the car heel over sideways, and is only resisted by the road springs. This heeling-over is harmless in itself, but may be rather disconcerting to the driver if the throttle is opened or closed suddenly.

On Blue Bird the springs are so set that when the engine is not pulling the car is heeling over slightly in the opposite direction, so that when the power is applied the car is more nearly on an even keel. In addition to this, the road springs are sufficiently strong and the shock absorbers sufficiently powerful to make this torque reaction nearly un-noticeable to the driver.

Up till recently the space available at Daytona Beach has been sufficient to enable a car to cover the measured mile and to pull up fairly comfortably without any very violent application of the brakes.

Speeds are now getting so high, however, that the ordinary type of

brake, as fitted to Blue Bird, is only just capable of stopping the car before it reaches the end of the Daytona track. There is no difficulty in designing brakes that will do what is required. The problem is to find means of cooling them without putting up the air-resistance of the car and so spoiling its performance.

This particular difficulty is only just beginning to make itself felt, and it is to be hoped that before long some place will be found with at least fifteen miles of perfect surface, so that future record attempts may not be hampered by the need for elaborate braking

systems and their possibly attendant risks.

The fuel used in the Rolls-Royce engine is rather different from the ordinary petrol of commerce, but is much the same as that frequently used in racing cars.

It is sometimes thought that the mere use of these special fuels enables any engine to give more power than with petrol. This is quite wrong, and most unfair to the ordinary commercial spirit, which is for all ordinary purposes the better and more economical fuel of the two. It would be more nearly correct to say that special fuels enable a specially powerful engine to develop its power without getting excessively hot inside and so damaging

itself, and that this advantage must necessarily be gained at the expense of economy.

The fuel tanks on Blue Bird hold twenty-eight gallons. It is estimated that the amount of fuel used in warming up and in one run up and down the course will not exceed twenty gallons. Some idea of the rate at which fuel is pumped to the engine may be gained from the size of the petrol pipe, which is one inch in diameter.

A good many people have expressed surprise at the use of an ordinary car-type honeycomb radiator on Blue Bird, suggesting that the "surface" type offers less wind resistance, and quoting Schneider Trophy machines as proof. At first sight this seems very sound, and the reasons why the honeycomb was used may be of interest. To start with, a surface radiator, as its

name implies, should form part of the external surface of the car, and as the total area on Blue Bird which could be used in this way is well under half the total area that would be required, additional radiating surface would be needed in any case. Secondly, it is impossible, in any case, to get anything approaching a perfectly streamlined "nose" for the car, due to the "interference" of the ground and the front wheels. Therefore, the addition of a suitably shaped honeycomb radiator increases the already high head-resistance only slightly.

There are, of course, several ways of cooling the engine for a short period without any external surfaces at all,

but the amount of experimental work required weighed against their adoption on Blue Bird.

The last sentence furnishes the death-warrant of ninety-five per cent. of the brain-waves that one would like to try out on cars like Blue Bird. When it is borne in mind that the driver may have to wait for days or weeks until the Beach is in a suitable condition for even a trial run, and that he may want to go for the record half an hour afterwards in case the Beach is never right again, the need for eliminating any experimental element becomes obvious.

When once one is reasonably confident that the car is sufficiently fast to beat the record, any further alteration is frowned upon, even if it is likely to give another 20 m.p.h., so long as it contains an experimental element which might require three or four trial runs to perfect.

Of course, there are bound to be many experimental features before one can be reasonably sure that the car will do the speed, but they are kept as far as possible in the "definitely right or wrong" category. Anything which by its nature is likely to need much trial and adjustment is avoided like the plague.

Stabilising Fin

Head Rest

Petrol Tank Filler

Pratt

Propeller Shaft driven by Layshaft

Brake Compensation

3-Speed Indirect Drive Gear Box

A SUGGESTED SIX-WHEEL DESIGN FOR RAISING

It is generally conceded that to raise the world's land speed record to 300 m.p.h. or over, wheel adhesion must be improved.
four rear wheels, so providing good adhesion and at the same time permitting of lighter construction and better acceleration
horizontal plane, so as to assist in keeping the tail down and also to provide directional stability. The radiators, as in the case
complete encasement of the driver by a detachable cover, wheel discs enclosing the hub caps and air scoops for the

wing by Bryan de Grineau depicts a suggested design for a potential record-breaker. The car, a six-wheeler, is driven on all
ody, bearing a resemblance to the famous "Golden Arrow," carries at the rear extremity a vertical stabilizing fin and a
Golden Arrow," are mounted between the wheels and at their extremities incorporate fairings. Other features are the
arger intake to the 12-cylinder Vee-type Rolls-Royce Schneider Trophy engine. (Inset) A side elevation of the car.

THE REBUILT BLUE BIRD

Windage Reduced and Wheel Adhesion Improved by Many New and Ingenious Features. Novelties Include Air Brakes, Controlled Streamlining and Twin Rear Wheels. World's Land Speed Record to be Attacked Next Month

(Above) A view which gives a good impression of the great length of Blue Bird (28 ft. 3 ins.) and the smooth contours of the panelling. The two humps represent the overhead-valve covers of the V-type engine.

Sir Malcolm Campbell seated at the wheel of the great car; note the substantial windscreen.

ALTERED almost beyond recognition, Captain Sir Malcolm Campbell's Blue Bird in its latest form has been rebuilt to give a maximum speed of slightly more than 300 m.p.h.

Given seven miles in which to accelerate and an equal distance for braking, Sir Malcolm is confident that this speed could be reached. At Daytona Beach, however, where the attempt is to be made, the course measures but little more than 10 miles, and Sir Malcolm tells us that he is doubtful whether this will prove sufficient. The record which he set up in 1933 was 272.46 m.p.h. over a kilometre.

The series of Blue Bird models now extends back to 1926, and the latest edition is by far the most impressive car ever prepared for a world's speed record attempt. The design reflects great credit upon Mr. Reid A. Railton and the car has been constructed throughout at Brooklands by Messrs. Thomson and Taylor. Exclusive drawings of the car and components

are reproduced on an art-paper inset in this issue, together with the principal measurements and engine specification.

The most striking changes in outward appearance are found in the nose and in the extension of the "bodywork" at each side to the full width of the wheels. As will be seen from the photographs reproduced, both front and rear wheels (the latter fitted with twin tyres this year) now turn in recesses formed in the sheet metal fairing. The nose is of double construction, so providing a slot extending to the full width, which forms a path for the air on its way through an enclosed Serck radiator honeycomb.

The front end of this air slot is fitted with a balanced flap-plate connected by an Arens control to a spring-loaded lever placed on the right of the driver. Just as he approaches the start of the measured mile, Campbell will tip the lever, so closing the slot and reducing the air resistance experienced by the car.

The power unit is once again a 12-cylinder Rolls-Royce aero engine of the V-type, and is mounted just behind the front axle. The panelling fits this unit like a glove, and the bulges which will be noticed along the top surface are the actual overhead-valve covers fitted to the two banks of cylinders. Between the power unit and the radiator there is a large tapering header tank holding a supply of water, and just beneath this there is an intake pipe, facing forwards, through which air passes on its way to the centrifugal supercharger.

Another novel feature is an air brake arranged just behind the rear wheels, which consists of a pair of flaps normally fitting flush with the fairing. When the brake pedal is depressed a valve is opened connecting the suction side of the engine with a very large Clayton-Dewandre cylinder carried in the tail. The piston rod fitted to this cylinder acts through a chain and lever upon a stout tubular cross shaft, and so lifts the flaps out of their recessed positions.

Effect of the Air Brake

It will be appreciated that the flaps hinge upwards like the elevators of an aeroplane, so that in addition to acting as an air brake tending to stop the car, they provide a downward force on the rear wheels, assisting stability.

While the engine, clutch and gearbox are the same components as were used last year, the back axle is an entirely new job. A very interesting point here is the use of two final drives; an arrangement which results in the offside rear wheel being placed about 1½ ins. ahead of the near-side wheel. Consequently, the car may be said to have two "wheelbases" according to the side on which the measurement is taken.

A diagram reproduced on the art-paper inset makes the arrangement quite clear. From this it will be seen that the split steel casing which is used

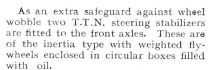

The most impressive of the series of Blue Bird models: the new car which is to commence its journey to Daytona this week.

to house the final drives provides space for two bevel pinions mounted on the propeller shaft. One of these drives a bevel gear connected to the offside wheel and the other meshes with an independent gear driving the near-side wheel. The offset of 1½ ins. is required to give clearance for the teeth. No differential is employed. The cross-shafts are housed in trumpet tubes bolted to each side of the steel housing.

The propeller shaft is enclosed in a short and massive torque tube which is pivoted by a large spherical joint to the rear end of the gearbox. It will be recalled that the box provides an indirect drive on each of the three forward ratios, so that the propeller shaft is offset to a considerable amount as compared with the centre-line of the engine. This arrangement enables the driver to be seated in a low position between the torque tube and the offside frame channel.

To suit this driving position the steering column is brought inwards at an angle from a Burman-Douglas steering gearbox mounted on the side of the frame adjacent to the engine. The column takes the form of a part of a Hardy-Spicer tubular propeller shaft with a universal joint just above the steering gearbox to allow for the slanting position. The rear end of the column is carried in a bearing just in front of the dash and terminates in a Bluemel spring-spoked wheel.

The duplicated steering gear employed last year has been discarded in favour of a straightforward system with a drag link and track rod arranged just as in an ordinary car. The front axle is also entirely new, and has been specially designed to ensure the utmost stability at the ultra high speed which is contemplated. It is a forging of circular section.

Instead of being bolted to the springs in the usual manner, the axle is carried in bronze bearings which, in turn, are supported by housings secured to the semi-elliptic springs. Consequently, brake reactions tending to turn the axle cannot produce a twisting effect upon the springs. In order to prevent the axle from turning under these reactions, it is fitted with a special structure at the centre, the upper part of which is pierced to clear a cross-member of the frame. This structure is pivoted to the centre of the axle and is connected at the top to a pair of stout radius arms.

(Right) The cockpit and steering wheel. The large dial at the top of the facia is a revolution speed indicator with coloured segments for quick reference.

(Below) Like a deep-sea monster; an unusual front view which shows the controlled slot through which air gains access to the enclosed radiator. The central square orifice is the air intake to the supercharger.

As an extra safeguard against wheel wobble two T.T.N. steering stabilizers are fitted to the front axles. These are of the inertia type with weighted flywheels enclosed in circular boxes filled with oil.

The rear axle tubes are carried in bronze bearings fitted to the semi-elliptic springs in much the same style as in the front axle. The frame is underslung at the back, stout steel hoops being provided which encircle the axle tubes at points where these members are fitted with rubber buffers; the maximum frame movement is thereby limited.

The Springing System

The front semi-elliptics are carried beneath the side members, the channels being kicked up to provide clearance for the axle; the rear springs are outrigged and are carried by shackles at each end. These springs, incidentally, are all of the patented Woodhead type and are damped by Andre-Silentbloc frictional shock absorbers. Four of these shock absorbers are employed at the back and six are used at the front. Of the latter set two are outrigged to provide a powerful control of axle movements as shown clearly in one of the drawings reproduced.

The frame is extended forwards and is built up into a structure of considerable strength to carry the radiator and to form the nose of the machine. Here there are bearings for the special flap which closes the air slot when the driver's hand lever is operated, as already explained. Four sockets are fitted at the front and rear of the frame through which jack screws can be run down when it is desired to lift the car for wheel changing. Dunlop tyres are again being employed fitted to bolt-on steel wheels An interesting point is that although the section is the same throughout, the diameter of the two front tyres is somewhat greater than that of the four tyres fitted at the rear.

Double Braking System

The braking system comprises expanding aluminium shoes carrying Ferodo linings, which operate in large ribbed drums fitted to each wheel. Cables connect the brakes to a servo-assisted pedal. As already explained, air flaps are automatically operated when the pedal is depressed.

The panels which form the fairing and "body" have to withstand terrific air pressures and are, therefore, securely mounted upon a structure of welded tubing, which forms a steel skeleton within the outer skin. The space available between the wheels is utilized on the near side to house a 40-gallon fuel tank connected to pumps on the engine by Petroflex tubing. Detachable under-shields are fitted from end to end of the chassis.

The facia fitted immediately in front of the steering wheel carries in the centre a large revolution speed indicator of Smith manufacture. Another large dial records water temperature and smaller instruments show super-charge pressure, oil pressure and temperature, the quantity of fuel in the tank, etc.

In addition to the usual pedals the driver has two hand controls: one to adjust the throttle while warming-up the engine and the other to control a petrol cock. A screw-down valve enables him to cut off the suction if the wind brakes are not required.

A close examination of this remarkable car reveals fine workmanship and extraordinary care for details in every component. It represents a great engineering achievement redounding to the credit of British skill and enterprise, and its courageous driver will have everyone's best wishes when he tries its paces in America.

*   *   *

Apart from the components mentioned by name in the course of this account the following parts are employed :—Dunlop wheels and tyres, Ace discs, Tyzack clutch plates with Ferodo linings, Hoffman bearings, K.L.G. sparking plugs, E.N.V. back axle gears, D.B.S. gearbox gears, Moseley Float-on-Air upholstery, Hadfield front axle and rear axle forgings, shafts, etc. Castrol oil, Guest, Keen and Nettle fold's bolts and nuts, B.T.H. magnetos, and chassis frame by John Thompson Motor Pressings, Ltd. The fuel has been prepared by Pratts' and fire-fighting equipment has been supplied by Pyrene.

An Interesting Forecast

WE reproduce on this page a drawing by Bryan de Grineau of an imaginary record-breaking car, capable of 300 m.p.h., which was published in *The Motor* dated October 17, 1933. The marked similarity between the shape of this car and that of the latest Blue Bird will be noticed.

One of the two flaps which form a wind brake, shown in the raised position.

In order to provide sufficient wheel adhesion Bryan de Grineau proposed the use of four driving wheels on two axles, whereas in the new Blue Bird the wheels are paired at the ends of a single axle. There are other minor differences, but in the main the drawing provides a remarkable forecast of the form which Blue Bird has now taken, 15 months later.

That world-famous designer of high-speed cars, Mr. Reid A. Railton, read a paper before the Institution of Automobile Engineers in December, 1933, in which he described the details of previous Blue Bird models. In the course of the discussion he was asked by Maurice Platt, M.Eng., Technical Editor of *The Motor*, to state an opinion upon the possibilities of four-wheel driving for future attempts upon the record. Mr. Railton replied :—

" Four-wheel drive for racing cars is an interesting proposition. The limit of adhesion on the rear wheels only is being approached, and therefore additional adhesion must be obtained from the front wheels. Acceleration, maximum speed and braking should all be improved, but possibly the chief objection would be the natural hesitancy on the part of the driver to trust a car of new design at high speed. All that would be necessary to design a four-wheel-drive car would be to study the beautiful picture of 'The Future Record-breaker,' a six-wheeler, published in a recent copy of *The Motor*."

The picture to which Mr. Railton referred was the prophetic drawing by Bryan de Grineau, reproduced on this page.

BRYAN DE GRINEAU'S PROPHETIC DRAWING, MADE IN 1933.

NOVEL DETAILS
OF THE
BLUE BIRD
CHASSIS

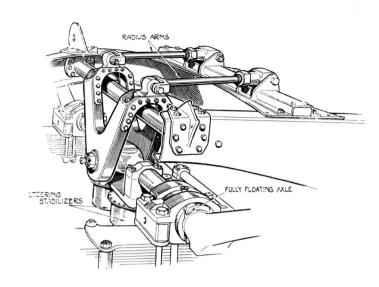

(Right) The front axle floats in bearings formed in the spring anchorages, but its movements are limited by a pair of radius arms pivoted to a cross member of the frame. Steering stabilizers of the inertia type are secured to the axle and are coupled to the track rod.

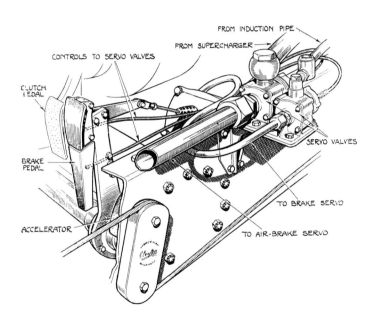

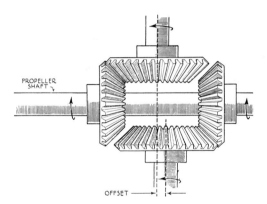

(Above) A diagram which shows the ingenious layout of the duplicated final drive; no differential is used. To provide clearance for the gears, the shafts which drive the rear wheels are offset slightly, as shown.

(Above) The foot controls, showing how the accelerator is tucked away in the side channel of the frame. When the brake pedal is depressed, valves are opened which enable the engine to exhaust air from a servo cylinder, which assists the driver, and from a large cylinder at the back which operates the air-brake flaps.

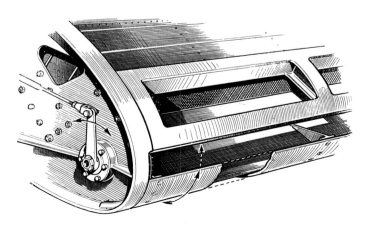

(Right) The slot in the nose which admits air to the enclosed radiator is fitted with a flap. By operating a hand control the driver can close the slot as the car enters the measured mile, so improving the streamlined flow of air past the nose and reducing wind resistance.

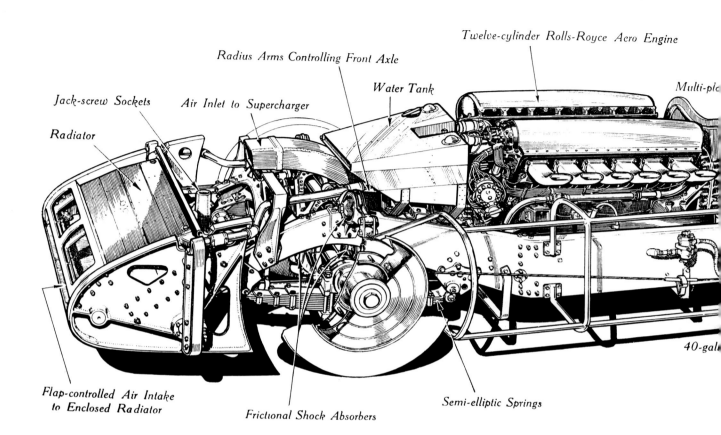

Twelve-cylinder Rolls-Royce Aero Engine

Radius Arms Controlling Front Axle

Water Tank

Multi-pl

Jack-screw Sockets

Air Inlet to Supercharger

Radiator

40-gal

Flap-controlled Air Intake to Enclosed Radiator

Frictional Shock Absorbers

Semi-elliptic Springs

IN the cut-away drawing displayed above the skeleton structure of steel tubing which carries the panelling is shown, but the panelling itself has been omitted in order to reveal the mechanical details. The shape of the completed car is made clear by the sketch reproduced on the right. It will be noticed that the fairings extend to the full width over the wheels and wind-tunnel tests have shown this shape to be most effective in reducing windage. Another novel feature is the provision of a control by which the driver can close the air intake to the radiator, so as to improve the streamline flow when covering the measured mile.

A supercharged Rolls-Royce engine of the famous Schneider Trophy type is again employed and the gearbox and clutch remain unchanged. New transmission features include the use of twin rear wheels and a duplicated final drive, details of which are given on the page which follows.

The immense strength of the frame will be noticed ; the side members pass beneath the rear axle and are upswept forward of the engine to clear the front axle. The latter component is controlled by radius arms. The car is carried by semi-elliptic springs, damped by powerful frictional shock absorbers The driver's seat is mounted in a low position alongside an offset torque tube.

To cope with the relatively short distance available for retardation after covering the measured mile, the mechanical braking system is supplemented by air flaps which are operated by a large vacuum servo cylinder mounted in the tail. These rise out of recesses into the airstream when the brake pedal is depressed and create a downward thrust on the rear wheels in addition to producing an effective resistance to motion. Full details of this most interesting car are published elsewhere in this issue.

Special Facilities were accorded to " The Motor " to prepare the exclusive mechanical drawings reproduced in this inset.

MALCOLM CAMPBELL'S NEW CAR

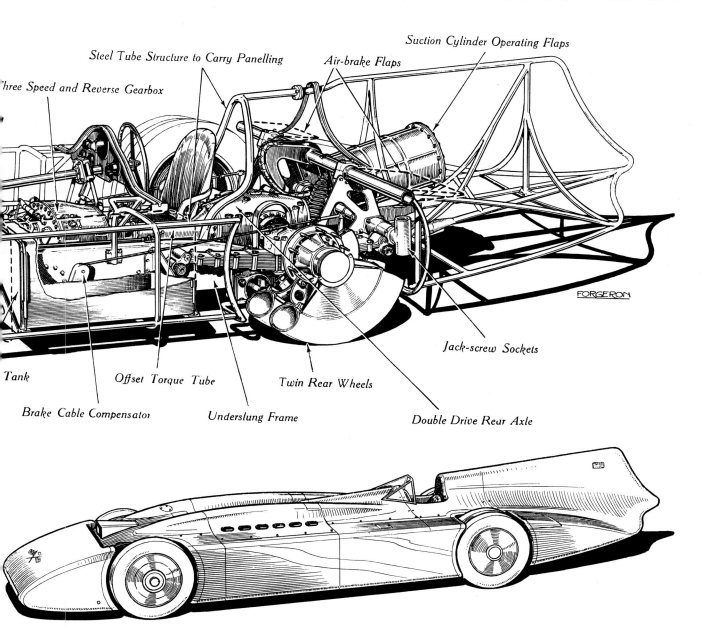

Suction Cylinder Operating Flaps

Steel Tube Structure to Carry Panelling

Air-brake Flaps

Three Speed and Reverse Gearbox

FORGERON

Jack-screw Sockets

Tank

Offset Torque Tube

Twin Rear Wheels

Brake Cable Compensator

Underslung Frame

Double Drive Rear Axle

ENGINE: Supercharged Rolls-Royce, twelve cylinders, 152.4 mm. bore by 167.64 mm. stroke; capacity 36,582 c.c., R.A.C. rating, 173.28 h.p., approx. output 2,500 b.h.p.; net weight, 1,630 lb.; length, 7 ft. 7½ ins.

TRANSMISSION: Multi-disc clutch; indirect-drive gearbox giving three forward speeds and reverse; enclosed propeller shaft; double final drive with a ratio of 1.19 to 1. Engine speed, 3,200 r.p.m. at 300 m.p.h. approx.

BRAKES: Internal-expanding shoes on all four wheels operated in conjunction with air flaps. Vacuum servo motors used in each case. Both systems controlled by a single pedal.

DIMENSIONS: Wheelbase, 13 ft. 8 ins.; track, 5 ft. approx.; overall sizes, 28 ft. 3 ins. by 6 ft. 11 ins.

WEIGHT: All on, including lead ballast, about 5 tons.

ALL EYES ON "BLUE BIRD"

THE GIGANTIC CAR WITH WHICH SIR MALCOLM CAMPBELL IS TO MAKE AN ATTEMPT TO REACH THE COLOSSAL LAND SPEED OF 300 M.P.H. CLOSE ATTENTION TO DETAIL WORK SHOWS THE IMMENSE AMOUNT OF PREPARATION REQUIRED.

THE mere man in the sports car, so to speak, can only stand in silent wonder before the impressive appearance of " Blue Bird," and his admiration extends to the intrepid man who has already held the world's flying mile and kilometre records on more occasions than anyone else.

When " Blue Bird " was pushed out of Sir Malcolm Campbell's private shed in the Brocklands Paddock on a foggy day in January, it presented a very different exterior from the car which set up the existing record of 272 m.p.h. two years ago. The chief alteration lies in bringing out the sides of the body to the full width of the car, so that the wheels are now completely inset. The " nose " has been correspondingly widened, and the result is a complete transformation. The tail, too, has received attention, and the total effect is a really magnificent example of advanced streamlining.

From End to End.

Let us examine the car, from end to end. The huge nose consists of a Serck radiator, the header tank of which is situated over the front axle. The air intake is in the form of a narrow aperture, and it is in connection with this intake that we come to the first of " Blue Bird's " many ingenious features. A good deal of windage is naturally formed by the aperture, and in order to give the car every chance to attain its maximum speed, mechanism has been provided whereby Sir Malcolm can close a sliding flap over the intake. He will, of course, resort to this action only when the car is about to enter the measured mile, so that the radiator is deprived of its cooling air-stream for the shortest possible time. On the last visit to Daytona the mile was covered in 13.23 seconds, not long enough for any damage to be done by overheating. The flap is operated by means of an Arens control and a spring-loaded lever is placed to the right of the cockpit. It is essential that the process should be a quick and

easy one, for the driver's hands should not leave the wheel for longer than is absolutely necessary.

Ahead of the engine, and projecting through the body proper, is the air scoop leading to the supercharger. This intake curves down below the header tank, behind which we come to the massive Rolls-Royce 12-cylinder engine. The two banks of overhead camshafts are the highest points of the car ahead of the cockpit, and the bonnet fits over them with only a very small clearance, thus forming the two ridges between which the driver has his forward vision. The drive of the 2,350 h.p. engine is taken to the 3-speed gearbox by means of a multi-plate clutch, and thence to a double-drive rear axle of a most ingenious layout. The propeller shaft carries two bevel wheels. The first one drives the right-hand road wheels, while the second is placed so that it just clears the teeth of the right-hand half-shaft bevel. Instead, it connects with the bevel of the left-hand half-shaft. This arrangement results in the rear-wheels being offset to the extent of 1½ inches, an altogether unusual departure.

Behind the cockpit is situated the colossal suction cylinder which operates the air-brakes. The tail itself consists of a light steel tube framework, smoothly panelled. Such is the rough layout of " Blue Bird." Now let us turn our attention to details.

Power !

The Rolls-Royce engine is exactly the same as that used in the victorious Schneider Trophy seaplanes. It is a Vee 12, with a bore and stroke of 156.4 mm. and 167.64 mm. respectively, giving a total cubic capacity of 36,582 c.c. On the basis of the R.A.C. rating the horse-power is 173.28 h.p., and it is calculated that at 300 m.p.h. the engine would be turning over at 3,200 r.p.m., and giving an output of 2,350 h.p. This concentrated power plant weighs 1,630 lbs.

The stubby exhaust pipes, six each side, emerge direct through ports in the bonnet.

The chassis frame, like every component of the car, has been designed to give a wide margin of safety even under the abnormal conditions in which it has to function. Accordingly, it is of exceptionally massive construction and of great depth. It is upswept over the front axle, but dips under the rear axle, which is underslung. Attached to the side members at various points is the framework of steel-tubing which carries the panelling of the body to the full width of the car. The space between the front and rear wheels, outside the chassis frame, is occupied by a 40-gallon petrol tank, the fuel being delivered to the engine by means of Petroflex tubing. Incidentally, a special consignment of Pratts fuel has already been shipped to Daytona from London.

The front axle is a new design. It consists of a circular forging, and is attached to the semi-elliptic springs by means of bronze bearings which, in turn, are carried in housings on the springs. Thus the front axle is fully floating, and the risk of brake reactions twisting the springs is completely eliminated. The axle itself is anchored by a Vee-shaped girder, pivoted at the apex to the axle and attached at each end to radius rods leading to a special cross member.

The springs, both front and rear, are of Woodhead pattern, and are assisted by a veritable battery of Andre-Silentbloc frictional shock absorbers, six in front and four at the rear. With the object of combating excessive axle movements two of the front shock absorbers are outrigged. The rear axle is attached to the springs in the same way as is the front, and in order to limit the amount of frame movement strong hoops are used in conjunction with rubber buffers attached to the axle itself.

Steering Stability.

In an attempt of this sort every part of the car plays a vital part, but certainly no component is more important than the steering gear. On its last run, it will be remembered, " Blue Bird " was fitted with a duplicated steering gear, but this has now been abandoned. In its place we find an orthodox layout of drag link and track rod. A Burman-Douglas steering box is mounted on the chassis frame, and is connected to the Bluemel flexible steering wheel by way of a miniature Hardy-Spicer tubular propeller shaft. The driver sits in a very low position, thanks to an offset transmission, obtained by taking the final drive off the lay shaft, and this necessitates an exceptional slant in the steering column. This is overcome by the use of a Hardy-Spicer universal joint next to the steering-box. The other end of the column is carried in a stout bearing just ahead of the dashboard.

No step must be left undone in designing a car to attain such a colossal speed, and the precaution has been taken of fitting two Titan steering stabilizers on the front axle. These interesting devices work on the inertia system, two small weighted flywheels being contained in circular boxes, and working in oil. Their outstanding merit is that they ensure steering stability without the stiffening in operation which results from the usual pattern.

Sir Malcolm's chief difficulty lies in the all-important question of acceleration and braking. The former is limited by the numerous small shells, with knife-like edges, which unfortunately abound at Daytona. The tyre treads are of necessity extremely thin, not more than 1/16th inch, because a greater thickness would be torn off by centrifugal force. If too much wheelspin is experienced in an effort to make as much use of the available distance as possible, the result might easily be a punctured tyre—an eventuality to be avoided at all costs. This year twin rear wheels are being used, giving greater wheel-grip and less tyre wear. The wheels are covered with Ace discs to assist streamlining.

Wonderful Tyres.

The importance of tyres in this record attempt is paramount, and it is not too much to say that without the special Dunlop tyres the existing record would have been impossible. The greatest possible credit is due to the Dunlop research department in the production of accessories on which the driver depends for his very life.

Now we come to braking. The ideal distance for the record attempt would be 14 miles, for the great car takes seven miles to get into its fastest gait. The acceleration stretch of sand has been improved this year by removing one of the supports of the pier, beneath which the car has to pass. But Sir Malcolm is still left with only three miles in which to pull up his flying steed.

Obviously, heavy pressure on the brake pedal, while the car is travelling at 300 m.p.h. is likely to result in the most untoward eventualities — even though Ferodo brake linings are, of course, being used. You must remember that the car is no normal vehicle in weight, for it scales five tons, including its lead ballast !

For the initial checking of speed, the car is equipped with air brakes in the form of hinged flaps just behind the rear wheels. Once again a servo-system has been brought into play to assist the driver in his difficult battle with wind resistance. The considerable strength required to raise the flaps to a vertical position is derived from a huge Clayton-Dewandre vacuum cylinder carried in the tail. The piston-rod of the cylinder works the flaps by means of a chain and lever on a massive cross-member. Thus the driver will be able to apply a gentle pressure to the brake pedal and the flaps will promptly rise to the vertical. The remainder of the pedal movement is taken in the ordinary way by the servo mechanism of the wheel brake. The latter consist of aluminium shoes with Ferodo linings in great ribbed drums on each wheel. The operation is carried out by cables.

The process of slowing a rapidly moving car is always a tricky one, for the car is deprived of the steadying effect of the engine driving the rear wheels. In the case of " Blue Bird," however, the air-flaps will make up for the loss of this effect. Like the elevators of an aeroplane, they will tend to force the tail of the machine downwards, thereby giving the rear wheels a firm grip on the sand.

Normal Controls.

The cockpit of the car is protected from wind pressure by a stoutly constructed sloping widscreen. The driver sits in a normal bucket seat. Facing him are the Smith instruments, and dwarfing all others is the large rev-counter. One cannot imagine the driver being able to find much time to glance at the rest of the instruments, but they will serve their purpose when the car comes to rest at the end of each run. They consist of a water-temperature gauge, supercharger pressure, oil temperature and pressure, and petrol gauge.

The controls consist of the usual clutch,

brake and accelerator pedals, the latter being tucked away on the inside of the chassis frame. In addition there is a petrol cock, the lever which closes the air stream slots in the nose, a hand throttle for the engine, and a screw-down valve which cuts out the wind-flaps should they not be required.

" Blue Bird " is a masterpiece. All those who have had a hand in its design and construction are to be heartily congratulated on a production—nay, a creation—which reflects the greatest possible credit on British engineering skill. Mr. Reid A. Railton has designed many fine cars in his short career ; certainly he has never designed a more impressive one than " Blue Bird." The same can be said for the firm which has built the car from his designs, Messrs. Thomson & Taylor, of Brooklands.

As for Sir Malcolm Campbell, we can

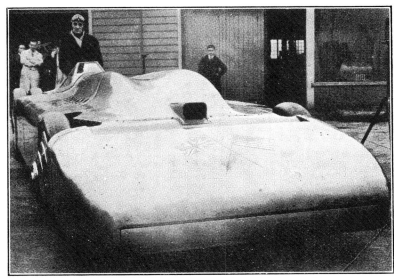

From this angle, " Blue Bird " bears only a faint resemblance to an automobile ! The cooling slot for the radiator is shown here in the closed position.

only join in the general good wishes of all British sportsmen for his complete success in an epic adventure. No man is better equipped for the task, for he has already confirmed many times over his reputation as a driver of skill, determination and courage.

May good luck attend him !

The Components.

Here is the full list of components and accessories used in the construction of " Blue Bird." Every one is of vital importance to the success of the venture, and the mere fact of their being used places a " hall-mark " on them : —Dunlop wheels and tyres, Ace discs, Tyzack clutch plates with Ferodo linings, Hoffman bearings, K.L.G. sparking plugs, E.N.V. back axle gears, D.B.S. gearbox gears, Moseley Float-on-Air upholstery, Hadfield front axle and rear axle forgings, shafts, etc., Castrol oil, Guest Keen and Nettlefold's bolts and nuts, B.T.H. magnetos, chassis frame by John Thompson Motor Pressings, Ltd., Pratts Ethyl fuel, Pyrene fire-fighting equipment.

BRAVO!
SIR MALCOLM TRIUMPHS AGAIN

After Waiting Five Weeks for the Daytona Beach to Smooth Out, Sir Malcolm Campbell Averages 276.81 m.p.h. and Secures World's Land Speed Record for the Eighth Time

Sir Malcolm Campbell. A new portrait by R. E. Poulton, of "The Autocar."

Once more man has travelled faster than man ever travelled before on land. At Daytona on Thursday, March 7th, Sir Malcolm Campbell, with his world-famous "Blue Bird," beat his previous record by 4.35 m.p.h., obtaining a mean speed of 276.81 m.p.h.

It is an extraordinary business, this record, when you come to think of it. Far away, in Florida, five tons of monstrous car, created for this and this alone, makes a run of a few seconds, first in one direction, then the other, in front of a large and enthusiastic crowd and on the very edge of the ocean.

A moment's calculation while the reading of the electrical timing apparatus, whose accuracy is vouched for by international standards, is checked, then the news goes forth by wire all over the world, speed in one direction 272.72 m.p.h., in the other 281.03 m.p.h., average time—not, mark you, speed—giving a record speed of 276.81 m.p.h. Just for those brief seconds the car has been alive, for the rest of the year it is merely inert metal save, perhaps, for a minute or two's exhibition

run. For that over a hundred men have worked hard for quite a number of months.

For the eighth time Campbell's name appears on that long list which gives to history the names of the men who made a motor car go faster than anyone else had travelled before them. It is a wonderful record possessed by no other driver, which will stand in history for ever, and probably no other driver has desired that this should be so more than Sir Malcolm, whose whole energies of recent years have really been concentrate l on this record, and this alone.

It is curious to think of those days of long ago when only almost by an accident was it possible to find out that the maximum speed ever recorded for a car had been beaten, when only a few fervid enthusiasts knew the name of the driver, and scarcely one ordinary man the name of the car. It is a far cry from that to the immense organisation of to-day of talking films, and photographs, and speeches, and banquets, and almost every incident before and after the record being flashed across the ocean to serve as a news paragraph for the nations. In the matter of publicity this record surpasses everything else on earth, which is why, in a way, it is so interesting that the car is sponsored by no particular manufacturer, is, in fact, a monstrous engine with no entailed responsibilities.

When man reached 60 miles an hour the old tale that he was daring the gods, would, in fact, be unable to breathe if he went any faster, was revived ; when Segrave achieved the then miraculous figure of 200 m.p.h., the same story held at his attempt. It has been said again but recently of Campbell ; it will be said when 400 m.p.h. is in prospect.

People will challenge the usefulness of this record, will argue that the risk should not be taken, yet the plain fact still remains that those brief seconds of very high speed are immensely satisfactory ; that the thrill of increased speed does not lessen, but increases, with experience ; that, when all is said and done, there is nothing in the world quite like it. Probably man first had the feeling right away in those distant days when he first rode a horse, and probably it was just as satisfactory.

Sir Malcolm has had really no light task. Daytona, with all that the A.A.A. could do—and they, as usual, did much—is over small for this sort of speed. It was not quite possible to say, even with all Dunlop's reputation, that the tyres could stand the stress. The wind brakes were a novelty, and novelties beget uneasiness. There are too many unknown factors in this attempt for any man to feel comfortable beforehand, and when it is done the credit does not only rest on the designer or the driver, great though their share may be, but is spread also to those responsible for every part of the machine, to the men whose financial aid allowed this attempt to be made, and to the little group of mechanics who worked desperately hard to make sure everything was right.

Early Speed Kings and Cars

The commencement of all this was practically a private battle between the fiery and excitable Jenatzy on an electric car which resembled a large, fat, short torpedo as much as it resembled anything, and the Count Chasseloup-Laubat with another electric car rather like an upturned punt in outline. These two, in the park at Acheres in France, put up, first one then the other, the first flying kilometre times, and started that world's record list which was to grow beyond the wildest calculations of the enthusiasts of those days, just as the speed was to soar far beyond anything the wildest thinking pioneer would have prophesied as possible.

It is a far cry from those queer electric machines capable of one short run before utterly exhausted batteries put an end to further movement ; but how interesting technically are the cars that have followed those two in the list, cars driven always to record the highest speed so far attained on land.

Early ideas of streamlining followed the theory that wind cutting, that is, a wedge driven point forward,

must be the best form of body ; hot and strong was the argument thereon, as first one type then another took the record, and the discussion was the more lively because at regular intervals some utterly unstreamlined car was the fastest for the moment.

The shock created when a Stanley steamer away at Daytona put the record up many miles an hour—its speed is in the accompanying table—can be imagined quite easily, for in one short rush, at the utmost pressure the engine could carry, that comparatively well streamlined machine put the record out of reach for a time. Had that happened in Europe the excitement would have been immense ; as it occurred in America, at Daytona, there instantly arose the suggestion that the timing was wrong, and weird assertions were made as to the length of an American mile, but the facts were indisputable when they were available at last. This was the last great effort of steam, however ; thereafter the petrol engine established a marked superiority.

Queer Methods

There was the Gobron-Brillié which was a great car of its day, and odd because it had two opposed pistons in each cylinder, the upper ones operating a crank where most people now put a camshaft, and the crank being connected to the main crankshaft, on which were the big-ends of the other pistons. Much merit was claimed for this, since the explosion occurred between the two pistons and not between a piston and the stationary head of each cylinder.

It is quaintly told of those days that people used to wait for a day when a strong wind could be used to help the car, and there is an odd story of one man who even with this help could not get his car to beat the record, whereupon those responsible moved one kilometre stone of the course nearer to the other, carefully planting new grass and watering the same until no one would notice the modification, whereupon the record was attempted once more, this time successfully.

But in those days people were not so meticulously careful as they are to-day, when every decimal and every certificate is checked again and again.

In their turn most of the Grand Prix cars took a hand, each in turn raising the record, and then the matter was left to America for the duration of the War. America, by the way, has had a lot of interest in this record, for no less a person than Henry Ford once took the land speed record with a car named " 999," and did it on a frozen lake.

After the War the procedure of records was very much organised, and the business with a strong wind was

BLUE BIRD, the fastest car in the world.

Publicity surrounds every little incident of the record attempt. A curious crowd and camera men follow Blue Bird as it is towed to the beach.

This year the delay before the record could be made was exceptional, the beach was in its worst mood, the elements, as it were, against the attempt. Sir Malcolm arrived on January 31st, and had to be content with what amounted to trial runs in the intervening weeks. These, at all events, allowed him to try out the air brakes, which were successful, and the effect of a black line marked in oil along the centre of the course, which was only moderately so. A slight displacement of the cowling gave the driver an unpleasant shock, as fumes and smoke developed in the cockpit, the exhaust flames giving the impression that the car might be on fire.

The difficulties of a record attempt which is, unfortunately, also regarded as an entertainment, were very strongly emphasised when Sir Malcolm desired to make a run, but the Mayor of Daytona refused to sanction any attempt at all. The possibilities, or otherwise, of the weather and beach conditions at the moment can only be judged accurately by Sir Malcolm and the officials of the A.A.A.   S. C. H. D.

*   *   *

A very good idea of Sir Malcolm's long period of waiting and the world-wide publicity attached to his every move is given by this collection of headlines from the English daily Press :—

JAN. 28th. Sir M. Campbell lands to-day. Off to Daytona at once. JAN. 29th. Sir M. Campbell on his record bid. Tells U.S. "We don't worry." JAN. 31st. Ovation for Sir Malcolm. Daytona hails him as "human bullet." FEB. 3rd. Sir M. Campbell's safety line. Eleven miles long. Blue Bird goes astray. FEB. 5th. Sir M. C. pilots air liner. Visit to Florida

eliminated by making the car run first one way, then the other over the course, and only counting the average in time. Thus arose a misunderstanding, for inquisitive people added up the speeds in miles an hour and so obtained an average differing from the official, which was *concerned solely with time.* In other words, the *speeds* of two runs added together and divided by two does not produce the same mean as the mean of two *times* afterwards converted to speed.

Then, too, came the monsters—first the big twelve-cylinder Sunbeam which Sir Malcolm was afterwards to convert and use again, the big Benz, the Higham, aeroplane-engined cars because war aeroplane engines were easy to get; and so, by degrees, the even more monstrous machines of to-day with as much engine as can be obtained at the moment, and the need for some miles of ground instead of the two kilometres or so of Acheres all those years ago.

There was misunderstanding about the rules at times, some people thinking that a reverse was necessary, whereas it is not by the record rules and must only be fitted if the car attempts the record on a road governed by the ordinary law of the country concerned. That resulted in the weird sight of an American record-breaker carrying two extra rear wheels, driven by a starting motor solely to make the car go backwards enough to satisfy the officials, and, in another case, the arrangement of a small roller between the face of the flywheel rim and a special disc on the cone clutch. By jamming the roller between the two, the car was made to move slowly backwards, the unfortunate roller doing 30,000 r.p.m., but it sufficed.

And so, little by little, man's endeavour to go faster still has been recorded on a sheet of paper.

Daytona beach is narrow for over 200 m.p.h., and in an attempt to give a guide an oil line was marked down the centre. Sir Malcolm superintends.

Fair. FEB. 6th. Blue Bird damaged. Sir M. C.'s anxiety. FEB. 8th. Blue Bird's trial run on Monday. Overhaul complete. Hazards of the beach. FEB. 10th. Sir M. C.'s "slow" test run to-day. To do a mere 200 m.p.h.

FEB. 11th. Blue Bird's test held up. Campbell breaks two records, but track unfit for Blue Bird. FEB. 12th. Plague of worms. Speed attempt held up. Daytona phenomenon. FEB. 14th. Blue Bird flies at 200 m.p.h. FEB. 17th. Sir M. C. still waiting.

FEB. 22nd. Daytona improvement. Sir M. C. still hopeful of record attempt. FEB. 28th. Blue Bird dash likely to-day. Beach "ironed out." MARCH 1st. Record dash likely to-morrow. MARCH 3rd. Campbell misses death twice in two days. Blinded by slipping goggles in 270 m.p.h. "nightmare." MARCH 4th. Beach too bad for Blue Bird. Record dash postponed. MARCH 5th. Lady Campbell stops husband. Drive would have been suicide. MARCH 8th. 276 m.p.h.

BLUE BIRD'S EQUIPMENT

THE equipment of a car designed for a record of this description is more than usually interesting, and it is therefore given in full.

THE WORLD'S LAND SPEED RECORD			
DATE.	DRIVER.	CAR.	SPEED. m.p.h.
1898	Chasseloup-Laubat	Jeantaud	39.24
1899	Jenatzy	Jenatzy	41.42
1899	Chasseloup-Laubat	Jeantaud	43.69
1899	Jenatzy	Jenatzy	49.42
1899	Chasseloup-Laubat	Jeantaud	58.25
1899	Jenatzy	Jenatzy	65.82
1902	Serpollet	Serpollet	75.06
1902	Vanderbilt	Mors	76.08
1902	Fournier	Mors	76.60
1902	Augières	Mors	77.13
1903	Duray	Gobr'n-Brillié	84.21
1903	Ford	Ford	91.37*
1904	Rigolly	Gobr'n-Brillié	93.20
1904	de Caters	Mercédès	97.26
1904	Rigolly	Gobr'n-Brillié	103.56
1904	Barras	Darracq	104.53
1905	Hemery	Darracq	109.65
1905	Bowden	Mercédès	109.75*
1906	Marriott	Stanley	121.57*
1909	Hemery	Benz	125.9
1910	Oldfield	Benz	131.72*
1911	Burman	Benz	141.73*
1919	de Palma	Packard	149.87*
1920	Milton	Duesenberg	156.04*
1922	Guinness	Sunbeam	129.17†
1924	Thomas	Leyland-Thomas	129.73†
1924	R. Thomas	Delage	143.31†
1924	Eldridge	Fiat	145.90†
1924	Campbell	Sunbeam	146.16†
1925	Campbell	Sunbeam	150.86†
1926	Segrave	Sunbeam	152.33†
1926	Thomas	Higham	169.23†
1926	Thomas	Higham	171.09†
1927	Campbell	Napier-Campbell	174.88†
1927	Segrave	Sunbeam	203.79*†
1928	Campbell	Napier-Campbell	206.95*†
1928	Keech	White Triplex	207.55*†
1929	Segrave	Irving Special	231.44†
1931	Campbell	Napier-Campbell	246.09†
1932	Campbell	Napier-Campbell	253.96†
1933	Campbell	Rolls-Royce-Campbell	272.46†

* Over 1 mile. † Average of runs in two directions.

The engine was made by Rolls-Royce, and is very much of the same type as the machines used in the Schneider Trophy seaplanes; the tyres, of course, were manufactured by the Dunlop Rubber Company, who were also responsible for the wheels. The special fuel used was prepared by the Anglo-American Oil Company, Ltd., the oil was Castrol, the clutch plates were made by Tyzack and lined with Ferodo, which material was also used for the brake linings. The big special shock absorbers were manufactured by T. B. Andre, the steering gear by Burman and Sons, Ltd., the steering damper by T.T.N. Patents, the wheel itself by Bluemel. Then the instruments, many of which have specially marked dials, were made up by S. Smith and Sons, the controls by Arens Controls, Ltd., and the brake servo, including the big air cylinder at the back, by Clayton-Dewandre. All fuel piping was Petroflex, the plugs were K.L.G., David Brown and Sons responsible for the gears, and John Thompson for the specially deep side members.

Serck radiators were employed, both for the radiator proper and for its tank. The front and rear axles, with the necessary shafts, were of Hadfields' steel, the road springs were by Jonas Woodhead, Triplex made windscreens and goggles, Cornercroft, Ltd., the wheel discs, while David Moseley's were responsible for the cushions, Guest, Keen and Nettlefold's for all the bolts and nuts, and the British Thomson-Houston Company for the magnetos. Hoffmann made the ball bearings, the E.N.V. Company the rear axle gears, Tecalemit the chassis lubrication system, and Young the accumulators.

From horizon to horizon rushes a machine unlike any other car! F. Gordon-Crosby's impression of Sir Malcolm Campbell's Blue Bird during its record-breaking run.

304 M.P.H. !

SIR MALCOLM CAMPBELL has once again proved to the world the unapproachable superiority of British materials and workmanship, and the matchless determination, courage and skill of British record-breakers.

For the past eleven years, Sir Malcolm has visited the far corners of the earth searching for the course which would enable him to realise his life's ambition to be the first man to travel on land at 300 m.p.h.

The moment he received a report on the unique suitability of the Bonneville Flats for his venture, he made plans to take the " Bluebird " there.

He shipped his famous car over there eight weeks ago, following on the *Majestic* when George Eyston, Staniland and Denly left on their 24 hours records venture.

After the briefest of preliminary trial runs on Monday, September 2nd, Sir Malcolm expressed himself as not only satisfied with " Bluebird " and with the surface, but as extremely optimistic of attaining his goal.

He announced his intention to attempt the new record the following day and at the same time asked the A.A.A. officials to keep both ends of the course clear of spectators in case he should have to swerve in pulling up, should his air-brakes prove ineffectual owing to the altitude at which the course lies.

At the breaking of dawn over the Rockies, 45 miles distant on the horizon, next day, hun-

dreds of private cars could dimly be discerned threading their way to Salduro, and by the time " Bluebird " was brought out, the course was lined by many thousands of enthusiastic onlookers.

Just before clambering into the cockpit, Sir Malcolm gave instructions for the tyre-pressures to be increased all round, as the course was a little soft at either end.

A few minutes later the great car started off on its epic run, the short exhaust pipes emitting flames and black smoke and a mighty crackling rising steadily

This is the sort of film which was taken of " Bluebird's " instruments during her record-breaking dash

to a roar whose note varied as each gear was engaged.

Unbelievably quickly, " Bluebird " drew away to vanish in the distance, its note being plainly audible long after the car itself was out of sight.

The time for that run over the measured mile was 11.83 seconds, and the average speed was 304.311 m.p.h.—the first time man has ever attained five miles per minute on land and within a fraction of the United States aeroplane record of 304.98 m.p.h.

At the end of the first run, one of the front tyres burst at about 280 m.p.h., and the lay press has made much of this incident in a manner which might well prove detrimental to the prestige of British workmanship. But the fact remains that the Dunlop Rubber Company is the only tyre firm in the world which can produce a tyre which makes an achievement such as Campbell's a possibility ; and no praise is too high for the theoretical and practical skill which results in the production of tyres which will stand up to such a gruelling test.

The tyres were changed before the return run and on this the mile was covered in 12.08 seconds at a speed of 298.013 m.p.h.

Thus the mean speed for the two runs works out at 301.1292 m.p.h. against a mean time of 11.955 seconds, and so Sir Malcolm has realised the ambition of his life.

Owing to a number of mistakes, the wrong figures were at first announced which credited Sir

Malcolm with a mean speed of something over 299 m.p.h., but yet short of the 300 m.p.h. goal he had set himself.

Consequently, he planned to make a further attempt on the record the following day ; but happily the necessity for this was obviated by the timely discovery of the timekeepers' error and the figures on the opposite page are those finally issued and which are now lodged with the International body for official confirmation and recognition.

During this magnificent achievement the " Bluebird " carried a small movie camera which recorded the story of the run as told by the dials of the instruments on the dashboard. The camera, a specially made Cine-Kodak Eight automatically " shot " a film, thus making a continuous record of the instrument readings.

This unique idea was Sir Malcolm's own and has never before been tried.

Interviewed shortly before he set sail for America, Sir Malcolm said :
" When I am travelling at

chassis as on the test bench."

The apparatus is in a cabinet 3 feet long, 8 inches wide, 10 inches high. One end of this has a duplicate chronometer, revolution counter, oil and supercharger pressure gauges mounted on facia board which is illuminated by three 24-watt lamps, the current being supplied from a 6-volt accumulator.

The camera is driven by an electric motor and can be instantly removed from the cabinet for reloading with film or testing,

necessary electrical connections.

The pressing of a dashboard switch suffices to bring the apparatus into action.

The film used is Kodak Super-sensitive Panchromatic and is 100 feet in length which will give 8,196 separate pictures each .173 inch by .130 inch. The exposure is made at f/3.5 at eight frames a second, instead of the usual sixteen frames a second, so as to provide as long a run as possible without changing the film.

One loading of the camera will last 16 mins., which was more than ample for Sir Malcolm's purposes, as his run of thirteen miles was done in less than four minutes.

Here is a list showing how Sir Malcolm Campbell has built up his world record speeds since 1923 :—

Date.		Speed. m.p.h.	Place.
June 1924	...	146.40	... Denmark
June 1924	...	150.25	... ,,
Feb. 1927	...	174.22	... Pendine Sands
Feb. 1928	...	206.79	... Daytona Beach
Feb. 1931	...	245.73	... ,,
Feb. 1932	...	253.968	... ,,
Feb. 1933	...	272.108	... ,,
Mar. 1935	...	276.816	... ,,
Sept. 1935	...	301.129	... Salduro, Utah

high speeds it is absolutely impossible for me to watch the instruments. It is taking a terrible chance to take my eyes off the course even for a moment.

" This is unfortunate because the instruments record tremendously important data. I took my problem first of all to the instrument makers, but they were not able to help me, and then I consulted the Kodak people in London, and they have now fixed me up.

" I expect valuable results. For one thing I shall discover whether the engine is giving exactly the same power in the

without breaking any connections, as it is fixed in position by a special type of plug which not only locates the camera so that it is in correct focus, but, in addition, makes the

A New Course

Sir Malcolm Campbell glanced at his watch as he leaned over the rail of the transatlantic liner on his way home from Daytona in 1932. His action underlined the thought running continuously through his mind, like an obsession: the time for the flying mile record he had just set up was only just over two seconds slower than that for 300 m.p.h. The target of the neat round figure of 300 m.p.h., so exasperatingly close, yet actually so far away, was a challenge he found the utmost difficulty in resisting. Besides—and rumours of possible foreign challengers flashed through his mind—he wanted to make quite certain that Britain kept the record. By the time he reached Southampton, his mind was made up: he would try to become the first man to go faster than 300 m.p.h. All his resolution was to be needed, though, if he was to overcome the difficulties, and the disappointments, he was to encounter in endeavouring to reach his elusive goal.

His target of 300 m.p.h., he believed, would require more than one attempt if he was to be successful in achieving it. As a first step, he started to reconstruct *Blue Bird*. The surest way to go faster was to use more power. A much more powerful engine was therefore fitted to *Blue Bird*. This was a Rolls-Royce "R" aircraft engine similar to that used in the Schneider Trophy race. The power output of this sprint type engine was about 2,300-2,500 b.h.p. at 3,200 r.p.m. The cubic capacity of the 12-cylinder supercharged engine was 36,582 c.c. Now that the power had been so considerably increased, the reduction of wheelspin became even more important, and pieces of lead were mounted near the rear axle to help the rear wheels to grip the sands more firmly.

The redesign of *Blue Bird* was the responsibility of Reid Railton. The length of the body was increased, to 27 ft., and the front was modified to improve the streamlining. The changes in design were so major that the Campbell Special *Blue Bird* was largely a new car.

The big increase in the power of *Blue Bird* emphasised, in Sir Malcolm Campbell's thinking, the limitations of Daytona: the shortness of the course was even more disadvantageous now that an even longer run was required to get up the higher speed that the more powerful engine would make potentially possible; and the bumpiness of the surface would dissipate much of the increased power through wheelspin. Despite his misgivings, however, Campbell took *Blue Bird* out to Daytona early in 1933 because he knew of nowhere better to go. While Campbell did not expect to achieve 300 m.p.h. in this first step, he did hope that the greater power of the new engine would take him a good part of the way towards his goal.

The disadvantages of Daytona made themselves apparent, confirming Campbell's earlier fears, as soon as he arrived in Florida. The course was already too short, but storms had reduced its length by almost 2 miles. The weather was so bad that he had to wait 12 days before he could make his first trial run, and, even then, the surface was so bumpy that much power was lost through wheelspin.

The supercharger was so big that difficulty was experienced in streamlining the body, to cut down wind resistance. However, no wind tunnel tests had been carried out during the design of the body, and, as soon as Campbell made his first trial runs, he realised that the streamlining was unsatisfactory; the air currents hitting him in the cockpit told him that the flow of air over the body was not smooth. Not only did the bumpy surface cause wheelspin, but the poor streamlining made the

wheelspin start at a slower speed, about 200 m.p.h., than previously. To make matters worse, he strained his left arm when changing gear on his first run, so that afterwards he had to steer largely with his right arm. In addition, he experienced difficulty in breathing owing to exhaust fumes in the cockpit. Another disadvantage of Daytona was that the temptation existed to make a run, even though conditions were not really suitable, purely to avoid disappointing the big crowd of spectators.

The weather was bad, and the surface was bumpy, on Wednesday 22 February 1933—but Campbell made his attempt around noon despite his reservations, to live up to his announcement of the previous day, so that the crowd did not go away disappointed. Campbell took about 4 miles to get up speed on his first run, travelling south. He found difficulty in seeing too far ahead, owing to the haze; he simply kept his eye on the marker flags, which merged into a solid line, and hoped that no obstacle would appear suddenly out of the mist. The surface was so bumpy that he experienced difficulty in holding *Blue Bird* straight, and he realised the dangers of so narrow a course as he swerved back and forth between the dunes and the Atlantic breakers. His task of holding *Blue Bird* on course despite the bumps was not made easier by his reliance principally on his unsprained right arm; his left arm was so painful that he found difficulty in changing gear. Owing to the bumpiness of the run, he was not able to get the car up to maximum power until shortly before he entered the measured mile. Spray flung up off the sand, and exhaust fumes in the cockpit, did not make it easier to control the wildly swerving car.

The bumpiness of the sand continually threw him upwards and forward against his straps. As he fought to hold his right foot fully down on the throttle pedal through the measured mile, even though he was being bounced about in his seat, he noticed that the rev.-counter indicated a reading showing that the rear wheels were turning at the equivalent of just under 330 m.p.h. However, after he finished his run, he was disappointed to learn that his actual timed speed over the ground was only just over 273 m.p.h. Wheelspin, resulting from the bumps, caused this huge loss of potential speed. The spinning was so great that, throughout his runs, he was seriously worried that the rear tyres might burst. The strain on their thin rubber was increased by a stream of sand and shells thrown back on to them by the front wheels, and, afterwards, some tyres were found to have been cut to a depth of $1/4$ in. by sea shells; but they did not burst. Wheelspin, Campbell clearly saw, was stopping him reaching his goal of 300 m.p.h.

Nevertheless, Campbell set up a new world's land speed record with a mean two-way speed of 272.46 m.p.h. for the flying kilometre. His mean two-way speed for the flying mile was 272.11 m.p.h. He also established a new flying 5 kilometres record of 257.3 m.p.h.

Campbell had taken his first step towards his target of 300 m.p.h. He had pushed up his own existing land speed record by 18.49 m.p.h.—and, not surprisingly, back in England he was toasted by H.R.H. Prince George at a dinner in the Mayfair Hotel. However, Campbell was dissatisfied with his achievement. The new Rolls-Royce engine had clearly demonstrated that it possessed the power he needed—the rev.-counter having indicated an r.p.m. that was the equivalent of well in excess of the 300 m.p.h. for which he was aiming. The main problem was how to reduce the wheelspin that wasted so much of this power. Serious doubts arose in Campbell's mind as to whether the limitations of Daytona as a course would permit *Blue Bird* to achieve on the Florida sands the far higher speeds of which the powerful new engine made the car potentially capable.

In preparation for Campbell's next attempt to reach his target of 300 m.p.h., engineering modifications were now carried out in an effort to make *Blue Bird* as technically sound as possible. The redesign was again the responsibility of Reid Railton. Because the existing adhesion was clearly unsatisfactory, four wheels were substituted for the usual two, at the rear, in an endeavour to reduce the wheelspin and so increase the acceleration. A serious effort was made to improve the streamlining: wind tunnel tests were employed to guide the designers in cutting down wind resistance, and the streamlining of the wheels was made better. In addition, an air brake was fitted at the tail.

The shortcomings of Daytona as a course again quickly became apparent after Campbell arrived in Florida with the modified Campbell Special *Blue Bird* early in 1935. The course was now curved in places because the sea had eaten sections of the beach away. The weather was bad when he arrived, and he had to wait some weeks before the tides were suitable to make the sands hard. The surface was also rippled by worms under the sand. When Campbell did make some trial runs, he encountered clutch slip at more than 100 m.p.h.; fumes came into the cockpit when the exhaust ports became obstructed, making breathing exceptionally difficult; and flames came out of the engine. Once, at something like 270 m.p.h., his goggles were knocked down over his mouth when he was bounced up into the airstream, making it extremely difficult to see, and the surface of the sands was always extremely bumpy—one cause, on his previous attempt, of his failure to reach maximum potential speed.

Finally, following the frustration of waiting several weeks for the poor condition of the beach to improve, he carried out his attempt on the record on Thursday 7 March 1935. Because of the unsatisfactory state of the course, he made up his mind only at the last minute to tackle the record. The surface was extremely bumpy when he made his first run, and sand was thrown up on to the windscreen from wet patches. Nevertheless, even though the wind was against him, he set up a one-way speed of 272.727 m.p.h.—fractionally faster than the record he was trying to beat.

On his return run he narrowly missed hitting the supports of the pier as he raced between them at not too much less than 200 m.p.h. The surface was so bumpy that, at one point, the wheels of the car left the ground altogether for a considerable distance. The impact of the tyres on the sand ripped the casings off, and the heat burnt right through the rubber, leaving the casings hanging loose. After passing the end of the measured strip the car swerved violently when it hit a bump and almost ran into the soft sand on the left. Campbell, however, by his usual superb driving, held the car on its course. The wind was behind him on this return run, and he achieved a speed of 281.030 m.p.h.

Sir Malcolm Campbell had broken the world's land speed record again by setting up a mean two-way speed of 276.82 m.p.h. for the flying mile. His mean two-way speed for the flying kilometre was 276.160 m.p.h. and that for the flying 5 kilometres was 268.47 m.p.h. However, despite the efforts put into modifications of *Blue Bird*, to reduce wheelspin and improve streamlining, the margin by which his record had gone up was no more than 4.36 m.p.h.

The target of Sir Malcolm Campbell still remained 300 m.p.h. As he sailed home, he was obsessed by the thought that his time through the measured mile for his fastest one-way run was less than one second slower than that for 300 m.p.h. He continued to ponder what was stopping him reaching his goal—and finally concluded that the great power of the Rolls-Royce engine was potentially capable of enabling *Blue Bird* to reach 300 m.p.h. but that the limitations of Daytona as a course were probably among the handicaps preventing him from achieving that goal (although he was, of course, extremely grateful for the exceptionally generous assistance he had always been given at Daytona). To find out for certain whether unsatisfactory conditions at Daytona were among the factors at fault, he therefore decided to try out a new course.

Bonneville Salt Flats, Utah, first attracted the attention of Sir Malcolm Campbell after the American racing driver Ab. Jenkins broke world's long-distance records there. The bed of the lake, which was dry during part of the year, appeared to offer Campbell definite advantages over Daytona Beach as a record-breaking course. First, the salt surface was smooth, once the network of ridges was scraped off; this smoothness suggested that wheelspin would be reduced, thereby saving loss of power, which would be used to make the car go faster. Secondly, the salt of the surface was extremely hard, particularly early in the morning following the hardening effect of the cool night air; acceleration therefore promised to be good. Thirdly, the wideness of the course—a width not too far short of 4,000 ft.—suggested a reduction of the dangers inherent in the narrowness of the course, between the dunes and the sea, at Daytona Beach; moreover, the danger to the spectators always had to be borne in mind at Daytona, but, at Bonneville, the spectators were in safety some 2,000 ft. away. Fourth, the run used was perfectly straight for about 13 miles. Fifth, the course was so level that its elevation was exactly 4,218 ft. above sea level at its beginning, middle, and end, even though it was so long. Lastly, delays waiting for favourable wind and tide at Daytona would largely be eliminated at Bonneville; the weather at the salt flats, in any case, usually consisted of bright sunshine. Actually his long delay at Daytona waiting for favourable conditions before he made his last attempt was the factor that finally tipped the scales when Campbell made up his mind to try out Bonneville, to see whether the salt flats provided a better course for breaking the world's land speed record than did Daytona Beach.

The disappointments he had experienced at Verneuk Pan were still fresh in his mind, and, despite his misgivings about Daytona, he also had certain reservations about Bonneville when he first arrived in Utah with the Campbell Special *Blue Bird* in August 1935. Wheelspin resulting from bumpiness caused by ridges in the sand had been one reason why his speed had not been faster at Daytona. A network of ridges of salt existed across Bonneville Salt Flats, and, when Campbell first inspected the salt surface of the course, he was disappointed to find that, even though these salt ridges had been scraped, their height was still sufficient to cause serious bumps, and, hence, wheelspin. He was less worried after the ridges were scraped again, making them almost level with the salt surface of the course, but he was still anxious to find out just how much wheelspin would actually be encountered during a run. The thinner air at so high an altitude, he was also aware, would reduce the power of his engine by about 18 per cent; against this loss of power, though, had to be set a reduction in wind resistance of about 14 per cent; the net loss in power caused by the altitude at Bonneville therefore amounted to something like 4 per cent. The effect of the hard surface of the salt, and of the great heat of the sun, on the tyres, was another problem that worried him. The danger from his tyres, as it turned out, was a problem he was never to forget.

How to increase acceleration at high speed was still one of his major worries. The actual speed over the ground at Daytona had not been as fast as the careful calculations of the engineers following wind tunnel tests suggested it should be, and he decided to measure the performance of *Blue Bird* at high speed scientifically to endeavour to find out whether there were any faults in the car. No record existed of the readings of the instruments during a record run: Campbell could do no more than occasionally glance down at the instruments. To provide a permanent record of the readings of the instruments throughout a record run, a movie camera was mounted in the car to photograph a duplicate set of instruments. This continuous record of the readings could then be analysed afterwards to find out where the cause of the lack of acceleration at high speed lay, if in fact it was the car that was at fault.

The straining of Campbell's left arm on a previous run was still not completely better, adding to the difficulties of steering, and a bandage was put around his left forearm to help support the muscles, before he made his first trial run at Bonneville at dawn on Monday 2 September 1935. Many questions about how the car would perform on the salt filled Campbell's mind, and his worries were not lessened when salt became packed hard against the fairings, raising the possibility that the front wheels might become jammed completely at speed, causing a nasty skid. Parts of the fairings were therefore removed, to reduce the risk of the front wheels jamming. As Campbell started his run he anxiously wondered whether changing courses from Daytona to Bonneville would at last permit *Blue Bird* to go faster. As it turned out, his run on the salt proved to be much smoother than on the sand at Daytona, and the wheels gripped the surface much better. Campbell was so impressed by the reduction in bumpiness that he decided to make an attempt on the record next day.

The brilliant glare off the white salt caused Campbell to screw up his eyes, even though he was wearing dark glasses, when he got ready to make his first run shortly after seven o'clock on the morning of Tuesday 3 September 1935. The salt surface was hard in the cool morning air, assisting acceleration, Campbell reflected, and wind resistance was at a minimum so early. The dry air was so clear that Pilot Peak appeared to be astonishingly close even though it was actually several score miles away. As he slid behind the wheel of *Blue Bird*, he hardly had time to think about the possible danger from his tyres.

Campbell watched black smoke coming out of the exhaust ports after the Rolls-Royce engine was started by the external gas compressor engine. The start was delayed when the car of a spectator crossed the timing wires, necessitating the preparation of the timing equipment all over again. Waiting impatiently, Campbell felt the heat on his cheeks as the sun rose higher above the peaks. The glare would be in his eyes as he made his first run.

Campbell got away to a fast start when he finally received the signal to go, and acceleration continued to be good as the speed built up. He concentrated his entire attention on following the black line of Diesel oil sprayed on the salt to guide him —his only reliable point of reference. The black line, he was intrigued to notice, vanished out of sight beyond the curvature of the earth. Apart from this black line, he could see nothing but glaring white salt, with mountains all around, and he felt absolutely alone.

In his isolation, he was reassured to see the first mile board coming up: a big figure 6 was painted on its side, indicating that he was 6 miles from the start of the measured course. The other mile boards came up in rapid succession. When he saw the red boards indicating the start of the measured course coming close he moved a lever in the cockpit to close the shutter over the radiator. The boards went by, a red blur. As his wheels crossed the timing wires, he knew, a mark was made on the moving timing tape.

His object in closing the shutter over the radiator was to increase the speed. His action, though, was quickly followed by two dangers for which he had not bargained: exhaust fumes filled the cockpit, making breathing difficult; and a film of oil spread rapidly over the windscreen, causing him difficulty in picking out the black line; visibility became worse as the oil grew thicker, and salt was also flung up on to the windscreen. As the fumes in the cockpit increased, Campbell became conscious of a dull aching in his head: the supply of oxygen was getting lower. Nevertheless, he kept his right foot hard down until the second red board, marking the end of the measured mile, went past. A second mark, he knew, had been made on the moving timing tape. Suddenly his nearside front tyre burst—at a speed of around 300 m.p.h. Sheer instinct saved him. Somehow he managed to hold the car, which did not turn over—partly, at least, because the wheel did not sink into the hard salt. He put on the air brake, and managed to stop without further mishap. The blue body was covered with lumps of white salt when he climbed out, and the burst tyre was on fire.

His compensation, though, came when he was told that his time for this first run, north-east, was 11.83 seconds—a one-way speed for the flying mile of 304.311 m.p.h. His speed for the return run, though, would probably be slower: the wind would be slightly against him, instead of assisting him as on the first run; and he had half a mile less in which to get up speed because he had slowed down before the end of the course owing to the burst tyre. It would therefore be touch and go as to whether his two-way mean speed would be slightly faster than 300 m.p.h.—or slightly slower.

Time was pressing, as only one hour was allowed for the turn-around. All six tyres had to be changed, but the mechanics had to wait for the rubber and metal to cool. Only a quarter of an hour remained when Campbell was told there was a hold up because a snag had developed in the timing equipment. When he eventually received the signal to go, the engine refused to start: the plugs had oiled up. He finally roared off on his return run only five minutes before the statutory hour was up.

On his return run he decelerated too suddenly—and skidded at about 250 m.p.h. He also had trouble in breathing and in seeing where he was going, as on the first run. The distance in which to pull up was too short, and he stopped the car only a few hundred feet from the embankment at the end of the course.

Had he gone just slightly faster than 300 m.p.h.—or just slightly slower?

An official came up. The two-way mean speed he had set up was 299.874 m.p.h.—a mere 0.126 m.p.h. slower than 300 m.p.h. He made up his mind to tackle the record again next day, despite the danger of another burst tyre.

Shortly afterwards the timekeepers apologised. A mistake in subtraction had been made. His correct time for the second run was 12.08 seconds, not 12.18 seconds as hurriedly recorded in the rush to get the result out. His actual mean speed for the two runs over the flying mile was therefore 301.1292 m.p.h.

After his initial doubts wore off, Campbell accepted the truth: he had passed 300 m.p.h., the first man ever to do so.

This was the last time he broke the world's land speed record, and afterwards he concentrated on tackling the world's water speed record. However, by breaking the world's land speed record no fewer than nine times, he had earned the title of fastest man on earth more often than any other man in the history of the record, before or since.

His decision to try out the new course had paid off brilliantly —and Bonneville Salt Flats were to be used for many more attempts on the world's land speed record.

One of the first people to congratulate Sir Malcolm Campbell was his son Donald, then aged 14. Twenty-five years later Donald Campbell carried on his father's tradition by endeavouring to break the world's land speed record on those same salt flats on which Sir Malcolm Campbell had, through sheer perseverance, at last successfully achieved his ambition of becoming the first man to go faster than 300 m.p.h.

CAMPBELL SPECIAL BLUE BIRD SPECIFICATION

COUNTRY OF MANUFACTURE. Britain. ENGINE. Rolls-Royce "R" Schneider Trophy aircraft type. Cylinders: V12. Bore: 152.4 mm. Stroke: 167.64 mm. Cubic capacity: 36,582 c.c. Compression ratio: 6:1. Power at r.p.m.: 2,300-2,500 b.h.p. at 3,200 r.p.m. Single centrifugal supercharger. TRANSMISSION. 3-speed gearbox, indirect drive. STEERING. Each front wheel steered separately. WHEELS. Type: steel disc. TYRES. Dunlop 35 x 600. Pressure: more than 100 lb. per sq.in. Tyre r.p.m. at record speed: 2,430 r.p.m. WEIGHT. 95 cwt. DIMENSIONS. Length: 27 ft. Fuel tank capacity: 28 Gallons.

THE NATIONAL MOTOR JOURNAL

301.129 M.P.H.

Sir Malcolm Campbell's Own Story

Behind the Scenes at Utah—The Full Facts of "Blue Bird's" Historic World's Record Revealed for the First Time. Trials and Difficulties which Led to the Final Triumph

At the banquet given by the Daily Mail *in his honour, Sir Malcolm Campbell informed us that the inside story of his World's Land Speed record of 301.129 m.p.h. still remained to be told. It is, we think, of considerable interest both from a scientific point of view and as a record of a venture which marks the attainment of his life's ambition*

to be the first man to exceed on land the speed of 300 m.p.h. With the consent of the Daily Mail, *of which he is the motoring editor, Sir Malcolm agreed to write the story in detail for* The Motor. *The first instalment appears below.*

SINCE I returned from my successful pursuit of that elusive 300 miles an hour, many people have expressed surprise that I had apparently never heard of the salt beds of Utah before I set out. As a matter of fact, my attention had been drawn to them some years ago, but the bitter experiences I met with at Verneuk Pan in 1929 had given me to think that it is probably better to deal with the devil you know rather than with the one you don't.

Hence Daytona.

That is why I chose to go to Daytona for so many successive years. At least I knew what the difficulties to be encountered there were like, but the problems I should have to meet in Utah were a sealed book.

It was really almost a counsel of desperation which impelled me to go to Utah. I had always realized that a beach course left much to be desired, but it required all those weeks of weary waiting early this year to convince me at last that the

Sir Malcolm Campbell at Utah, preparing to make his successful bid for the 300 m.p.h.—or more, as it proved to be—on September 3 last.

time had come when we must look elsewhere for a track if that 300 m.p.h. were ever to be reached. The sands of Florida had served their purpose, but speeds had outgrown their capacity and it was essential that we should find a better and safer course.

The Daytona course had been adequate until 1933, but it was then that it showed up its weakness. Prior to that year, the maximum horse-power we had been able to install into "Blue Bird" was 1,350, but on that run we used the Rolls-Royce engine which developed over 2,350 h.p. and which was ultimately to give us the speed we were definitely aiming at, namely, something over 300 m.p.h.

Disillusion.

In theory, we ought to have attained that speed two years ago and it was with cheerful confidence that we looked forward to the 1933 attempt. Nothing but disillusionment lay in wait for us—as is now a matter of ancient history.

Under its best conditions, the beach was so uneven that we suffered terribly from wheel-spin.

How bad this actually was may be judged from the fact that on

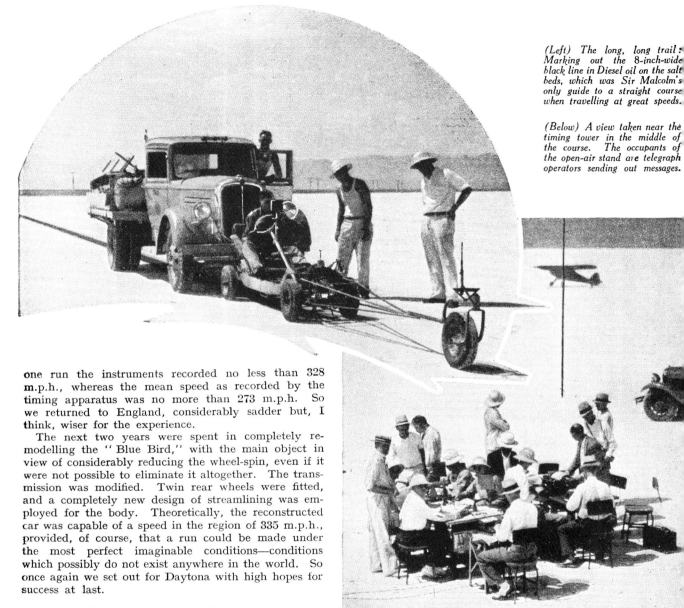

(Left) The long, long trail: Marking out the 8-inch-wide black line in Diesel oil on the salt beds, which was Sir Malcolm's only guide to a straight course when travelling at great speeds.

(Below) A view taken near the timing tower in the middle of the course. The occupants of the open-air stand are telegraph operators sending out messages.

one run the instruments recorded no less than 328 m.p.h., whereas the mean speed as recorded by the timing apparatus was no more than 273 m.p.h. So we returned to England, considerably sadder but, I think, wiser for the experience.

The next two years were spent in completely re-modelling the "Blue Bird," with the main object in view of considerably reducing the wheel-spin, even if it were not possible to eliminate it altogether. The transmission was modified. Twin rear wheels were fitted, and a completely new design of streamlining was employed for the body. Theoretically, the reconstructed car was capable of a speed in the region of 335 m.p.h., provided, of course, that a run could be made under the most perfect imaginable conditions—conditions which possibly do not exist anywhere in the world. So once again we set out for Daytona with high hopes for success at last.

Weeks of Waiting at Daytona

It was not to be, however. After weary weeks of waiting for the conditions that simply would not come, at last the beach had improved to an extent which made the risk of a trial at least justifiable. The condition of the beach was really bad, but it was the best we could hope for and, after repeated efforts, the highest speed we could attain in one direction only was 281 m.p.h. So uneven were the sands that the car continually left the ground completely, but even so I thought we should have travelled faster than we did.

The most disturbing factor was that, although we had now stopped the wheel-spin—excepting when the car left the ground—our acceleration curve, instead of going right up, flattened out completely. Many months had been spent in carrying out the most careful tests in the wind tunnel, with results which seemed to be conclusive, but the difference between the deductions thus arrived at and the actual speed of the car on the sands was sufficiently wide to give rise to the conviction that there must be something wrong somewhere. There was a number of possible reasons to explain the discrepancy, but as no single one of them could account for it, it may be of interest if I refer to them in detail.

Missing : 50 m.p.h. !

In the first place, there was the possibility that the engine did not give off the same brake horse-power when installed in the chassis as it had shown while under test on the bench. This might have been due to wind-eddies interfering with the air-flow through the main intake to the supercharger, thus cutting down the boost pressure. So we decided on the next attempt to take a photographic record of the supercharger pressure and the reading of the other instruments, as it is obviously impossible for the driver to watch them at speed.

Then it was possible that our wind-tunnel calculations were not accurate, so these were very carefully checked, with the result that we found them to be correct within one per cent. Of course, we realized that it is a practical impossibility to build a body that actually corresponds exactly to the model used in the wind-tunnel. The latter, being solid, is entirely free from air leaks, while the body which is built from it obviously cannot be so. Still, this factor could not by any means account for so large a margin as over 50 m.p.h. in actual car-speed.

Again, as we were now using twin wheels and had materially strengthened the transmission, our unsprung weight had been increased. This, however, could only be contributory to the loss and could certainly not be regarded as the main cause of the trouble.

Lastly, the course itself might be to blame, as it was quite possible that an abnormal amount of horse-power was being wasted in overcoming rolling resistance consequent upon the heavy nature of the sands. It was decided, therefore, on the next occasion to carry an accelerometer so as to ascertain the amount of power actually absorbed in overcoming wind and rolling resistance.

Having considered the whole matter very fully, I came to the decision that it was essential to try out "Blue Bird" on the salt flats so as to ascertain definitely

Sir Malcolm Campbell's World's Land Speed Record

FLYING MILE.
Mean speed, 301.1292 *m.p.h.*
Time—North-east run, 11.83 *secs.* (304.311 *m.p.h.). South-west run,* 12.08 *secs.* (298.013 *m.p.h.)*

FLYING KILOMETRE.
Mean speed, 301.473 *m.p.h.*

FLYING FIVE KILOMETRES.
Mean speed, 292.142 *m.p.h.*

whether the course was at fault or whether we must look elsewhere for the causes of failure. I realized that, in any case, even if we did not succeed in reaching our objective, we should obtain such valuable data that would ensure that the next attempt would make its attainment a matter of practical certainty rather than a problematical one.

Salt Lake City lies approximately 2,600 miles west of New York, close up to the foot of a mountain range that is really a part of the Rockies. The Bonneville Salt Flats, which were the scene of the record attempt, are about 120 miles west of the City, but the excellent roads characteristic of Utah State render the Flats easily accessible—there is one stretch alone which boasts of 40 miles dead straight, over a wonderful surface.

We fixed our headquarters at a village some 6½ miles from the course. It is called Wendover, but anything more unlike the familiar town of that name in Bucks it is impossible to imagine. There is a railroad station, one or two wayside cafés, the usual petrol filling depots, a couple of garages and a block of cabins where the passing traveller can find food and shelter for the night. Incidentally, Wendover is just over the border between Utah and Nevada. "Blue Bird" we housed in the larger of the two garages, where it created great interest and was always a centre of attraction.

Under the shade of an improvised tuning shed, "Blue Bird" is prepared for the record runs.   On the extreme right, the compressed-air cylinders for starting can just be seen.

Never shall I forget my sensations on first seeing the salt flats. I had heard a great deal about them and had seen many photographs of them and the surrounding country, but the actuality was totally different from all the impressions I had formed.

A Desert Plain of Salt

These salt beds extend over an area of more than 300 square miles and are cut in halves by the railroad and a parallel highway which run through the centre of this vast desert plain. In the summer months the heat is intense, temperatures exceeding 115 degrees Fahr. in the shade being often registered, and, as the surface is composed of pure, white salt crystals, the resulting glare must be seen to be imagined. Needless to say, it is extremely trying to the eyes.

In the far distance can be seen a range of mountains, but so clear is the atmosphere that they seem almost on top of you. In spite of the high temperatures, the heat is not oppressive. The flats are some 4,230 ft. above sea level, the air is dry and the combination renders the heat far less uncomfortable than the thermo-

was assailed by very grave doubts as to whether the tyres would obtain the necessary adhesion. The ridges were still some ½-in. high and it seemed to me that these would set up tremendous vibration and would, moreover, prevent the tyres from gripping the surface, owing to their continual deformation. When I pointed this out to the authorities, they were most helpful and suggested going over the course again with a heavier scraper than the one used originally. This was done, and proved highly successful. In fact, I am certain that if this had not been done we should never have succeeded in our attempt.

In the light of the experience gained at Verneuk Pan, I knew that it was essential to have a black line painted down the centre of the entire length of the course, as without some such marking it would be utterly impossible to keep the car dead straight. I had already advised the Chamber of Commerce of this, and the work was in progress when we arrived. The line was 8 ins. wide and the material employed was Diesel oil, which, being black, showed up extraordinarily well on the white surface.

Salt packed tightly in the fairings and rubbed the wheels when the car was first towed out—to prevent its recurrence the bottom lips of the fairings were cut.

meter reading would naturally lead one to believe.

The surface, although flat, is completely covered with ridges of hard salt, an inch or so high. These ridges, I was told, are caused by the strong winds which prevail during the winter months. The Junior Chamber of Commerce of Salt Lake City, who were sponsoring the record attempts, had surveyed a large area of the desert and had finally selected the best course available, and the ridges referred to had already been partially removed by means of a mechanically drawn scraper.

This stretch extended for a distance of about 13 miles, running approximately N.E. and S.W. At the northern end the surface of the salt rapidly became soft, while the southern end was bounded by the highway which I have already explained cut the plain practically into halves. Owing to some freak of Nature, the thickness of the salt varies considerably, so that notwithstanding the enormous area of the region only this 13-mile straight is available for record-breaking purposes.

When I made my first examination of our course, I

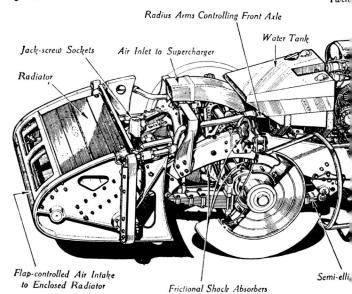

Radius Arms Controlling Front Axle

Water Tank

Jack-screw Sockets   Air Inlet to Supercharger

Radiator

Flap-controlled Air Intake
to Enclosed Radiator

Frictional Shock Absorbers

Semi-elli

Twel

"Blue Bird" had arrived by rail from New York, and my loyal band of mechanics were busy preparing the old car for her first test run. By Sunday evening, September 1, work on the course was finished and, as the car was ready and the timing officials of the A.A.A. had arrived, I announced that I would make a trial on the following morning at dawn. At daybreak, therefore, "Blue Bird" was towed out to the course. A huge crowd had already assembled, notwithstanding the early hour and the fact that we were 120 miles from the nearest real civilization.

A Preliminary Hitch

We were obliged to pull up before reaching the starting point to remove the salt thrown up by the wheels, which, having collected and packed up tight in the fairings, was rubbing the wheels. This was a contingency we had not allowed for, so to safeguard against the possibility of the front wheels becoming locked while at full speed we cut away the bottom lip of the fairings, thus effectively preventing the salt from piling up.

At each end of the course we had erected a shelter, so that the car and tyres should be protected from the heat of the sun while awaiting the "All Clear" signal from the officials. There was a considerable delay that morning before we were told the course was clear, the reason apparently being that the timing apparatus was not functioning properly. Eventually word came down that we could proceed. The time was now 8.30 a.m., the sun was well up and the heat had become intense.

Never shall I forget my sensations as the car got off the mark! Would the rear wheels grip, or would the car begin to slither about when we reached a certain speed? Nobody could tell and we had to find out in practice. My mechanics had suggested that I should keep the speed inside the 180 m.p.h. mark in this first test, as the car had not been run since its last overhaul and the clutch required bedding in. On the other hand,

Four of Sir Malcolm's trusty mechanics—men who have helped him in so many successful records: (left to right) W. Hicks, Leo Villa, Harry Leach and A. E. Poyser.

I could learn little about the course or how the car was likely to handle unless I went considerably faster than than that.

We made a perfect start, changed up from first to second at 90 m.p.h., then into top, and before I realized we were properly away we had reached the maximum speed suggested by my staff.

A Wonderful Sensation

The course appeared to be perfect and the temptation to let the car go was more than I could resist. However, I kept bringing back my foot, keeping the engine revs. at about 2,700, i.e., 240 m.p.h. It was the most wonderful sensation I have ever felt. Here we were, skimming over the surface of the earth, the black line ever disappearing over the edge of the horizon; the wind

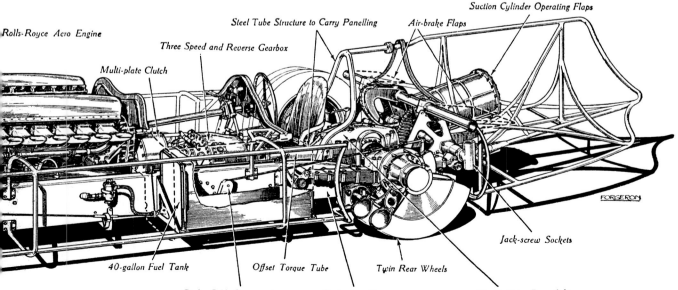

Rolls-Royce Aero Engine · Three Speed and Reverse Gearbox · Steel Tube Structure to Carry Panelling · Air-brake Flaps · Suction Cylinder Operating Flaps · Multi-plate Clutch · FORGERON · 40-gallon Fuel Tank · Offset Torque Tube · Twin Rear Wheels · Jack-screw Sockets · Brake Cable Compensator · Underslung Frame · Double Drive Rear Axle

A detailed and informative skeleton sketch of "Blue Bird," in which all the parts are clearly indicated. The panelling of the body is built up on the tubular steel framework.

whistling past like a hurricane; and nothing in sight but the endless sea of salt with the mountains 50 miles away in the distance.

We shot over the end of the measured mile all too soon and I started immediately to apply the wind-brakes. On and on we went, the air-brakes seemingly having little effect, so eventually I had to bring the mechanical brakes into action. By the time the end of the course was reached we had slowed sufficiently to enable me to turn the car round and drive straight under the shelter, where the mechanics were awaiting me. I felt highly elated as I jumped out of the car. The course seemed to be perfect; the car was running magnificently; and I felt that, given any degree of luck, we should reach our coveted goal on the next morning.

When the remaining mechanics who had followed up in a touring car arrived and had looked over the car, they pronounced everything to be perfect, so we decided to let well alone and "Blue Bird" was towed back to Wendover.

The two outstanding impressions that remained were, first, the extraordinary and really wonderful sensation of skimming over the black line—there was none of the awful vibration I had so often experienced at Daytona as the car leaped off the ground and came crashing to earth again.

Chasing a Disappearing Horizon

The surface was smooth, so smooth, in fact, that I could have discarded my safety strap altogether. Earlier this year, at Daytona, I had to employ two straps—one to prevent my being thrown forward and another to keep me glued into the seat. What a pleasure it was to drive under such altered conditions! Secondly, I could never see the black line for more than a hundred yards ahead of the car, as all the time it seemed to be disappearing over the edge of the horizon. It was like chasing an endless ribbon. I felt, too, that we were skimming along over the top of the world and the earth appeared to be acutely round, if one may be allowed the apparent paradox. It was a wonderful experience and one I shall never forget.

Could I Pull Up in Time?

Another not quite such pleasurable sensation was that of wondering if I should be able to pull up "Blue Bird" before reaching the end of the course. At Daytona we had a five miles run on each side of the measured mile. Here we had six, but, owing to the rarefied atmosphere and the lesser rolling resistance, it was a question whether the greater distance would prove sufficient. There was small danger of getting into real trouble when running from south to north, as the worst that could happen was that the car would run off into soft salt and might become bogged. It was, however, a very different proposition when running in the reverse direction, because if I could not pull up in time I should have to charge the embankment of the highway, unless I could swerve and run parallel with it. It was owing to this reason that I therefore had made up my mind to make the first run to the north.

The remainder of that day we spent in checking over the car, and going carefully over all the arrangements for the morrow. We decided that it would be wise to make an even earlier start to avoid the intense heat, so we asked the A.A.A. officials to have everything ready for getting off the mark not later than 6 o'clock on the following morning.

(TO BE CONTINUED.)

Next week Sir Malcolm Campbell will conclude his personal narrative of "Blue Bird's" 300 m.p.h. record. This instalment is a record of what no man has ever done before, an achievement which sets up a milestone in the history of motoring—relating how a tyre burst at 280 m.p.h., how the driver was almost asphyxiated by engine fumes and of how, on the return run, he applied the brakes at 250 m.p.h., and pulled up only just in time at the far end of the course.　　**See page 94.**

Overture: "Blue Bird" streaking across the blinding white expanse of the vast salt beds at 280 m.p.h. in a practice run the day before the actual record attempt. The mountains which loom in the background are actually about 50 miles away—their nearness an optical illusion due to the rarefied atmosphere and intense heat of the desert over 4,000 ft. above sea level.

Continued from page 22

Campbell's New Daytona Car.

and blends with the tail and is padded at the front end.

Actually, the body consists of two streamline forms, one rising, then falling in front and behind the driver's head, and having on it a glass windscreen at an acute angle, the other rising over the engine then sweeping down alongside the driver to the tail. The tail projects considerably behind the rear axle, partly because the wheelbase had to be fixed, while the length of tail depended on the assumed speed of the car.

In front of each tyre is a nose-piece; behind is what amounts to a separate tail, and the space between the body and these streamline casings is filled by another streamline plane. The wheels are extremely heavy, very strong steel discs held to the hubs by ten bolts, and the hubs project to receive the attachment for discs covering the wheels, while the tyres will

have practically no tread, since the tread would be flung off by centrifugal force, and no pattern or ribs.

One of the problems of the record is that the car has to run one way over the measured course, stop, turn round, and come back again within half an hour, and in that time it is also desirable to stop the engine, replenish the water tank, and change all four wheels.

No Joke !

Now changing wheels on this car is no joke; the discs and tyres combined are almost as much as two men can lift. Ten nuts have to be undone for each wheel, then done up again, while the disc covers must be removed and replaced, and the car jacked up and unjacked—a fairly lengthy process.

Campbell may decide to risk it on the same set of tyres, but in case he does not, big bosses with a heavy in-

ternal thread are mounted on either side of the frame at the front and at the rear, and into these bosses can be screwed stout steel shafts with holes in their heads for a bar. If the lower end of the shaft is placed on a hard sheet of material and the bar screwed down, the wheels are lifted off the ground, a system of jacking which is the only one possible when the streamline covers conceal every other part of the axle or frame.

Underneath the car runs the flat aluminium underpan. The arrangement of weight is such that approximately two tons are on the rear wheels and 1½ tons on the front, the balance being obtained by huge masses of lead inside the frame channel at the back in order to gain adhesion. The bevel ratio is 1.58 to 1, and the engine will be running at something like 3,500 r.p.m., its supercharger at 28,000 or 30,000 r.p.m.

BLUEBIRD IN IT'S LATEST FORM Continued from page 44

shaped air intake pipe between the blocks faced forward, and about two pounds additional pressure was produced by the forward motion of the machine. On the Blue Bird the supercharger end of the engine is in front, so the air intake will come from behind the radiator. In the space now made available between the cylinder blocks, six car-type carburettors have been installed.

The engine of the Blue Bird also differs from that shown in the illustration in not having the propellor reduction-gear.

The Schneider Trophy engine was rated to give 2,350 h.p. for one hour, but as each 10 mile run at Daytona only takes about 3 minutes, the output has been brought up to 2,500 h.p. The engine speed is between 3,200 and 3,600 at which speed the centre main bearing is under a strain of about 9 tons.

The extra length of the power unit has

made it necessary to lengthen Blue Bird's chassis, and the total length is now 27 feet. The side members have been prolonged to form supports for the radiator, which is no longer separated from the body shell. The cooling air therefore passes into the bonnet and will escape through enormous louvres in the sides. The header tank, which is connected to the radiator by two pipes passing over and under the very deep front chassis cross member, is tapered in front and cut away at the back to clear the supercharger casing.

The steering lay-out, in which independent steering rods, with steadying links near the front, were actuated by separate steering boxes has been retained. The front axle is positioned by a flexible radius rod, and the friction type shock absorbers are now arranged across the chassis.

The clutch has been re-designed to cope with the increased power output and the three speed gear box is offset to bring the propellor shaft in line with the final drive. This of course is also offset, so that Sir Malcolm sits on the right of the car below the level of the shafts.

A Dewandre vacuum-servo cylinder applies the brakes, and the drums are almost hidden inside the disc wheels. Needless to say Dunlop tyres will be used.

The Rolls Royce engine develops 2,500 h.p. against the 1,450 of the Napier formerly fitted. The power required to propel a vehicle increases at the square of the velocity, so with an extra 40% power one may expect about 6% increase in speed or an additional 18-20 m.p.h. The streamlining and other factors have been altered, however, so we will take refuge in the good old tip of "Wait and see."

The Record Achieved—The Sensatio
Minute—Moments when th
Gassed by Fumes—
the Scenes at Uta

**"Blue Bird" gets away for the actual record run. The running
mechanics have just helped to push the car off.**

*WHAT HAS GONE BEFORE.—In last week's instalment of Sir Malcolm
Campbell's exclusive article, the great driver described something of the trials and disappointments attending his repeated attempts to reach 300 m.p.h. on Daytona Beach, and
how he was constrained to believe that it was the unsuitable surface that robbed "Blue
Bird" of its known speed.*

    *Came the journey to Utah, the comparatively unknown, with speculation as to wheel
grip on the sun-baked salt of the 4,000-ft.-high lake bed . . . then the first trials with
complete success at a mere 240 m.p.h. . . . and the recognized danger of so little space in
which to pull up. The stage was set.*

RECORD DATA

Flying mile, mean speed: 301.1292 *m.p.h.*
Flying kilometre, mean speed: 301.473 *m.p.h.*
Faster run: 304.11 *m.p.h.*
Maximum water temperature: 90 *degrees Centigrade.*
Maximum oil temperature: 85 *degrees Centigrade.*
Supercharger pressure: 17 *lb.*
Maximum engine revolutions: 3,500 *r.p.m.*
Tyre pressures: Front, 125 *lb.; rear,* 110 *lb.*

SOME OF THE EQUIPMENT

*6 h.p. engine, multi-stage air compressor for the air
  bottles (used for starting the engine).*
Complete air-bottle set.
Two petrol-driven compressors.
500 K.L.G. plugs.
58 tyres.
200 gallons of special Esso-Ethyl fuel.
125 gallons of Esso-Ethyl alcohol fuel.
400 gallons of Wakefield Castrol oil.
One complete spare Rolls-Royce engine.
Six large cases of tools and spares.

AT last the great day had arrived and the stage was
set. Once more "Blue Bird" was towed out
to the course, this time before the sun had appeared over
the horizon. The wheels were changed, the engine
started and warmed up to the required temperature, and
then we all stood by waiting to receive the "All Clear"
signal. These long waits are to me very reminiscent of
the war—waiting for "zero hour"—when everybody's
nerves get keyed up to the highest pitch.

    It was not until 12 minutes past seven that we got
the word to go, apparently a motorist had driven into

...ell's Own Story

...t Five Miles a
...river was
...ehind

Flat out! A magnificent photograph of "Blue Bird" actually breaking the record at 301 m.p.h., dead astride the black line of Diesel oil. A moment after this picture was taken Sir Malcolm closed the radiator shutter and was almost overcome by fumes.

...ccelerating flat out for the start of the measured mile. The car had to shoot between the telegraph posts seen on the extreme right.

I revved up to full speed, changing into second at 100 m.p.h. and into top at 200 m.p.h., and now the car was getting hold of it as she had never done before.

At the beginning of each mile I had large numerals painted on boards, signifying the number of miles that were left before reaching the measured mile, on the reverse side of which I had marked the distance left for pulling up. This was an idea I had thought out some years before and now it proved invaluable.

Closing the Radiator Shutter—and the Result

We appeared to be flying over the ground; up and up soared the needle of the rev. counter; no sooner had we passed one mile sign than another seemed to shoot

and broken some wires during the night, and the sun by now had risen high and it was already beginning to get hot.

Away we shot, this time in dead earnest. There was no time to think of sensations or thrills—the only thing that mattered was to get going as quickly as possible. I had just time to remember to turn on the two switches operating the electrically driven Cine-Kodak and the accelerometer as we tore away on first gear. This time

---

Some Facts About "Blue Bird"

Engine: 12-cylinder supercharged Rolls-Royce aero-type unit in two banks of cylinders. Power output: 2,500 b.h.p. approx. Length of engine: 7 ft. 7½ ins. Weight: 14½ cwt. Supercharger speed at 3,200 r.p.m. engine speed: 30,000 r.p.m.

Complete car weighs nearly 5 tons.

Wheelbase: 13 ft. 8 ins. Track: 5 ft. Overall length: 28 ft. 3 ins.

300 m.p.h. is equivalent to 440 ft. per second.

About 90 per cent. of the 2,500-odd horse-power available was required to overcome wind resistance—120 lb. per sq. ft. of frontal area.

Centrifugal force at the tread of the rear wheels was about 2 tons per lb. of rubber.

Transmission was via a normal clutch, through a three-speed "crash-type" gearbox (all ratios indirect) to a solid back-axle via a double propeller-shaft.

This is the eighth time Sir Malcolm Campbell has held the World's Land Speed Record, which has been raised from 39.24 m.p.h. in 1898 to 301.129 m.p.h.

by. I had decided to close the radiator shutter when two miles distant from the measured mile, and as the mark loomed in sight I glanced for the last time at my rev. counter. It showed 3,200 r.p.m., equivalent to 280 m.p.h., and was mounting rapidly.

I knocked forward the lever controlling the shutter. Up to now, everything had been going perfectly, but no sooner was the shutter closed than my troubles started in earnest. Instantly a slight film of oil began to cover the windscreen and I commenced to inhale the exhaust fumes from the engine, which was now turning over at a really high speed. The farther we went, the more opaque became the screen and the more obnoxious the fumes.

Gassed

By this time we had shot over the timing strips marking the commencement of the measured mile. Halfway along the distance I began to experience an awful sensation of pins and needles being driven through the top of my head, and I realized that at any moment I might pass out. My visibility was reduced to a minimum and I could barely see the black line in front of the car.

At last the red banners marking the end of the mile flashed by and I commenced to ease my foot off the accelerator as quickly as I dared. By this time I had lost the black line altogether, but now that the engine

Sir Malcolm Campbell examines the black line, which he used at Daytona and Utah, to guide him on a straight course.

was shut down the fumes and oil ceased to come into the cockpit. I applied the wind-brakes, realizing I had not much space in which to pull up and, spotting the black line a little to my right, started to ease the car over to it.

Suddenly there was a tremendous report. The nearside front tyre had blown and the car instantly swerved to the left, but responded at once to the correction. We "snaked" for a short while, but then the car seemed to settle down, although the steering became heavier and heavier and bits of the tyre were flying off in all directions. Now that the car was again under control, I knew I must pull up as soon as possible and started to apply the mechanical brakes, wondering at the same time how long the wheel was going to stand up to the terrific punishment it was getting. The next I saw was that the remains of the tyre were well alight!

Braking Heavily

I then began to brake heavily and eventually pulled the car up about half a mile away from my mechanics who were waiting for me at the end of the course. At first they did not appear to realize what had happened, so I stood up in the cockpit and waved for them to come to me.

A considerable delay now occurred, as after dashing out in a car to see what had happened they had to go

Starting up. Final preparations before the momentous first run for the record. On the right can be seen the compressed air starting apparatus which rotates the engine before the ignition is switched on. The tent-like erection is to shield the car and the mechanics from the terrific heat which reaches as much as 115 degrees in the shade.

back, load all the tyres, jacks and engine gas-starter into a lorry and come out to me again. By this time I had got my Pyrene to work on the tyre and my other mechanics, who had followed me in a touring car, had arrived.

Both runs must be accomplished within the hour, and more than half an hour slipped by before we had all four wheels changed; more valuable time was lost in cleaning the oil off the windscreen and my goggles. Then a motorcyclist came tearing up to tell us that our first run had been accomplished at the rate of 304.11 m.p.h.

Valuable Minutes Slipping By

This was certainly good news, but I wondered whether the tyres would be able to stand up once more to the terrible gruelling they would receive. At last we were ready for the return journey. The engine was started up and just as I was about to get away an official ran up and told me to wait as one of the timing wires had broken and was now being repaired. I switched off the motor, as the water soon boils if the engine is allowed to run for long while the car is stationary.

I saw by my watch that we had barely 15 minutes left before our hour was up. Valuable minutes slipped by as I sat in the cockpit, with the full glare of the sun beating down upon the car, waiting for the word to go. It seemed an eternity before the " O.K." signal was given. This wait had been certainly the greatest trial of all, and then, to make matters worse, the engine refused to start! At long last we got going again, with a bare five minutes to spare—ample, of course, to cover the seven miles, provided the engine did not stall.

Curious Effect of Centrifugal Force

I had decided that it would be folly to close the radiator shutter on the return run, because of the consequences I knew must ensue. I felt, moreover, that we could just about reach the 300 without the added assistance of the closed shutter. As we tore along, I kept glancing at my front tyres and, to my amazement, I could see plainly that the tread of the off-side tyre had become pointed and appeared to be transparent! The centrifugal force generated by the rapidly revolving wheel was so great that it threatened to throw the tyre from the rim. At each revolution the cover became elongated to an ellipse.

We were travelling at about 290 m.p.h. when I last looked at the off-side wheel—and a most unpleasant sight it was! We had now flashed past the entrance to the measured mile and only a few seconds seemed to have passed—actually it was 12.08 secs.—before we had left it at the finish.

Broadside at 250 m.p.h.!

Realizing I must slow down as quickly as possible if

These Contributed to the Ultimate Success :

'Blue Bird" was constructed by Thomson and Taylor (Brooklands), Ltd., to the design of Mr. Reid A. Railton.

Components included: Rolls-Royce engine, Dunlop wheels and tyres, Ace wheel discs, Tyzack clutch plates with Ferodo linings, Clayton Dewandre servo-motors, Ferodo brake linings, Hoffmann bearings, Young accumulators, B.T.H. magnetos.

K.L.G. sparking plugs Serck radiator, E.N.V. back axle gears, D.B.S. gearbox and gears, Hadfield front-axle and rear-axle forgings, shafts, etc., Burman-Douglas steering-gear, T.T.N. stabilizers, Arens controls, Jubilee hose-clips, Bamberger's timber.

Hardy-Spicer steering column, Woodhead road springs, Andre Silentbloc shock absorbers, Guest, Keen and Nettlefolds bolts and nuts, chassis frame by John Thompson Motor Pressings Ltd., Smith instruments, Petroflex tubing, Pyrene fire-fighting equipment, Triplex windscreen and goggles, car finished in Belco, with Moseley Float-on-Air upholstery.

Fuel: Special Esso-Ethyl. Oil: Wakefield Patent Castrol.

I wished to pull up the car without hitting the highway embankment, I took my foot off the accelerator much sooner than I should, with the result that the car went into a broadside skid. Once more she responded perfectly to the steering and I soon had her on her course again.

On this run I did something I have never done before. I had already brought into action the wind-brakes and I now started to apply the mechanical brakes while still hurtling along at a speed of some 250 m.p.h. These brakes responded magnificently, and I could feel the power they were exerting. Still the question remained: could we pull up in time?

Right up to the last mile I was in doubt and just as I was preparing to swerve off to the left I saw that we should just about be able to stop in time. Actually, I suppose I had about 250 yards to spare. Little enough in all conscience, and if the brakes had failed—well, the situation would have been far from pleasant.

I was greeted by a most enthusiastic crowd when I pulled up under the shelter, and, judging by my instruments, I felt pretty confident that this second run was so close to the 300 mark that the average would work out slightly over that figure. There was a long wait before any figures were announced by the official who was standing by the telephone communicating directly with the timing officials.

My mechanics by this time had arrived on my touring car, and my son, in his anxiety to see how we had fared, jumped out of the car while it was still moving quickly. Of course, he fell heavily, but fortunately was not hurt. To add still further to the excitement, as the car pulled up beside " Blue Bird," I noticed smoke and flames coming from under the bonnet. We quickly produced Pyrenes and the blaze was extinguished before any material damage had been done.

At last we were told that the second run had been covered at the rate of 299.8 m.p.h., and, as the first had been timed at 304.11 m.p.h., we had therefore raised the record to a speed of about 302 m.p.h. The excitement was intense, not only amongst my own party, but it was shared equally by the many hundreds of spectators surrounding us, and for the moment I felt I was the happiest man in the world.

The Timing Error

I have said " for the moment," because there was bitter disappointment to come almost immediately. The news came through that it was the average mean speed of both runs which had worked out at 299.8 m.p.h. and that the second run had only been made at a speed of slightly over 296 m.p.h.

Our disappointment can be imagined. Our efforts, although we had beaten the old record by a handsome margin, all seemed to have gone for nothing and we should have to start all over again. It was then I realized that I had a most appalling headache, brought on, no doubt, by inhaling the poisonous exhaust fumes during the first run.

We towed " Blue Bird " back to the garage and notified the A.A.A. officials that we should be ready to make another attempt on the following morning. Then I had a conference with my staff, with the object of finding out why the action of closing the radiator shutter should have caused oil to spread over the inside of the windscreen and why the exhaust fumes had penetrated into the cockpit. After a thorough examination of the car, we arrived at the best means of overcoming the trouble.

The cause of the trouble was at once obvious—and very easily curable. Down by my feet in the bottom of the cockpit was the engine crankcase breather. Now, we had very carefully done all we could to make the cockpit airtight, because in some of the previous bodies used on " Blue Bird " the rush of air through the cockpit itself nearly lifted me out of my driving seat.

In practice, it is impossible to seal the cockpit completely against the tremendous pressure of air at over 250 m.p.h. and the tiny leaks past the bulkhead served to carry away the oil from the breather.

Problems of Streamlining

Of course, as soon as I closed the radiator, this air pressure was cut clean off and, in response to the suction of the air rushing past the cockpit, an oil mist floated up all over the inside of the wind shield.

The same reason accounted for the fumes coming into the cockpit. The streamlining of the car is such that the air, and with it any fumes, clings to the outside contour of the body until it leaves at the tail. With the cockpit practically airtight, owing to the radiator being shut, the flow of fumes past my head found an area of negative pressure as it were, and streamed into the cockpit in the form of eddies on the fringe of the main air stream.

The solution to the oil mist problem would simply have been to lead a pipe away to the rear and so out of the car. The cure for the fume-trouble was to cover-in the whole cockpit, and as a matter of fact my mechanics were actually at work beating the aluminium panel for the following day's attempt. Had we used this covered-in top, we knew we should have gained a clear 15 m.p.h. straight away.

While our discussion was taking place and we had settled to start work on preparing the car for to-morrow's attempt, I was asked, some two hours after the finish of the two runs, to step round and have a word with the chief official of the A.A.A.

When I met him and his confrères, I could see that they were very upset about something. This, they explained, was in consequence of the discovery that an error had been made in their calculations and that in reality the correct average speed for the mile was 301.129 m.p.h. and for the kilometre 301.473 m.p.h.

Wanted to Have Another Try

Strange to say, when I heard this I did not feel in the least elated. In fact, I suggested that they should tear up the timing strips and that I should have another try, as I had already announced, on the following morning. This they would not hear of, and pointed out that in any case the mistake in their calculations was such a simple one that it would have been discovered on their check up, as well as by the authorities in Paris when the papers were sent up for verification. I therefore decided that no useful purpose would be served by making a further attempt on the record, as we had achieved our objective. I am nevertheless convinced that had we done so an even higher speed would have been recorded.

After many attempts we had at last succeeded in reaching our goal. There was a time when I wondered whether we should ever get there, and I so well recollect imagining how delighted my little crew and I would be if only we could win through. Yet such were the circumstances that the first taste of bitter disappointment had been too much for us all and had robbed us of the joy that would otherwise have been ours, and which I do think we had deserved.

There was, however, one factor which pleased me perhaps more than any other and that was that our run had proved conclusively that our design was correct in every respect. " Blue Bird," on her first attempt, had reached a speed of 304 m.p.h. and our photographic records prove that had the course been longer the ultimate speed would have been higher. I am positive that with a few minor alterations she could improve her present record by at least a further 15 m.p.h. Taking into consideration that we were losing 18 per cent. of our power in consequence of the high altitude and gaining only 14 per cent. in lessened wind resistance, it means that our original calculations were not far wrong.

I cannot conclude without a passing reference to the tyres. No praise I could ever bestow upon the Dunlop concern who made those tyres could ever be adequate. How this wonderful organization can manufacture tyres that will withstand the tremendous strains and stresses imposed upon them during these tests is beyond my imagination. A driver has only to look at the deformation which takes place at very high speeds to realize to the full the wonderful skill and superb workmanship that have been displayed in their making.

And now after all these years I have said that I am retiring. I do so with the utmost regret, but having made a promise I intend to keep to it. It is not easy to tear oneself away from an almost lifelong hobby, but we must all be philosophers and realize the fact that all things must at last come to an end.

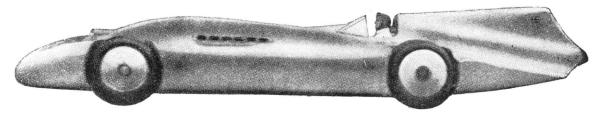

301.13 m.p.h for One Mile.   159.30 m.p.h. for One Hour

HISTORIC RECORDS ESTABLISHED BY SIR MALCOLM CAMPBELL AND G. E. T. EYSTON

Undoubtedly the most outstanding records of the year are those made at Bonneville Salt Flats, by Sir Malcolm Campbell on September 3 and by Capt. Eyston on September 6-18.

Sir Malcolm drove "Bluebird" over the measured mile at 304.33 m.p.h. in one direction, and returned down the course at 298.01 m.p.h., thus setting the World's Flying Mile Record at 301.13 m.p.h. More than that, Sir Malcolm is the first man in the world to exceed 300 m.p.h. on land, having attained at last the speed which has been his ambition since he first attacked the Land Speed Record with the old "V12" Sunbeam in 1924. It is understood that Sir Malcolm has now promised Lady Campbell that he will retire from this class of record-breaking, unless another country should produce a car that betters "Bluebird's" figure.

It is a tremendous tribute to Sir Malcolm's skill and experience and to the abilities of Reid Railton who designed the car, that this historic record was established almost without a hitch. On the faster run a tyre burst at 280 m.p.h., but Sir Malcolm contrived to maintain a steady course. After all tyres had been changed the return run was safely completed, and at first an error in estimating the actual speed made it seem that an average of 300 m.p.h. had just been missed. The error was soon corrected and the historic news released to the world—that a motor-car had covered a mile in 12 seconds !

"Bluebird" is now so well known that a full description is quite unnecessary. Built at Brooklands by Messrs. Thompson and Taylor Ltd., the giant car has a Schneider Trophy type, supercharged 12-cylinder Rolls-Royce engine developing 2,300 h.p. and the complete machine weighs over 4 tons. That it established the record on its first runs at Utah is a great tribute to all concerned. "Bluebird" was actally built in 1927, when it had a Napier engine. Since then it has undergone very extensive modification on a number of different occasions, and each time it has set up a new Land Speed figure, with one exception only, when the car established 5 mile and 5 kilo records at Verneuk Pan. It is, perhaps, significant that the present design retains rear-wheel drive and an open cock-pit. This time ingenious air-brakes assisted Campbell to check speed after the 300 m.p.h. sprint, and, as before, the venture would have been quite impossible without the special tyres supplied by Dunlops.

Always, after a record of this nature, there is someone who suggests that far too much is made of the achievement, in view of the proportionately much greater speeds attained by small-engined racing cars. The same thing invariably crops up in air-racing ; indeed, has occurred just recently when Howard Hughes did 352.46 m.p.h. in a 1,000 h.p. landplane, against M. Delmotte's 343.30 m.p.h. in a similar type of aeroplane of only 380 h.p. The matter was very nicely summed-up by "The Aeroplane," which said : "If we were arguing about comparative efficiences

. . . that would be a justifiable point to raise. But in talking about absolute speeds, regardless of conditions, the argument is useless and stupid." Exactly the same applies to the "Motor-car Speed Record" (as the lay-press term it), what it feels like to drive at over 300 m.p.h. only Sir Malcolm can know, but those of us who have felt unusually daring and "he-manish" after driving at a mere 100 m.p.h. would do well to try and imagine how we would have felt had the car accelerated to three times that speed !

Summing up, it is significant that Sqd.-Ldr. Orlebar, himself experienced in ultra-high-speed-travel, said in his book "Schneider Trophy" at a time when Sir Malcolm had reached only 250 m.p.h., that he fully appreciated the colossal task of controlling a machine travelling at this rate on the ground, and suggested that "Bluebird" must have been very nearly air-borne at that speed.

Turning to Eyston's records, one's greatest admiration is for the manner in which the front-drive, Rolls-Royce engined "Speed-of-the-Wind" was taken straight out to Utah, and, an experimental car running far from its "base," functioned perfectly at phenomenal speeds. The World's Hour Record has always been one of the most coveted, calling as it does for sustained running at speeds which could scarcely be held for one-mile only, ten years ago. To average 159.3 m.p.h. for an hour on a vast, salt lake course calls for immense fitness of both car and driver, and such an achievement deserves the highest admiration. Coveted as the "Hour" has always been, it was only a few years ago that it was raised to a speed beyond the capabilities of normal racing cars, indeed, it seems only a short time ago that Thomas astonished the motoring world by covering just over 110 miles in an hour on a Leyland-

Thomas. Now we have Eyston's figure of over 159 miles.

As we close for press we learn that Eyston, and his co-drivers, A. Denby and Chris Staniland, have broken the World's 24-Hour Record at 140.19 m.p.h., collecting numerous other records during the run.

Distance. Kiloms.	New Record. m.p.h.	Old Record m.p.h.
50	158.52	144.12
100	161.13	148.49
200	159.18	151.46
2,000	144.15	143.51
3,000	144.08	138.79
4,000	142.15	133.89
5,000	140.434	135.07
Miles	m.p.h.	m.p.h.
10	167.09	164.08
50	160.38	147.16
100	159.59	150.72
2,000	142.70	138.53
3,000	140.75	134.78
Hrs.	m.p.h.	m.p.h.
1	159.30	152.15
12	143.97	139.84
24	140.52	135.47

The following equipment was used for these records :—

"Bluebird."

Engine—Rolls-Royce ; Tyres—Dunlop ; Fuel—Esso Ethyl special ; Oil—Patent Castrol ; Clutch lining—Ferodo ; Brake linings—Ferodo ; Shock absorbers—T. B. Andre ; Steering—Burman ; Steering damper and wheel—T.T.N. & Bluemel ; Instruments, etc.—S. Smith & Sons ; Brake servo—Clayton-Dewandre ; Sparking plugs—K.L.G. ; Gears—David Brown ; Frame members—John Thompson ; Finish—Belco ; Radiators—Serck ; Axles and shafts—Hadfields steels ; Springs—Woodhead ; Glass—Triplex ; Wheel discs—Cornercrofts ; Cushions—Moseley ; Magnetos—B.T.H. ; Axle-gears—E.N.V. ; Accumulators—Young.

"Speed of the Wind."

Engine—Rolls-Royce ; Tyres—Dunlop ; Fuel—B.P. Ethyl ; Oil—Patent Castrol ; Brake linings—Ferodo ; Shock absorbers—Andre-Hartford ; Steering—Adamant ; Wheel—Dover Wheel ; Instruments—Jaeger ; Brakes—Lockheed brakes ; Plugs—G.M.S. ; Gears—Armstrong, Siddeley pre-selector box ; Frame members—L. T. Delaney Ltd. ; Radiator—Gallay ; Axles—Miller-type drive shafts ; Springs—Herbert Terry ; Whee discs—Ewarts ; Cushions—Moseley ; Magnetos—B.T.H. ; Axle gears—E.N.V. ; Accumulators—Lucas.

At Bonneville the timekeepers and their instruments occupy a lofty perch overlooking the course. Judging from the first announcements of the Campbell records, an adding machine was not included amongst their equipment.

301 MILES AN HOUR ON SPECIAL

ESSO ETHYL

It is typical of **SIR MALCOLM CAMPBELL'S** thoroughness that he had his own supplies of special Esso Ethyl shipped from England to Utah — 6,000 miles — for his magnificent achievement in setting up his recent sensational world's record. The Ethyl anti-knock used in blending this phenomenally powerful fuel was identically the same as is used in Esso Ethyl, available to motorists everywhere.

ANGLO-AMERICAN OIL COMPANY, LTD. *Established 1888.*

SIR MALCOLM CAMPBELL RETIRES —

"PROVISIONALLY"!

ON the night of Thursday, September 26th, a gathering of more than 600 well-known people met at the Dorchester Hotel, as guests of the *Daily Mail*, at a banquet given as a tribute to Sir Malcolm Campbell's achievement in attaining 301.129 m.p.h. on Bonneville Flats, Utah.

The Hon. Esmond Harmsworth, who presided, read congratulatory telegrams from His Majesty The King and His Royal Highness The Prince of Wales, which were greeted with enthusiasm by the guests, many of whom were members of the British Racing Drivers' Club.

After the chairman had outlined his career of speed and paid tribute to his personal qualities, he presented him with a gold plaque on behalf of the *Daily Mail*.

In replying, the Guest of Honour declared that his new record was really an Anglo-American affair, belonging equally to the two countries, since, without their incomparable course at Salduro and without their unstinting aid and co-operation, the establishment of such a record would be an absolute impossibility.

The speaker went on to pay another obviously heartfelt tribute, this time to Leo Villa, Harry Leech and others of "that loyal and enthusiastic band of fellows, my mechanics, without whose help I should never have been able to realise my life's ambition to be the first man to travel at 300 m.p.h. on land."

After stressing the very great importance internationally of such efforts as those involved in breaking the World's Land Speed Record, and the extent to which the prestige of a successful nation benefits, Sir Malcolm described the interesting and valuable results obtained at Utah by the fitment in the cockpit of a Ciné-Kodak apparatus which "shot" the instrument dials throughout his successful sprint.

An interesting fact was that at 300 m.p.h., centrifugal force resulted in the tops of his tyres assuming a totally different shape, being pointed instead of flat.

With regard to his future plans, Sir Malcolm said : "I promised my wife that when I had done 300 I would retire, and it is my intention to keep my promise— but with this one reservation, that if a foreign car should beat my record, and if no other British car be available to attempt to recapture it, then "Blue Bird" will again be in the field. But," added Sir Malcolm, "if any British driver makes an attempt on "Blue Bird's" record, I shall be happy to give him all the assistance that I can in every way and to give him the benefit of my experience."

Lastly, Sir Malcolm paid a moving tribute to the selfless devotion of his wife, a tribute which evoked tremendous applause.

Earl Howe, President of the B.R.D.C., was the next speaker.

After he had assured Sir Malcolm of the high esteem in which his fellow-drivers would always hold him and Lady Campbell, and had reminded all those present of the very real importance of a man like their Guest of Honour as an ambassador of this country's industry and sport, he presented to Sir Malcolm, on behalf of his fellow-members of the B.R.D.C., a Gold Star bearing the inscription : "Presented to Sir Malcolm Campbell, the first driver in the world to exceed 300 miles per hour on land. 3 : 9 : 35."

SERVICING "BLUE BIRD" UNDER AN AWNING, BETWEEN HER RECORD-BREAKING RUNS.
Taken on Kodak Panatomic Film at Bonneville Salt Flats, Salduro, Utah, U.S.A.

MORE CURIOSITIES OF RECORD BREAKING

By R. KING-FARLOW

A car designed in 1932 by Monsieur Stapp to attack the World's Land Speed Record. It was wrecked in a preliminary try-out at La Baule sands

THE two-way timing of short-distance records was first laid down by the A.I.A.C.R. in 1909, but it was four years before this ruling was put to a practical test. The standing half-mile and kilometre records taken by Hemery on the Benz at Brooklands in December, 1913, were the first runs to be timed in both directions. A curious situation over the Land Speed Record arose owing to this new regulation. Prior to the new rule being made, the record stood to the credit of Hemery's Benz at 125.9 m.p.h. As time went on, however, very much higher speeds were achieved in America, culminating in Tommy Milton's Duesenberg record of 156.04 m.p.h. in April, 1920. Since these American records were only timed in one direction, they were not recognised by the A.I.A.C.R., so that when Kenelm Lee Guinness clocked 133.75 m.p.h. over the kilometre at Brooklands in 1922, he officially took the Land Speed Record, at a time when the American National Record stood nearly 23 m.p.h. higher. Although irregular, the American speeds have been carefully verified, and now usually appear in lists of the history of the record.

*   *   *

American procedure was not finally brought into line with European methods until early in 1927, when the American Automobile Association formally joined the A.I.A.C.R., adopting all their rules concerning timing and measurements. One of the first results of this agreement was that Segrave was able to attack the Land Speed Record at Daytona under official conditions. Some of the American National Records set up prior to the A.A.A. joining the A.I.A.C.R. are extremely interesting. For example, at the end of 1926 the American 100 mile record stood at 133.709 m.p.h., a speed that was not achieved elsewhere until March, 1934, when Hans Stuck did great things with an Auto-Union at Avus. Again, in the 1,500 c.c. class, the 1926 American 100 mile record was 126.55 m.p.h., considerably higher than even the present-day record, held by Pierre Veyron's Bugatti at 119.01 m.p.h. It should, however, be noted that the American National Records are timed from a flying start, whereas World and International Class Records of over 10 miles are, of course, taken from a standing start. Nevertheless, the speeds set up in America in 1925 and 1926 are a very great tribute to the designers of both cars and tracks.

A curious machine built for record work was the four-cylinder 1,500 c.c. "razor-blade" Panhard, which appeared in 1926. This was one of the most ultra-streamlined racers ever produced. The front brake-operating mechanism was concealed within the tubular front axle, the drums being covered by the wheels' discs. There were no rear brakes, other than a transmission brake. The rear springs were attached to the centre of the axle, no part of them appearing outside the body shell. Most curious of all was the steering. The driver sat with his legs encircled by a large wheel, fitted on the outer rim with gear teeth that engaged a pinion projecting through the floorboards. The pinion shaft, after suitable gearing, operated the drop-arm connected to a rocking-arm which actuated the ends of the divided track-rod. A similar machine with a 4.9-litre engine was also built. The Panhard concern had very high hopes of their unorthodox creation, but in practice the radically new steering was not a success. In fact, while driving the larger car, Marcel Breton, the well-known French record breaker, completely lost control, crashed into the

MORE CURIOSITIES OF RECORD BREAKING

Montlhèry retaining wall and was killed instantly.

* * *

Another even stranger French vehicle was that designed and built in 1932 by a Monsieur Stapp "to attack the land speed record." Amongst other pleasing features it had three Jupiter engines of 800 h.p., an additional Voisin engine for starting purposes, electrical transmission and four-wheel-drive. Also, to complicate matters, the Jupiters were reported by Monsieur Stapp as having been converted by his especial genius into internal combustion turbines, although the method by which this was done was not revealed. The contraption also carried two spare wheels and a battery box strapped to the outside of the body and was registered for road use, details lacking in other recent world record cars. Pictures exist of it being driven about the Paris streets by its optimistic inventor, accompanied by a passenger wearing a bowler hat. M. Stapp tried out his "bolide" on the sands at La Baule, where it proceeded to burst into flames almost instantly, finally turning over and becoming a total wreck. Both driver and mechanic managed to jump clear, without serious injury.

* * *

The highest speed ever recorded officially on a road is 200.78 m.p.h., over the mile on the Firenze-Mare autostrada by Tazio Nuvolari with the bimotere Alfa-Romeo last June. At the time of writing, Nuvolari is the only living driver besides Sir Malcolm Campbell to have secured a record at over 200 m.p.h. There is little doubt, however, that the Mercédès and Auto-Union will endeavour to improve

on the Alfa's time in the near future.

* * *

In the early days world records were, naturally enough, almost invariably taken at Brooklands. Then came the turn of Montlhèry, with occasional long-distance runs at Miramas and Monza. For a brief interval it looked as if the Avus track at Berlin might win favour and probably develop an entirely new type of record breaker. Before this could happen, however, the

Sir Malcolm Campbell and the late Frank Lockhart, whose performances our contributor regards as the most meritorious in the history of record making

Utah Salt Beds came into the news, and every other venue instantly faded into the background. It is fairly safe to say that there is not a single world record under 24 hours, other than the standing kilometre and mile, that can at present be taken in Europe. In other words, anyone wanting to attack world records has got to start off by making a journey of several thousand miles, an added trouble and expense that will almost kill world records. Possibly a time will come when a new Avus-like track, or

combination of autostrada, will be available. Till then interest will probably centre on the International Class records.

The Class records are undoubtedly interesting, but are robbed of much of their attraction by their multiplicity. At the moment there are, besides the 217 World's Records, 607 officially recognised International Class Records, plus half-a-dozen Diesel records. Moreover, there is nothing to prevent a firm sending a car to roll round Montlhèry till it drops to pieces, creating new records as it goes. Surely if any extension over 24 hours was really necessary, 48 hours, seven days, 28 days and three months would have been ample, without distance records. The duplication of kilometre and mileage distances is also a pity, but is presumably unavoidable. The bulk of the Class records, being over 24 hours, are naturally held at Montlhèry. In fact, at present only 33 International records remain to Brooklands, 19 of them being in the smallest class of all, up to 350 c.c.

* * *

It would be a very invidious task to pick out any particular record as being the most meritorious on the list. Nevertheless, some guide may be taken from the advance any record-holder shows over the next best in his class. On these lines the palm for the best performance should go to Campbell for his 300 m.p.h. Land Speed Record, 70 m.p.h. faster than any other man has travelled, or to the late Frank Lockhart for his incredible 164.01 m.p.h. over the mile with a 1½-litre Miller in 1927. Probably the vote would go to Lockhart, for when he made his run, the World Record, established with a monster of 22.3-litres, was only 10 m.p.h. higher.

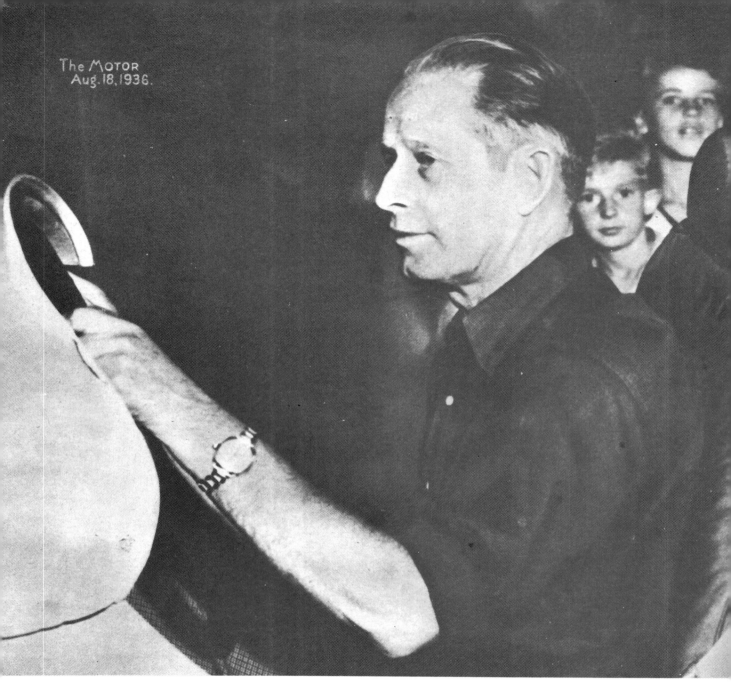

AMERICAN CHALLENGER

Here is Ab Jenkins, the American record breaking driver who hopes shortly to go out for records on the Bonneville Salt Flats, near Salt Lake City, Utah, aiming to lower the figures recently set up by George Eyston and Albert Denly with "Speed of the Wind." John Cobb will shortly be en route with the Napier Railton for the same purpose. Below is Jenkins's new car, which he hopes will be fast enough to break Sir Malcolm Campbell's 300 m.p.h. Land Speed Record as well as regain the records taken by Eyston. Known as "The White Ghost" it has a 12-cylinder engine and is said to have cost 40,000 dollars to build.

Designed For Over 300 m.p.h.

Captain Eyston's New Rear-engined Racing Car to Attack World's Land-speed Record

![Photograph of the rear-engined racing car chassis]

Towards an Unknown Region—Capt. Eyston's rear-engined 5,000-h.p. 24-cylinder car without its streamlined shell.

SO far as we are aware Captain G. E. T. Eyston has never attacked a record that he has not broken. As he is one of the most prolific breakers of class and world's records, this fact is a testimony to his engineering skill, to the care with which his car is prepared, as well as a demonstration of his capacity as a driver. When, therefore, it was known that he intended to build a car to attack the maximum land-speed record one waited with considerable interest to learn how he would approach the severe engineering problems involved.

The ordinary motorist can have little conception of the magnitude of the difficulties that present themselves. The present record stands to a speed of 301 m.p.h., and has been achieved by a car of good streamline form, having an engine developing approximately 2,400 h.p. Any new car built must, in view of the expense involved, have a large margin in designed speed available so that it can resist challenge for some time to come. If this margin is set at 50 m.p.h., i.e., a designed maximum speed of 350 m.p.h., the increase in power necessary is over 50 per cent., even with the equal frontal area and resistance. To raise the power by this extent is, in itself, difficult, and the problem is increased when one considers the transmission of around 5,000 h.p. without wheel spin.

Captain Eyston has tackled the matter with characteristic thoroughness by employing two Rolls-Royce engines, each of 12 cylinders and giving a total of not far short of 6,000 b.h.p. Following the latest practice in racing car design, these engines are mounted behind the driver, thereby concentrating the weight at the rear end of the car, and assisting wheel adhesion. Behind the engines is a train of spur wheels that join them to a huge centrally mounted three-speed gearbox, and behind this again is a bevel gearbox mounted on the frame. From this extend short transverse springs to the wheels that are located by wishbones giving a parallel motion. This form of suspension has proved thoroughly satisfactory in modern Grand Prix racing, and undoubtedly provides far better contact between tyre and track than the conventional axle used on previous record breakers.

A similar suspension scheme is adopted at the front end, but this is entirely novel in so far that there are four steering wheels all inter-connected by linkage to the steering mechanism, each one being separately sprung.

Captain Eyston has obviously given considerable attention to braking. The brakes are actually mounted, both fore and aft, on the sprung part of the car and driven (at the front end) by shafts from the "rear front" wheels. By this means unsprung weight is reduced considerably and, furthermore, the heat developed by braking is not transmitted to the tyres.

We should estimate the ultimate maximum speed of the car as 350-360 m.p.h., but, of course, it is not to be expected that such figures will be realized on the first run. There are many detail problems in a car like this that can only be solved in actual test and development, and a steady rise in speed is to be expected.

A detail which will, for instance, be of interest to the ordinary motorist is the fuel consumption. Even when not travelling at maximum speed this will be approximately eight gallons per minute, or six times as much as the average car consumes in an hour. A battery of approximately 75 electric petrol pumps of conventional type would be needed to pass the required volume.

All motorists will join in wishing Captain Eyston the best possible fortune in his bold attack, and congratulate him upon the audacious design which is evidenced in his new car.

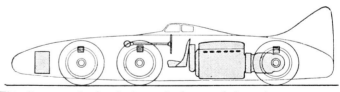

This diagrammatic sketch shows the layout of the main components in Capt. Eyston's new car. Note the transverse springs; rear mounting of the two 12-cylinder Rolls-Royce engines and use of tandem front wheels.

312 M.P.H.!

Eyston Breaks World's Records

New Figures for the Mile and Kilometre Records in One Attempt

THE RECORD SPEEDS

THE FLYING MILE. Northwards run : 305.34 m.p.h.
Time : 11.79 secs. Southwards run : 317.74 m.p.h.
Time : 11.33 secs. Mean speed : 311.42 m.p.h.

THE FLYING KILOMETRE (*World's Land Speed Record*) :
Northwards run : 305.59 m.p.h. Time : 7.32 secs.
Southwards run : 319.11 m.p.h. Time : 7.01 secs.
Mean speed : 312.20 m.p.h. Time : 7.165 secs.

FASTEST MAN ON EARTH: Capt. Eyston, who had never driven at much over 170 m.p.h. in his life before, last week quite calmly broke the World's Land Speed—

—Record with the "Thunderbolt" at 312.20 m.p.h. on Bonneville Salt Flats, Utah, thus beating Sir Malcolm Campbell's 301.13 m.p.h. with "Bluebird."

DRIVING his 5,000 h.p. Rolls-Royce-engined " Thunderbolt," Capt. G. E. T. Eyston broke the World's Land Speed Record last Friday. Hitherto held by Sir Malcolm Campbell's " Bluebird " at 301.13 m.p.h., Eyston pushed the record up (subject to the usual official confirmation) to the staggering speed of 312.20 m.p.h.—his mean speed of two runs over the flying kilometre.

Eyston actually broke both the world's mile and world's kilometre records in the one attempt, on Friday last—the news coming through shortly before 4 p.m. British time.

His speeds for the various runs are shown at the top of the page.

* * *

DOGGED by bad luck, held up by bad weather and irritating delays, Capt. G. E. T. Eyston, with his huge twin-engined, eight-tyred " Thunderbolt " at Bonneville Salt Flats, Utah, has given an exhibition of determination and singleness of purpose which would have covered him with glory even if his car had failed officially to break the World's Land Speed Record which he sought.

Eyston has been in Utah for several weeks, taking with him the older " Speed of the Wind " with single Rolls-Royce aero engine and front-wheel drive, and having the new " Thunderbolt " sent out to him a little later on its completion.

With the former car, hampered by bad weather, he eventually broke the world's 12-hour record at 163.3 m.p.h. in a breathing space between trials of the " Thunderbolt."

At the end of October Eyston made his first test run on full throttle with the " Thunderbolt," and clocked 309.6

m.p.h. in a northerly direction. He turned for the run south, and then the car developed trouble with one of the clutches—but Eyston had travelled faster on land than any other living man, although he had not officially broken the record which must be the mean of two runs.

To repair the defect both engines had to be taken out of the frame, and in the meantime Eyston broke the world's 12-hour record with " Speed of the Wind."

About a week later the car was ready again, and for the first time the run was broadcast from the spot and transmitted to the B.B.C., who relayed the commentary to listeners in this country. The microphone caught the roar of the car flashing over the dry salt lake in one run—sounding exactly like an aeroplane. Then Eyston turned for the run back again, and once again clutch trouble developed and once again he was robbed of the record. His one run was at just over 310 m.p.h.

Through all these disappointments " The Captain," as the American called him, remained completely cheerful, and was delighted with the handling of the car. Eyston had no awkward moments, and it is a tribute to his skill that although he had never travelled at even 200 m.p.h. in his life before, he quite calmly took the enormous machine over the salt beds at over 300 m.p.h. without batting an eyelid. Which, of course, is typical of the man.

The " Thunderbolt " was built with more speed and less limelight than any previous 300 m.p.h. car, and designed by Eyston himself, it embodies many new ideas. The power is derived from two Rolls-Royce supercharged aircraft engines, developing about 5,000 h.p. There are two pairs of front wheels, bogie fashion, both steerable, and the rear-wheel drive goes through twin wheels to reduce stresses on the Dunlop tyres. Suspension front and back is by transverse leaf springs of enormous power.

* * *

THESE SHARE THE CREDIT

Engines: Rolls-Royce, Ltd., Derby. **Tyres and wheels:** Dunlop Rubber Co., Ltd. **Bodywork:** Birmal Boats, Ltd., Southampton. **General assembly and manufacture of approximately 600 details:** Beans Industries, Ltd., Tipton.

Fuel: B.P. Ethyl. **Oil:** Castrol.

Gearbox: Beans Industries, Ltd. **Gearbox casing:** Birmingham Aluminium Casting Co. **Gear grinding:** The Gear Grinding Co., Ltd., Handsworth. **Radiator:** Serck Radiators, Ltd., Birmingham. **Road springs:** Jonas Woodhead and Sons, Ltd., Leeds. **Coil springs:** H. Terry and Sons, Ltd., Redditch.

Frame and engine suspension: John Thompson Motor Pressings, Ltd., Bilston. **Petrol tanks and piping:** John Marston, Ltd., Wolverhampton. **Brake gear:** Lockheed Hydraulic Brake Co. and Ferodo, Ltd. **Clutches:** John Thornycroft. **Gear change mechanism:** Burman and Sons, Ltd., Birmingham.

Steering gear: Burman and Sons, Ltd. **Bearings:** Hoffmann Manufacturing Co., Chelmsford. **Pipes from engine to radiator:** Petroflex, Ltd., London. **Certain parts of hubs and suspension:** Wolseley Co., Birmingham. **Various aluminium bronze castings for spring suspension:** T. M. Birkett and Sons, Hanley. **Friction metals for gearbox and clutches:** Ferodo, Ltd. **Gear steels:** United Steel Corporation. **Precision work:** Wolseley.

"*Thunderbolt*"

The fastest car in the World and its intrepid driver "on location"

Left: "Thunderbolt" being pushed off by a tender-car, on one of its runs, in order to save the clutch

Left: An unusual rear view of Capt. Eyston's monster car in full flight

Check-over. Mechanics swarming round the car to refuel, change wheels, replenish oil, et cetera, between runs, this work having to be completed as quickly as possible to prevent the engine growing cold

Captain G. E. T. Eyston chatting with Mr. T. E. Meyers, A.A.A. Timekeeper from Indianapolis, in between runs in the "Thunderbolt"

Hearty Congratulations, Capt. Eyston!

His car, "Thunderbolt," smashes Sir Malcolm Campbell's Land Speed Record after many vicissitudes

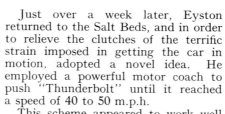

Just over a week later, Eyston returned to the Salt Beds, and in order to relieve the clutches of the terrific strain imposed in getting the car in motion, adopted a novel idea. He employed a powerful motor coach to push "Thunderbolt" until it reached a speed of 40 to 50 m.p.h.

This scheme appeared to work well and Eyston shot away to return 310.685 m.p.h. for the measured mile in a northward direction, despite the fact that there were several soft patches on the course.

On the southward run there was a recurrence of the clutch trouble, and Eyston again had to pull up before the measured mile was reached. In an interview, Eyston expressed the view that

of a second faster than Sir Malcolm Campbell had done in "Bluebird," yet his speed beat the previous record by no less than 11 m.p.h.!

Visibility was very poor at the time the run was made, but Eyston dared not wait longer, for there was a threat of imminent rain.

Already he is talking about another visit to Bonneville in 1938 to improve upon his new record.

"The car," said Capt. Eyston, "is still in its experimental stage. We have learned a mighty lot, but we hope to learn a lot more about the many

"Thunderbolt," Captain Eyston's wonderful 312 m.p.h. car

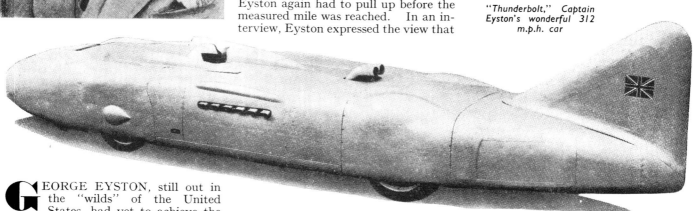

GEORGE EYSTON, still out in the "wilds" of the United States, had yet to achieve the ambition of his life by becoming the holder of the world's land speed record up to Friday, November 19th.

Ever since he arrived at the Bonneville Salt Flats he had been dogged by ill-luck, and so far his only success had been to capture world's records up to 12-hours from the American pair, Ab Jenkins and Lou Meyer.

Two attempts had been made on Sir Malcolm Campbell's record of 301 m.p.h. odd, and but for Eyston's bad luck the old figure would have been beaten by eight or nine miles per hour.

On the first attempt, "Thunderbolt," biggest and most powerful car ever constructed, covered the flying mile in one direction at the colossal average speed of 309.6 m.p.h. No man nor machine had ever travelled so fast on land before, for Campbell's highest speed for one run is 304.311 m.p.h.

The record thus looked a "sitter" for Eyston, but on the return run clutch trouble developed before the measured distance was entered, the car being taken back to Wendover and dismantled.

the repairs had been effected somewhat hurriedly and that the trouble ought to have been dealt with more drastically.

The runs, however, proved that "Thunderbolt" was wonderfully controllable; in fact, no previous record-breaker had ever shown better stability.

Eyston said that at least ten days would be required to cure the clutch trouble, but the biggest problem was whether the Salt Flats would be in good enough condition to permit of another attempt this year.

The matter was further involved by having to send the clutches to Detroit for re-construction.

On Friday, November 19th, however, Eyston essayed another attempt on the record, and although he covered the measured mile only one-hundredth

novel ideas incorporated in its design. Such knowledge can only be obtained at high speed."

On the record run, the two Rolls-Royce engines developed nearly 6,000 horse-power and it has been stated that they devoured eight gallons of petrol in under sixty seconds! Oil was pumped through at approximately the same rate.

The tyres revolved 2,520 times a minute, while centrifugal force increased the tyre diameter by no less than $1\frac{1}{4}$ inches.

"Thunderbolt's" equipment included Dunlop tyres, Wakefield Patent Castrol oil, Lodge Plugs, B.P. Ethyl petrol and Wolseley suspension and steering.

The car is 36 feet long and weighs approximately seven tons.

EYSTON'S NEW RECORDS				
The Kilometre			**The Mile**	
North : 7.32 secs.	... 305.59 m.p.h.		North : 11.79 secs.	... 305.34 m.p.h.
South : 7.01 secs.	... 319.11 m.p.h.		South : 11.33 secs.	... 317.74 m.p.h.
Average : 7.165 secs.	... 312.20 m.p.h.		Average : 11.56 secs.	... 311.42 m.p.h.

WHERE'S GEORGE ?

FINAL TRIUMPH OF G. E. T. EYSTON ON THE BONNEVILLE SALT FLATS.
"THUNDERBOLT" REACHES 319 M.P.H.

WHERE'S George ? At one moment he was at one end of a measured kilometre on the Bonneville Salt Flats, Utah, U.S.A. Seven seconds later he was at the other end, having travelled in his "Thunderbolt" at no less than 319.11 m.p.h. Then he was back again, this time averaging 305.59 m.p.h. A new world's land speed record had been set up, the mean of the two runs representing 312.20 m.p.h. !

Only slightly slower were the speeds over the measured mile. In one direction Eyston averaged 317.74 m.p.h., and in the other 305.34 m.p.h., giving a mean speed over this distance of 311.42 m.p.h.

The record runs took place in the early morning, and the light was by no means good. So dark was it, in fact, that Capt. Eyston on one of his runs was unable to note the distinguishing marks at the start of the measured distance, but had in any case, after a flying start of about five miles, attained sufficient speed for the record. He was further handicapped by his goggles blowing out of place just as he entered the measured distance on his fastest run. Quite unperturbed, Eyston removed one hand from the wheel at 320 m.p.h., and pulled the goggles straight again.

The surface at the Salt Flats has not this year been at its best. It is only for a few months during the year that the surface is ever really dry, and this year the water took longer than usual after the seasonal rains to evaporate. In consequence, Eyston had some poor conditions to overcome, especially on his earlier test runs. On the day of the record he was fortunate in finding the surface a little drier, after a short spell of fine weather, but it was not as good as one has reason to expect at this time of year.

The whole record was a fight against time, for it must be appreciated that the "Thunderbolt" incorporated many novel features of design, and there had been no opportunity to test the car as a complete unit before leaving England. Eyston arrived at the Salt Flats at the beginning of October, and found the salt crust still too soft to support his seven-ton car.

It was not until October 28th that a test run was possible over the ten-mile course, and on this occasion 309.6 m.p.h. was attained in one direction—a speed well above the old record set up by Sir Malcolm Campbell at 301.13 m.p.h. On the return run, however, the clutch gave trouble, and no time was recorded. While this trouble was being attended to, George Eyston took out his other car, "Speed of the Wind," and using a circular course instead of the straight eleven miles traversed by the "Thunderbolt," captured several long-distance records, including the world's 12-hour record at 163.68 m.p.h.

On November 6th, "Thunderbolt" was ready again, and this time reached 310.685 m.p.h. But again the terrific power from the two Rolls-Royce engines was too much for the clutch. The clutch was of interesting design, which must not be condemned merely through failure

Captain G. E. T. Eyston.

in initial experiments. The power was first transmitted by friction plates, which, after the principle of a synchromesh gear, synchronised the speeds of the clutch shaft and the crankshaft, and allowed spring-loaded dogs to engage and give the effect of a solid drive.

The trouble was not occurring in the friction part of the clutch, where the Ferodo linings stood up well, but in the rest of the novel principle involved. Capt. Eyston, who, while the car was being built at the Bean works at Tipton, Staffs., had personally supervised the whole operation, now showed his mettle as a designer, as well as a driver, by sitting down and redesigning the clutch. The drawings were rushed off by aeroplane, and new parts were made. On the final runs, when the world's record was broken no further trouble was experienced.

The car itself was built in under seven months. Its two supercharged Rolls-Royce engines, of Schneider Trophy type, have a total capacity of over 73 litres, and develop 5,000 h.p. The engines are set side by side amidships, and there is a three-speed gearbox. Eyston attained 100 m.p.h. in bottom gear, and accelerated up to 220 m.p.h. before changing into top !

Although the car is a six-wheeler, only the rear pair of wheels are driven. Both pairs of front wheels, however, are connected to the steering, while the driver sits just in front of the engines. All six wheels are independently sprung. The steering gear was of Burman-Douglas type, and the steering layout was built by the Wolseley company. The road springs were made by Jonas Woodhead, the well known Leeds firm which has supplied so many racing drivers. Andre shock absorbers were used, and Moseley Float-on-Air upholstery.

The tyre manufacturers deserve especial credit. It is only by the unflagging research of the Dunlop technicians that such speeds have become possible at all, one must remember that this is only the second time that the Salt Flats have been used for the land speed record, and that fresh calculations were necessary on the change-over from Daytona Sands to Utah, with a surface of an entirely different character. So great is the centrifugal force at 320 m.p.h. that the tyre diameter increases by no less than 1¼ in. ! For this reason extremely thin treads are necessary, or the rubber would be flung right off.

In spite of the five mile stretches for acceleration before entering the measured distance and for pulling up, both these operations require great skill, with the gigantic forces involved. It will be remembered when the late Sir Henry Segrave attained 200 m.p.h. for the first time, the brake shoes actually melted, and Sir Henry had to run into the sea to pull up. It is estimated that the stored energy to be dissipated at the end of

Continued on page 112

The complete rear brake mounted on the transmission at the rear of the chassis.

EYSTON'S OWN STORY

WORLD'S FASTEST DRIVER GIVES PERSONAL ACCOUNT OF HIS RECORDS AT THE SALT FLATS

SINCE his return to England in triumph from the U.S.A., the penalties of the successful record-breaker have fallen upon George Eyston. A whirl of social activity has occupied his time, for all kinds of bodies throughout the country have been anxious to do honour to the fastest man on earth.

George has certainly shown himself fully competent in this side of the record breaker's activities, which in modern times has become scarcely less important than skill at the wheel. One of the functions at which he must have felt most at home was the dinner at the Savoy Hotel, London, given in his honour by the British Racing Drivers' Club. At this dinner Eyston gave a most interesting account of his recent experiences at the Bonneville Salt Flats, and in his speech many hitherto unrecorded incidents were brought to light. The difficulties met with may well have been even greater than those mentioned in this personal account, for George is never one to make the most of his own exploits.

The chair was taken by Sir Malcolm Campbell, owing to the absence of the B.R.D.C. President, Earl Howe, in South Africa, and he and other speakers paid tribute to Capt. Eyston's career, in which he has already crammed so many successes. Eyston is only forty years of age, and the hope was expressed that he had at least another twenty years of record-breaking in front of him !

After going down from Cambridge, Eyston started his motoring career in 1923 with various hill-climbs. Lionel Martin, who was present at the recent B.R.D.C. dinner, sold him his first car, an Aston-Martin, which recalls the fact that the name of this famous make is derived from the Aston Clinton hill-climbs, which were prominent at the time, and from Lionel Martin's own surname.

Not long after this Eyston was married, and gave up racing for a time. In 1926, however, he could no longer be restrained, and, returning to racing, won the Boulogne Grand Prix in a Bugatti supplied to him by Malcolm Campbell. He continued with various other successes until in 1931 he turned seriously to record-breaking, a sphere of activity in which he has proved himself more proficient that anyone else in the world, having taken since that time approximately 250 records over distances ranging from one kilometre to 5,000 miles.

In 1931 Eyston was the first man to reach 100 m.p.h. in a 750 c.c. car, and later in the same year covered 100 miles in one hour with the same type. He has naturally had many thrilling experiences, but his only serious accident was also in 1931, when at Montlhéry his car caught fire and crashed. Eyston's forethought probably saved his life on this occasion, for he was wearing asbestos overalls. His famous car, " Speed of the Wind," was constructed in 1935, and embodied many interesting features to his own design, such as front wheel drive and independent suspension.

It was with this car, " Speed of the Wind," that Eyston arrived at the Salt Flats during the first week in September, 1937. The " Thunderbolt " was not yet quite ready and followed a month later. Ab Jenkins, the American, was already there, with his Mormon Meteor Special, in order to attack the 24 and 48-hour records.

Usually a twelve-mile circle has been used for these long distance records at the Salt Flats, but this course was in bad condition, for there was a kind of morass at one end of the lake. An eleven-mile circle was therefore marked out, and Jenkins had " first whack," putting up the 12-hour figure to just over 160 m.p.h., and the 24-hour to 157.27 m.p.h. On the very day that Jenkins finished his 24-hour record, it rained in torrents, and quite soon the entire surface of the lake was three or four inches under water.

A fortnight's wait ensued, to let the water evaporate. Eyston's luck appeared to be out, for when the surface had dried sufficiently, he took out " Speed of the Wind " and promptly seized up the front drive. Meanwhile " Thunderbolt " had arrived, and after a test run at 309 m.p.h., the clutch gave trouble on this machine as well !

However, " Speed of the Wind " was soon put right again, and at midnight George Eyston set off once more to attack the 24-hour record. The reason for starting at this peculiar time was that the prophets had promised fine weather, and no opportunity could be lost. But as dawn broke ominous clouds obscured the sky, and then a violent storm burst and swamped the lake again.

Eyston was prepared for this emergency, and changed over to a ten-mile circle, which had been marked out in readiness, and which was in better condition. Driving at 167 m.p.h., there was a considerable difference between the twelve and the eleven-mile circles, owing to centrifugal force, and even greater difficulty on the ten-mile circle, especially with the surface as slippery as it was. It was then that the vane on the front of the car, a device designed by Reid Railton, was of the utmost service, and Eyston was able to keep going at a speed above the record.

When only half-an-hour of the 12-hour period was left, a further storm broke over the lake, and it became imperative to slow a little. As a result, Eyston failed to get the 12-hour record by a decimal point. He went on for the 24-hour figure, and also during the run made an attempt on the hour record, lapping at 180 m.p.h.

After another wait for the water to evaporate, Eyston set out once more, and this time, lapping at 170 m.p.h., was more favoured by the weather, and got the 12-Hour record at 163.68 m.p.h. Then the supplies for " Speed of the Wind " which he had brought from England ran out, and for this reason only he had to abandon a further attempt on the 24-hour figure, which thus remained in the hands of Jenkins.

Another test run on " Thunderbolt " had been sandwiched in between the long-distance attempts, but the clutch again proved defective. Eyston paid a big tribute to his mechanics, who had to strip the complicated mechanism of the big car three times in all.

At last on November 19th " Thunderbolt " was ready, and the party were up at 2 a.m. It got light by about 7 a.m., and it was evident that there was no time to lose, for black clouds hung over the mountains. The great car was taken out to the record stretch, but then, to show how a hitch can occur even in the best laid plans, it was found that the special fairing to prevent fumes entering the cockpit had been forgotten !

While this was being fetched and fixed in position, Eyston chafed and fumed, for the clouds were becoming more threatening, and the oil was getting cold.

It took sixteen minutes to change all the wheels and refuel, and Eyston set off in the southward direction, a course that he had not previously traversed on either of his test runs. He said that the first indication he had that the speed was up quite a lot was a rag, which had somehow got lodged in the cockpit, dashing past his face, and immediately afterwards his goggles lifted, and he had to haul them back again.

The timed stretch for the kilometre was at the end of the mile, and for the former distance the speed was now 319.11 m.p.h., and for the mile 317.74 m.p.h. Thus it is seen that the car was accelerating right through the distance, and indeed Eyston said he was so exhilarated that he kept on accelerating long past the final mark post.

Eventually he got back to the garage at Wendover, and was just lifting a drink to his lips when someone told him there was a telephone call, and he was asked to broadcast to England, nearly 6,000 miles away. By this time it was raining cats and dogs, and an aeroplane arrived to take him to Ogden to the broadcasting station. He was pushed into the plane, still in his overalls, and at the other end got his talk over.

He thought that " Thunderbolt " still had speed in hand, but a mean speed of 312 m.p.h. was enough to be going on with. If anybody thought it was not real motoring, he recommended, " You go and try it ! "

Captain G. E. T. Eyston.

Caracciola's record-breaking Mercedes.

ACHIEVEMENT AND TRAGEDY

BERNDT ROSEMEYER KILLED ON THE FRANKFURT AUTOBAHN. CARACCIOLA'S AMAZING 271 M.P.H.

THE whole sporting fraternity has been struck with a sense of grievous loss by the sudden death of Berndt Rosemeyer, one of the three greatest road-racing drivers in the world.

The accident which cut off the champion Auto-Union driver in his prime occurred on the Frankfurt-Darmstadt *Autobahn*, scene of his triumphs during the record week last October. Earlier in the day Rosemeyer had seen his 253 m.p.h. records, which created such a sensation at the time, handsomely beaten by his friend and rival, Caracciola of Mercédès-Benz. It was in an attempt to regain the honours that he met his death.

Truly has it been said that the astonishing formula cars of 1933-37 have become almost too fast for any track. Rosemeyer's own 253 m.p.h. records were hailed as an unparalleled achievement, set up as they were on a road designed for ordinary motor traffic, and not specially built for record breaking purposes. The *Autobahnen*, it must be remembered, are divided into two strips, each less than 30 feet wide. It was only a short time ago that a broad stretch of sand, several hundred yards wide, and many miles in length, was considered essential even for 200 m.p.h. Rosemeyer and his colleagues added 50 m.p.h. to this speed without turning a hair, on a road narrower than the Barnet By-pass.

In the October record week there was an incident which might have resulted in disaster, when Caracciola's car, under the terrific wind pressure, tried to lift at the nose. Many years ago, tragedy overtook Frank Lockhart at Daytona sands for the same reason. It was a treacherous gust of wind which brought Rosemeyer to his doom. The horrified spectators, already thrilled by Caracciola's breathtaking speeds in the early morning, saw the Auto-Union swerve, saw Rosemeyer fighting madly for control. Then, like a flash, it was over. The super-streamlined silver car had given a vicious lurch, hit the stone parapet of a bridge over the *Autobahn*, and had leapt hurtling over the heads of the crowd, to lie a tangled mass of metal at the foot of an embankment. Ambulance men and doctors rushed forward, but Rosemeyer had been killed outright.

Rosemeyer was only twenty-nine years of age. He had had an astonishing rise to fame. The son of a garage proprietor at Lingen, he first took the wheel of a car at the age of nine, with special extensions bolted to the pedals. He started competitions as a motor-cyclist, and showed such promise that in 1934 he was engaged as a rider for the Auto-Union D.K.W. team.

He was not satisfied with motor-cycles, however, and at the close of the 1934 season managed to get a trial in the Auto-Union racing-cars at the Nürburg Ring. At once it was evident that a new star had arisen, and Rosemeyer made his début in the Avus races in 1935. Tyre trouble caused his retirement, and it was in the Eifelrennen of the same year that Rosemeyer first came into the limelight. After a stirring race, he lost to the already famous Caracciola by only 1¼ secs., after leading for the whole of the last lap till within a few hundred yards of the finish ! Later in 1935, Rosemeyer won the Masaryk Grand Prix, against the full force of the Continental drivers.

This paved the way for his greatest season, 1936, when with his Auto-Union he carried all before him, and won the title of European Champion. In this season he gained no fewer than seven victories, five of them in the biggest races of the year—the Eifelrennen, the German Grand Prix, the Coppa Acerbo, and the Swiss and Italian Grands Prix.

In 1937 he was almost as successful, though Caracciola regained the championship of Europe. However, Rosemeyer won the Eifelrennen, thus scoring his third consecutive victory at the Nürburg Ring, the Vanderbilt Cup, in America, the Italian Grand Prix, and the Donington Grand Prix. British spectators of this last race will always count themselves privileged to have witnessed his driving.

In October of 1937 Rosemeyer accomplished perhaps his most sensational performance, setting up a record for the standing start mile at no less than 138.68 m.p.h. ! For the standing start kilometre he averaged 117.24 m.p.h., almost as

R. Caracciola climbing into one of the super-streamlined Mercedes record cars.

fast as the previous record for the mile. Over the flying mile he averaged 253.708 m.p.h., and over the flying kilometre 252.487 m.p.h.

Rosemeyer was married during 1936 to Elli Beinhorn, the well known German airwoman. His wife was not present at the time of the accident, but at most of his races could be found in the pits, helping with a stop-watch. He leaves one little son, 2½ months old. To his family, to the Auto-Union team (which was robbed of another fine driver last July when Ernst von Delius was killed during the German Grand Prix), and to German motor sport as a whole, we extend our deepest condolences. A great driver has entered into Valhalla.

* * *

The tragedy followed one of the most startling performances ever made by a car and driver. Early that morning, at 5 a.m., the Mercédès-Benz équipe had been active, and as dawn broke over the *Autobahn*, Caracciola took his seat in the long silver car. The engine size was only 5.66-litres, or slightly smaller than that used last October, and the shape of the aerodynamic body had been modified to prevent the trouble of the nose lifting. The weather was splendid, and at this time in the morning the air was still.

After a short run, Caracciola expressed himself satisfied, and the attempt began, to regain for Mercédès-Benz the honours of the fastest speed on the road. On the first run, so steady was the car that spectators thought that Caracciola was having another practice spin, in order to warm up the engine. The engine, however, had already been warmed up to some purpose, for a gasp of astonishment went up when the speeds were announced—266.099 m.p.h. for the flying kilometre, and 268.086 m.p.h. for the flying mile.

At the far end of the record stretch Dietrich, the *Reifenmeister*, or Continental tyre expert, was waiting. Mechanics set to work, and tyres were changed as a precaution. Then the silver projectile began its return run. The engine note rose shriller and shriller. This time it was obvious that the Mercédès was travelling faster than ever before. There was an expectant hush while the timekeepers worked out the speeds. Neubauer, the Mercédès manager, could contain himself no longer, and hurried to the box. Then a great cheer went up—271.311

The late Berndt Rosemeyer travelling all out at the Avus Track in an Auto-Union similar to that in which he met his death.

m.p.h. for the kilometre, and 268.893 m.p.h. for the mile !

The full times and speeds for these amazing runs, which, subject to official confirmation, rank as International records in Class B, for cars up to 8-litres, were :—

Flying Kilometre :
Outward : 8.40 secs.   266.099 m.p.h.
Homeward : 8.24 secs.   271.311 m.p.h.
Mean Speed 268.712 m.p.h.

Flying Mile :
Outward : 13.43 secs.   268.086 m.p.h.
Homeward : 13.38 secs.   268.893 m.p.h.
Mean Speed 268.496 m.p.h.

Caracciola said after the records that the road-holding of the car was marvellous, and that he never had a moment's uncertainty. He was not, however, able to take full advantage of the power of the engine, which was reaching its maximum r.p.m. too quickly, owing to the gear ratio fitted. Immediate arrangements were made to take the car back to Unterturkheim for a higher gear to be fitted, but in view of the subsequent accident to Rosemeyer, it may well be that Mercédès-Benz will rest on their laurels.

In any case, Caracciola was of the opinion that speeds much in excess of 270 m.p.h. were impracticable on this particular stretch of road, owing to a bend which had to be negotiated. For higher speeds they would have to await the completion of the special road to be built for records near Dessau.

WHERE'S GEORGE ?—Continued from page 109

each run, converted into heat, would be enough to raise one cwt. of water from freezing to boiling point in 40 seconds.

The air brakes originally designed for the car were not used, and Eyston relied upon the friction brakes alone. These were of interesting design, for instead of the usual internal expanding type, disc brakes, similar to a plate clutch, were used. None of the brakes was on the wheels, for in order to keep the unsprung weight as low as possible, cardan shafts ran from the second pair of front wheels to the centre of the chassis, just in front of the driver's seat ; while, at the rear, the brakes were mounted on the end of the propeller shaft, *behind* the rear axle.

The brake operation was on the Lockheed hydraulic system, the stationary friction plates were manufactured by Borg and Beck, while the rotating spinners, also made by Borg and Beck, were lined with Ferodo, in which firm's laboratories the whole brake layout was tested. It was found that temperatures between 800 and 1,000 F. were developed, which means that the braking surfaces actually reached dull red heat.

Special B.P. Ethyl was used for the record, and the two engines burnt eight gallons a minute ! It is fortunate that at maximum speed Capt. Eyston took only just over 11 secs. to cover a mile ! The oil was Castrol, circulated by the pump on each engine at the rate of eight gallons a minute. Some ingenious person has also calculated that at 310 m.p.h a cylinder wall area of 2½ acres per minute had to be covered by lubricant.

Forty-eight Lodge sparking plugs, and B.T.H. magnetos, supplied the ignition. The delicate instruments needed were by Smith and Negretti and Zambra, and, as in previous record attempts, a T.T.N. steering stabiliser was fitted. The body, interesting in that all wheels were totally enclosed, as on the original 200 m.p.h. Sunbeam, was made of Birmabright metal, to Capt. Eyston's own design.

Eyston is expected back in England on the Aquitania, arriving on December 14th.

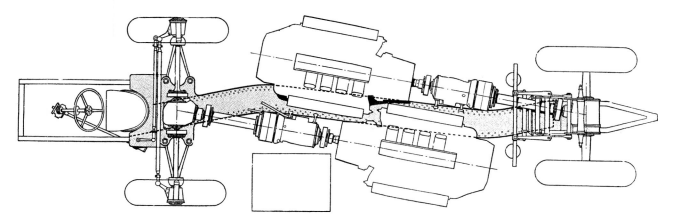

A plan view of the Railton chassis which clearly shows the angle of the engines and the two transmissions to front and rear wheels.

An Amazing New Record Car

The Unorthodox British Designed and Built Machine with Which John Cobb Will Attack the Land Speed Record

OF all the machines that have been produced to travel at the highest possible speed on land, right away from those wonderful days of Jenatzy and Chasseloup-Laubat with their weird electrical cars, none has been half so attractive as the new car, called the Railton, that the genius of Reid Railton has produced for John Cobb to drive over in Utah. Not only is the Railton fascinatingly unconventional, but there is a thrill in merely inspecting the mechanism, so well does it seem suited to the purpose for which it is created, so ingeniously have the various components been arranged for strict economy in weight.

Weight and Tyre Problems

The problem before Railton was not as simple as most people believe, having an eye to the performances recorded already by what are practically modified versions of the German road-racing machine. First, the engines that had to be used were already in existence, two supercharged Napier Lions naturally not of the most modern design nor even intended for car work. Secondly, the one tyre manufacturer who has tackled seriously the question of tyres suitable for these extraordinarily high speeds is Dunlop, and that firm naturally set a limit to the size of tyre that could be used, and to the amount of weight each tyre could carry. If the car was more than a certain weight, not four, but six, wheels would have to be used. So it came about that the new car had to be something completely out of the ordinary, and very out of the ordinary it is. Characteristically, Railton began by designing the body, then fitting the machinery into place, which materially affected the arrangement, as will be seen.

Conventional frame there is none, but instead a rectangular steel girder which forms the spine of the car and terminates at each end in a fork. On either side of this girder, roughly in the centre, are the two engines carried on outrigger brackets, which together give approximately 2,500 h.p. from 23,936 c.c. each. They are relatively simple engines with three blocks of four cylinders arranged broad-arrow fashion on a single crankcase, two

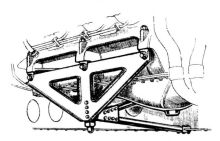

Since the frame is a "back-bone," each engine has an outrigger mounting.

bevel-driven camshafts close together overhead, and two lines of vertical valves. The cams operate the valves direct. The connecting-rods have plain bearings, the crankshaft roller bearings. One rod is the master, the other two articulated auxiliaries. The cylinder block itself is of light alloy with steel liners, the pistons being of light alloy also.

At one end of the engine is a very large centrifugal blower turning at something like 30,000 revolutions a minute. It is supplied by three large carburettors, the air intakes for which have to be carried to a point where they are not likely to pick up salt on the track. Two magnetos supply current for the plugs, of which there are two in each cylinder. The lubrication is on the dry-sump principle.

From the other end of the crankcase the drive is taken through a Laycock joint to a short shaft, and so to the gear box, the joints allowing a certain freedom of movement through rubber bushes.

Three-speed Gear Box

The gear box is very neat and comparatively small, has three speeds only, with straight toothed gears of great size, and at the rear end the drive passes to a brake drum with a broad contracting Ferodo band operating on the outer diameter and actuated by hydraulic pressure through a Lockheed cylinder. The band type of brake is used partly because it grips almost the entire surface of the drum, partly because it makes it easy to install a water-cooling system allowing water to flow to the inside of the drum when the brake pedal is pushed forward. Here it is held by centrifugal force and discharged eventually through a special outlet on to the track. Water is supplied from the main tank. Behind this drum is the propeller-shaft, with two Laycock joints, which for the left engine do not have to act as universal joints because the driving bevel and its casing are fixed to the frame.

All four wheels are driven. The right-hand engine drives the rear wheels, the left-hand engine the front wheels, each crankshaft turning towards the frame, and each transmission being complete with its own bevel and its own three-speed gear box. But the front axle has independent suspension for its two wheels. In front, therefore, the bevel and crown wheel, which have spiral teeth, drive through a differential to exposed shafts with constant-velocity universal joints of great size just behind the front hubs. The hubs are mounted on wishbone brackets that are almost of delicate fineness and have rubber-bushed joints.

Diagonally across the structure run the rods connected to the suspension. The suspension is housed in an almost cylindrical case. The first movement of the wheel is taken by a short sturdy coil spring, and further movement by a nest of large rubber discs. Mounted as part of the unit are the necessary stops, and another circular casing, which is part of the suspension, slides in a collar. This is held against the casing by pressure which can be adjusted so that this forms the shock absorber with very little additional weight. Be it noted that the actual movement of the wishbones and wheel is very limited.

The differential is necessary because the front wheels have to turn to steer the car. The track for this axle is 5ft. 6in.

At the rear the construction is different. The wheels are not independently sprung. There is an ordinary type of propeller-shaft. The spiral bevel is within a sturdy casing mounted on wishbone brackets top and bottom. There is no differential, and short steel tubes of considerable diameter project through the centre casing on either side to form the drive shafts. Again, the casing for the suspension acts as a shock absorber, the actual spring being partly metal coil, partly rubber disc. As the propeller-shafts enter their casings at an angle, both bevels and crown wheels are cut of special shape. The track of the rear axle is 3ft. 6in., very much less than that for the front wheels. Gigantic Dunlop disc wheels are used, but some saving in weight has been effected by altering the design and using steel instead of light alloy, while the tyres are of a special type of very small cross-section measuring 44in. in diameter, practically without tread. Experience has proved that these withstand best the very high centrifugal stress entailed. The Simmonds wheel

SPECIFICATION

Engines	..	Two Napier 12-cylinder, 5½in. bore, 5⅛in. stroke, 23,936 c.c., 1,250 h.p.
Gear box	..	Three speeds, top gear ratio 1.35 to 1.
Rear axle	..	Bevel driven.
Tyre size	..	44in.
Suspension	..	Independent front ; normal rear.
Fuel tank	..	18 gallon.
Oil tank	..	15 gallon.
Water tank	..	75 gallon.
Wheelbase	..	13ft. 6in.
Track	..	5ft. 6in. front ; 3ft. 6in. rear.
Overall length	..	28ft. 8in.
Overall width :	..	8ft.
Overall height	..	4ft. 3in.
Approximate weight		3 tons.
Approximate weight per h.p.	..	2.8 lb.

nuts have fibre rings which serve to lock the nut on its thread.

The driver in his cockpit is placed almost in the nose of the car, well in front of the engines. He is actually in front of the forward axle. The steering gear actuates the front wheels in the normal manner save that the steering column operates a bevel gear which drives a shaft, trailing backwards in a horizontal tube towards the axle, and, through this shaft, the drop-arm and steering-rod are actuated by a Burman gear. The spring wheel is of Bluemel design with three spokes in the form of a T.

Though the actual time for which the car will run and the distance it will travel are necessarily short, 18 gallons of fuel have to be carried in a light tank at one side of the frame, and 15 gallons of oil in another tank also at the side of the frame, tucked in beside an engine.

Then another point of interest is added. There is no radiator to break up the smooth nose of the streamlined body. The engines are just cooled by the 75-gallon water tank carried within the body and assisted by ice. It would be inadvisable to ice the whole of the water in the tank, so there is a separate compartment for the iced water. The contents of this are fed to the main supply for the engine by a thermostatically controlled valve in accordance with the temperature attained, the whole arrangement being entirely automatic.

Yet another point, and one of great importance, is the body. Some time before the German cars appeared with their beetle-shaped detachable bodies, this design of aluminium and

The driver's seat is positioned well in front of the forward axle with the gear lever in a gate at its side. There should be an appreciable impression of speed at over 300 m.p.h. from that cockpit !

" Alclad " was evolved, and it is certainly beautiful to look at, though totally unlike a car. Imagine a wonderfully smooth streamline shape that has much resemblance to a giant beetle but lacking any break in the flow of its lines, not even a fin. The cockpit cover, a streamlined metal hood with a window of Perspex—a patent material resembling glass—alone shows above the line. Even this projection is only slight, and gives the whole a curious animal appearance. Further consideration has led to four small humps, two on either side, to allow for the tyres, which are rather larger than those originally considered. But there is nothing else, and the whole of this body can be lowered on to the chassis like a cover, and removed equally easily. No mechanism is attached to the body at all. A fin, in Railton's opinion, is of no use whatsoever unless the car skids badly, in which case the little it could do would not avail to help the driver.

With the body in position and the flat, or nearly flat, underscreen, the wheels are almost invisible, which is one reason why the machine does not look like a car, and why it would be difficult to portray it pictorially at speed. The exhaust gases are discharged through short pipes from the top, at one side, and underneath the body, an ingenious scheme directing the blast from the lower pipes backwards instead of directly downwards.

The driver's control is relatively simple. There are the throttles working in unison from one pedal, and the brake pedal, which also controls a big flap which can be

Air brake, its actuating levers and twin vacuum cylinders in the " withdrawn " position.

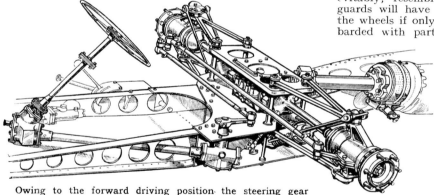

Owing to the forward driving position the steering gear is arranged with a connection from the bevel at the foot of the steering column to the special gear at one side of the frame.

caused to project from the top of the body and act as an air brake. The gear lever controls both boxes, operating them simultaneously through rack-and-pinion mechanism and Simmonds-Corsey controls. At the right-hand side there is also a brake lever connected mechanically to the pedal actuation.

The air-brake flap is mounted on two vertical H-section arms within the body, but held by four levers which together give a parallel action. The whole is actuated by a pair of vacuum cylinders with pistons controlled by the brake pedal at need. When the vacuum apparatus is operating, the levers carrying the flap are raised vertically, bringing the flap above the body. When not required the levers are lowered and the flap is carried entirely inside the body.

What this machine will accomplish in speed is a matter for trial—all its designer will say is that it is intended to beat the existing record—but it should be very fast, and it is not difficult to believe that one day a car of this type will record as much as 400 m.p.h. if tyres for this speed can be produced. As a piece of mechanism, which is

what has to be considered at the moment, it is one of the finest and most satisfactory that have been produced. Since the body can be detached in a few minutes, lifted and replaced by six men, the change of wheels and refilling between the two runs for the record are made much easier.

The driving cockpit is a rather weird and most unusual place. The driver has his seat inside the body, his head being in the metal conning tower or hood, and he can see clearly through the curved front window. At the back there is a bulkhead cutting off the engine compartment; beneath is the underpan, and at each side the huge wheels and tyres. The machine remotely, but nevertheless inevitably, resembles a submarine. It is probable that guards will have to be erected between the driver and the wheels if only to prevent the driver from being bombarded with particles of salt. The metal cowl of the windscreen forms part of a hatch which is raised to allow the man to get into position, and lowered and secured when he is in his seat.

The instruments, of course, include two revolution counters, one for each engine. Provision is made for starting the car with a lorry, a cross-member at the extreme rear end of the frame having a socket for what amounts to a push-bar attached to the front of the lorry, this being necessary because the projecting tail considerably overlaps the frame and is much too fragile to allow of it being pushed by any machine.

SUPPLIERS

Body material	Northern Aluminium Company, Ltd.
Brake and shock absorber lining	Ferodo, Ltd.
Transmission gears ...	David Brown & Sons, Huddersfield.
Universal joints... ...	Laycock Engineering Company, Ltd.
Steering gear	Burman & Sons, Ltd.
Steering wheel ...	Bluemel Brothers, Ltd.
Steering gear links ...	Automotive Products, Ltd.
Brake operating gear ...	Lockheed Hydraulic Brake Company, Ltd.
Air brake gear	Sir G. Godfrey & Partners. Ltd.
Frame	John Thompson Pressings, Ltd.
Steel tubes and light alloy extrusions	Reynolds Tube Co., Ltd.
High tensile steel ...	Firth Derihon Stampings, Ltd.
Cockpit window... ...	Triplex Safety Glass Ltd.
Instruments, thermostats and fuel pipes ...	S. Smith & Sons, Ltd.
Fuel gauge	Simms Motor Units, Ltd.
Special controls and wheel nuts	Simmonds Aerocessories, Ltd.
Tyres, wheels, seat cushion and rubber suspension	Dunlop Rubber Co., Ltd.
Suspension springs ...	Tempered Spring Co., Ltd.
Ball and roller bearings...	Hoffmann Manufacturing Co.
Oil seals	Super Oil Seal Manufacturing Co., Ltd.
Plugs	K.L.G. Sparking Plugs, Ltd.
Fuel	Supplied by National Benzole Company, Ltd.
Oil	Shell-Mex & B.P., Ltd.
Designer	R. A. Railton, B.Sc., M.I.A.E., M.S.A.E.
Builders	Thomson & Taylor (Brooklands), Ltd.

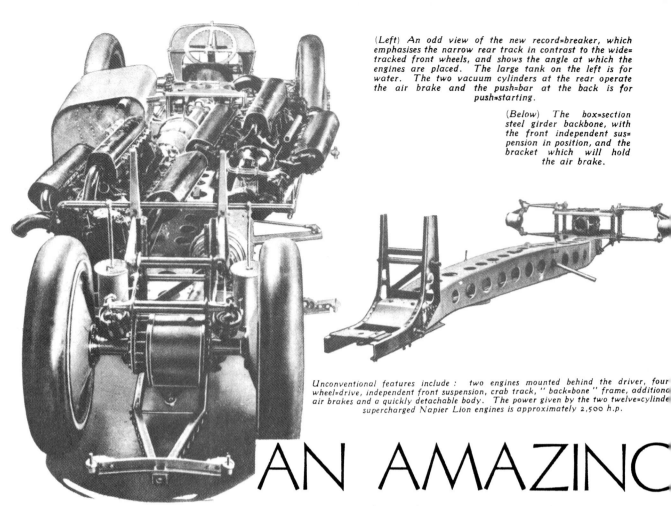

AN AMAZINC

The Railton : a Two-engined Machine Design

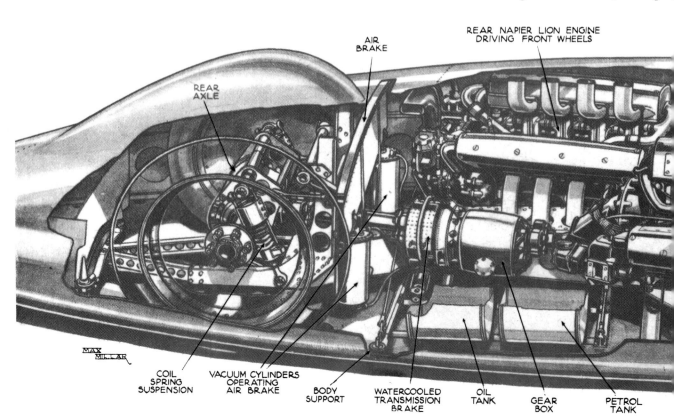

REAR AXLE

AIR BRAKE

REAR NAPIER LION ENGINE DRIVING FRONT WHEELS

MAX MILLAR

COIL SPRING SUSPENSION

VACUUM CYLINDERS OPERATING AIR BRAKE

BODY SUPPORT

WATERCOOLED TRANSMISSION BRAKE

OIL TANK

GEAR BOX

PETROL TANK

The three men responsible for the design, the driving, and the construction

Reid A. Railton, shown here at the Frankfort record week last October, has been associated as a designer with the famous Brooklands firm of Thomson and Taylor for many years. He has been responsible for many of Sir Malcolm Campbell's Bluebirds, besides the car which holds the Brooklands lap record.

John Cobb, like Reid Railton, is a quiet and unassuming person. He has been very successful as a driver, especi= ally with long=distance records, driving his single=engined Napier=Railton. He holds the Brooklands lap record at 143.44 m.p.h., and the fastest he has driven is probably about 180 m.p.h. He is now pro= posing to boost that up to some 350 m.p.h. or so !

Ken Taylor, the Taylor of Thomson and Taylor, is usually to be encountered at Brooklands himself helping in the workshops. "Before you say anything about me," he will murmur, "remember any credit that's going is due as much to the boys as to me." By the "boys," Taylor means the squad of mechanics who have worked so hard to com= plete the amazing new Railton.

NEW RECORD CAR

by Reid Railton for John Cobb and Completed in the Greatest Secrecy

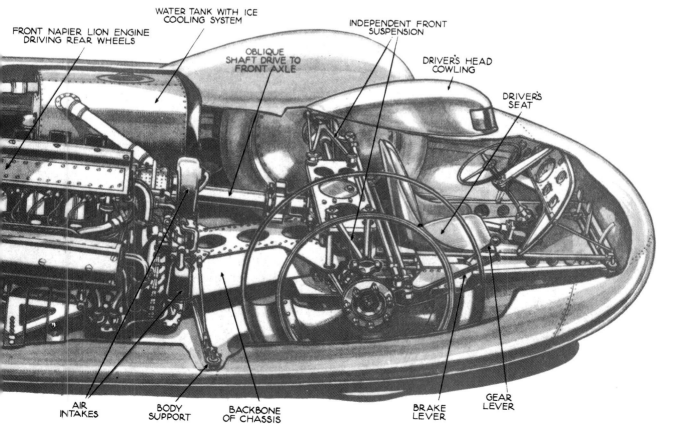

WATER TANK WITH ICE COOLING SYSTEM

INDEPENDENT FRONT SUSPENSION

FRONT NAPIER LION ENGINE DRIVING REAR WHEELS

OBLIQUE SHAFT DRIVE TO FRONT AXLE

DRIVER'S HEAD COWLING

DRIVER'S SEAT

AIR INTAKES

BODY SUPPORT

BACKBONE OF CHASSIS

BRAKE LEVER

GEAR LEVER

AIMING AT 400

Cobb's New World's Record
Challenger — Railton Designs
Car with a Twisted Spine

**THE
2,500 H.P.
3-TON
RAILTON**

A fine rear view of the low, turtle-backed car designed by Reid Railton for John Cobb's forthcoming attack on the World's Record. Cobb will sit in the "conning tower" in the nose. The projecting tyres will be covered under streamlined hoods.

IN deference to John Cobb's own wishes, I have held out on you about his new car destined to attack the world's land speed record. Last Tuesday, however, the ban was lifted and the car was shown for the first time—just too late for last week's issue of this journal.

The new Railton, as the car is named, after its brilliant designer, Reid A. Railton, of Thomson and Taylor's, is the most unorthodox record-breaker ever built anywhere.

At one blow, Railton has solved difficulties which have arisen for designers of other cars of this sort.

He had to commence with certain definite things — the two available engines, the tyres of a given size, for example. His solution does away with excrescences on the body for oil or petrol fillers, there is no radiator at all, no tail fins, the wheels are almost entirely enclosed, the cockpit is covered, there are only four wheels, and the total weight of the car is 62½ cwt.—a shade over 3 tons with empty tanks! Eyston's "Thunderbolt," for instance, weighs over 7 tons.

The first shock you get on seeing the chassis is that there is no chassis frame. The single girder-type backbone is curved like a flattened "S." On one side of the car, in a loop of the "S," goes one engine—a 12-cylinder supercharged Napier Lion aero unit, developing at least 1,250 b.h.p. from its 23.9 litres—and in the opposite "loop" on the other side of the chassis fits the second similar engine.

These engines face opposite ways and are set at an angle to the axis of the car, one driving forward to the front axle with its short propeller shaft almost diagonal to the line of travel, the other driving the rear axle.

Each prop. shaft has its own clutch and gearbox (three speeds) and on each

shaft is a large transmission brake, water-cooled. There are no brakes at all on the wheels. At the back provision is made for raising a wind flap.

A Seat in the Prow

The driver sits away out in front of the car, ahead of the wheels, with the back of his little bucket seat up against the front axle. In front of him is the instrument board with dials duplicated for each engine—blower pressure, oil pressure, fuel pressure, and revolutions per minute. The steering wheel is set at a flat angle, rather like a London bus.

The front axle (with differential) is independently sprung—chiefly, says Railton, because that was the simplest way of arranging things—and sprung very cleverly indeed. There are parallel horizontal wishbones upon which the half-axles swing. The back axle is fixed and has no differential.

Both at front and back the springing arrangement is the same—vertical coil springs, backed by a series of rubber rings low down under the "chassis" and inclined outwards at an angle of 45 degrees; these "cylindrical" springs compress or extend within guides which

embody a novel form of shock absorber roughly like a piston working inside a jam pot the sides of which are split and can be tightened on to the piston or slackened off at will.

The front track is 5 ft. 6 ins., but at the rear the wheels are very close together, giving a crabbed track of only 3 ft. 6 ins.! The wheelbase is 13 ft. 6 ins., the overall length of the extraordinary body is 28 ft. 8 ins., and the complete car is only 4 ft. 3 ins. high.

--------**THE RAILTON**--------

TECHNICAL DATA

Engines: Two Napier Lion aero engines, 12 cylinders, supercharged, 23,936 c.c., 1,250 h.p. each.

Gearboxes: One to each engine. Three speeds (top, 1.35 to 1), controlled by a single gearlever.

Brakes: Transmission brakes, water cooled, hydraulically operated.

Tyres: 44 ins. diameter.

Suspension: Front, independent; rear, normal fixed axle.

Axles: Rear, no differential; front, differential. Both bevel driven. Four-wheel drive.

Fuel tank: 18 gallons. On right of frame.

Oil tank: Alongside fuel tank; holds 15 gallons.

Cooling: From 75-gallon tank of water and ice.

DIMENSIONS

Track: Front, 5 ft. 6 ins.; rear, 3 ft. 6 ins. **Wheelbase:** 13 ft. 6 ins. **Overall length:** 28 ft. 8 ins. **Overall width:** 8 ft. **Overall height:** 4 ft. 3 ins. **Weight:** Approximately 3 tons.

M.P.H.?

Both engine throttles work simultaneously, and the single gear lever changes the gears in both boxes. The brake pedal likewise operates (hydraulically) the band brakes on the transmission. The design is such that the car can be stopped on these brakes alone, without a wind flap.

There is no radiator, with its attendant difficulties of weight and the rush of air through into the car. On the left-hand side of the backbone Railton has slung a 75-gallon tank containing ice, sufficient to cool the car during the few seconds of the record run. On the opposite side of the frame are slung the oil and fuel tanks.

The front wheels have a steering lock of only 15 degrees.

Now the body. This is in itself a wonderful piece of panel beating in duralumin. It is quite unlike anything ever used before, and covers the entire car, wheels and driver included. The wheels project above the top of the body through slits—so you can imagine

A frontal view of this extraordinary machine showing the driver's "conning tower." The spectators emphasize the low build of the car, which is only 4 ft. 3 ins. high. It is 28 ft. long, but the body weighs only 4 cwt.!

can lift the body on and off with great ease, and it can be fixed down in a matter of minutes. There are no detachable panels for access to tyres or engines—they simply whip the body off. Cobb gets into his cockpit from a little bridge which is placed across the car. He then slides down into his seat and the dome is fitted on top of him. He looks forward through a little curved window.

The engines have three banks of four cylinders, set clover-leaf fashion. There is a big centrifugal blower in front

and there are twin magnetos and twin carburetters.

The car is not yet completed and the body has still to be finished and painted. The Railton will go to Bonneville Salt Flats, Utah, U.S.A., in August, according to present plans.

Now we have an idea that the modified "Thunderbolt" of George Eyston will probably get somewhere around 350 m.p.h. if all goes well on his forthcoming visit to Utah. Railton confidently states that his new car will beat that. I can't see Cobb going to all this trouble to raise such a record by 10 m.p.h. Which train of thought brings us to very fantastic speeds indeed, in which 400 m.p.h. looms ahead.

The Technical Editor agrees with me, using what data we have and a sprinkling of shrewd estimates to assist in calculation. Assuming the Mercedes-Benz which did 260 m.p.h. had 700 b.h.p. and a frontal area of 18 sq. ft., he estimates that Cobb would need 1,400 h.p. to move his car at 260 m.p.h. with an estimated frontal area of 36 sq. ft. Which, by a process of slide ruling, indicates that, with the 2,500 h.p. which Cobb has under the turtle back of his Railton, the speed should be around 375 m.p.h. Now, supposing Cobb can persuade another 500 h.p. out of the engines—not very difficult, perhaps—the speed would rise to something not far off 400 m.p.h. And that is Speed! GRANDE VITESSE.

Close-up showing the front axle arrangement, where the wheels are independently sprung and are driven through a differential. The seat is seen in the foreground with the front-wheel-drive propeller shaft just behind. On the shaft can be seen the gearbox and transmission brake.

(Below) A view of the "works" showing the twisted back-bone and the staggered engines. The seat is seen in the nose, forward of the front wheels. The large tank on the right contains ice for cooling—there is no radiator.

how low the body is upon the ground.

"There is no tail fin," said the designer, " because I think a fin is useless unless the car gets into a bad slide, and even then its action is problematical. The line of the body is broken only by the dome over Cobb's head and the covers where the tyres project upwards. In order to use four tyres, we had to keep the weight down to 3 tons.

"People are bound to ask about the car tending to lift in front owing to wind pressure at high speed. The shape of the body has been designed to meet that, and any lifting will be negligible.

" Speed? It is only possible to say that the car has been designed to go faster than any car hitherto designed for the world's land speed record, or any car which will be in existence this year. The engines develop 1 h.p. for every 2.8 lb. of the total weight."

The body weighs only about 4 cwt. and is specially designed for quick attachment and removal. Six mechanics

Nearly Six Miles a Minute!

Eyston Breaks His Own World's Land Speed Record by 33 m.p.h. with "Thunderbolt"

RECORD BREAKER. George Eyston, photographed at Utah during Cobb's recent test runs. See the nose of Cobb's car in the background?

THE RECORD

THE FLYING MILE

	secs.	m.p.h.
Northward run ...	10.36	347.49
Southward run ...	10.48	343.51
Mean	10.42	345.49

FLYING KILOMETRE

	secs.	m.p.h.
Northward run ..	6.45	346.80
Southward run ..	6.50	344.15
Mean	6.48	345.21

The 1937 Figures

Flying mile: Mean, 11.56 secs., 311.42 m.p.h.
Flying kilometre: Mean, 7.165 secs., 312.0 m.p.h.

AGAIN Capt. G. E. T. Eyston has broken the world's land speed record, putting it up to the prodigious average speed of 345.49 m.p.h.—over 33 m.p.h. faster than the previous record which Eyston himself set up in November last. The times and speeds for the north and south runs and those of his 1937 efforts are given above.

He covered the mile in each run, on Saturday last, August 27, in less than 10.5 secs.—nearly six miles a minute!—a really staggering speed which it is impossible for the layman to visualize. Just think, London to Brighton (52 miles) in 8½ minutes.

After making several tests on the salt beds at Utah, Eyston decided to make a definite attempt on the record last Wednesday. His first run was timed at 347.155 m.p.h., but on the return the timing apparatus went wrong and no figure was recorded. Therefore the " Captain " had to have his second shot and a successful one it was. The timekeepers took every precaution to prevent a recurrence of the previous trouble and to ensure efficiency in the light-ray recording device, " Thunderbolt " was painted black; it was believed that the plain light colour of the car, the bright sun and the dazzling whiteness of the salt had something to do with the previous unsuccessful recording by the electric-eye.

The speeds for the mile were greater than those recorded over the kilometre, showing that the acceleration was being maintained right up to the time that Eyston crossed the final line: if he had a longer run, the figures recorded would probably be appreciably higher.

Great crowds, enthused by Wednesday's speeds, turned out on Saturday to watch Eyston, and at the conclusion of the run he received a terrific ovation.

" Thunderbolt " stood up to the runs perfectly and the performance is a magnificent tribute to the British design, materials and equipment generally, and, in particular, the personnel associated with its production.

It now remains to be seen what John Cobb will do with his car, the Railton. Cobb has already made some fast test runs and will go out for the record very soon; indeed, he may even have broken it by the time these words appear in print.

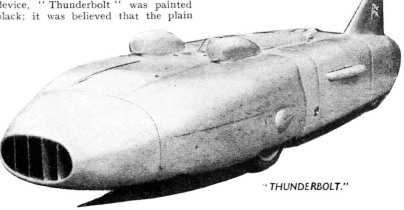

" THUNDERBOLT."

Eyston v Cobb

A battle of speed, to keep pushing the world's land speed record still higher, was now fought at Bonneville between two Englishmen: Captain G. E. T. Eyston and John Cobb. Eyston made the first attempt, in an effort to beat Sir Malcolm Campbell's existing record of 301.13 m.p.h.

George Eyston was a good mechanical engineer, as well as a famous racing driver—and he was not above working with his mechanics on the engines of his cars. He played an important part in the design of *Thunderbolt*, the car in which he tackled the world's land speed record, and, when trouble with the clutch twice prevented him winning the record at

Jon Cobb's *Railton* without body shell.

Bonneville, he personally was closely associated with the redesign of the clutch, so that new parts could be made in California—to give him the chance to try again.

Eyston was frequently breaking motor racing records, and was often getting more than one car ready for an attempt on some new records, at any given time: he tackled the world's hour record, long-distance records, and the world's 24-hour record, among others. His decision to attempt to break the world's land speed record was a natural culmination of his attempts on these other records, and it was his satisfaction with Bonneville when he broke the world's 24-hour record there that made him choose the salt flats for his attempts on the world's land speed record.

John Rhodes Cobb, his rival in competing for the land speed record at Bonneville, but also his friend, was a big, affable motor racing driver who had also broken many records, at Brooklands, Montlhery, and Bonneville, before he decided to tackle the world's land speed record. Like Eyston, John Cobb was a modest man who never boasted about his successes. He was, in fact, generally remarkably quiet. Once he was asked to appear before the newsreel cameras to celebrate a new record. He refused. When friends finally persuaded him to appear, he learnt a speech so that he would not be stuck for something to say. But, when he finally did appear in front of the cameras, he said practically not a word. He spoke very little when he

was on racing committees, too—unless he thought that someone had been wronged, when he spoke forcefully. Because of his modesty, honesty, calm good humour, and his serious interest in motor racing, he was extremely popular.

The car in which Cobb started racing at Brooklands was rather large, a 10-litre Fiat, but he coped quite easily. Later he won fame at Brooklands driving the V12 Delage in which Rene Thomas had broken the world's land speed record at Arpajon in 1924. The Napier-Railton which he later drove at Brooklands was so powerful that, even though he started at scratch, he was compelled to brake when he caught up his rivals. It was in this car that he broke the lap record at Brooklands and also the world's hour record and world's 24 hours' record at Bonneville. As with Eyston, his satisfaction with Bonneville when breaking these records made him choose the salt flats for his attempts on the world's land speed record.

Captain George Eyston made his first attempt to break the world's land speed record in the year before John Cobb challenged him in Utah. Eyston was handicapped in his endeavour to beat the existing record held by Sir Malcolm Campbell by the fact that Campbell had already used the most powerful engine that was available—the Rolls-Royce type "R" aircraft engine. To get the greater power he needed to go faster than Campbell, Eyston fitted two of these engines in his *Thunderbolt*, instead of the one used by Campbell. Both engines employed a single gearbox, and positive dog clutches were fitted to improve the transmission. Air brakes were incorporated, and a fin was mounted at the tail. *Thunderbolt* was built at the Bean factory at Tipton, Staffs.

The weight of the car was deliberately made heavy, to help reduce that old problem, wheelspin; the dry weight was 6 tons 17 cwt. This heavy weight imposed an even bigger strain on the tyres, so eight were fitted: twin driving wheels were employed at the rear, to improve adhesion, and four wheels were used for steering, at the front, to improve stability. Heating at high speed always reduced the life of the tyres, but the improvement of the streamlining around the tyres, compared with previous record-breakers, reduced the amount of cooling provided by the airstream; consequently, Dunlop had to design tyres able to withstand even higher temperatures. The tyres also had to stand up to an even greater centrifugal force than before, owing to the higher speed envisaged; and the speed of rotation of the tyres at record speed in 1937, as it turned out, was 2,480 r.p.m. The treads of the Dunlop tyres were therefore made exceptionally thin, to prevent tread stripping, and a nut was used to hold each valve on to the rim of its wheel.

Both the weather and mechanical difficulties were against Eyston at Bonneville. Rain fell so hard after he arrived that the salt flats were flooded to a depth of several inches, and he had to wait two weeks before he could try *Thunderbolt* at high speed for the first time. On 28 October 1937 he had the satisfaction of going faster than the existing record: he set up a speed of 309.6 m.p.h. for the flying mile—but only in one direction. However, on the return run the minor differences in speed between the two engines broke the dog clutches; consequently, no two-way mean speed was established—so that no new record was set up. His hopes were raised again on 6 November, when he once more beat the existing record on the outward run, this time reaching 310.685 m.p.h. But, on the run back, once again the dog clutches did not function properly—so that, for the second time, he failed to break the record. The threat of the approach of the winter rains, which would flood the course, meant that the clutch problem had to be solved speedily if the record was to be broken that year. Eyston himself therefore supervised the changes in the design of the troublesome dog clutches, new parts were manufactured in Los Angeles—and *Thunderbolt* was finally made ready for another attack on the record on 19 November 1937.

The knowledge that his time was running short, owing to the approach of the bad weather, was still at the back of Eyston's mind when he made his first run—and he wondered how the new dog clutches would perform. No trouble was experienced on the outward run, though, travelling north, and he set up a speed of 305.59 m.p.h. for the flying kilometre. On the return run he had a nasty experience, even though the dog clutches still gave no trouble: he had to steer with only one hand for a short distance, at a speed of about 300 m.p.h., when he had to use the other hand to move his goggles back over his eyes after they were blown upwards by the wind. Nevertheless, his speed for the run southwards was 319.11 m.p.h. for the flying kilometre, giving him a mean two-way speed for the flying kilometre of 312.00 m.p.h.—a new world's land speed record. Shortly afterwards, the weather broke, ruling out further attempts that year. He had smashed Campbell's record only just in time.

When Sir Malcolm Campbell was told that his record had been beaten he confirmed that he would not try to raise the speed while the record remained safely in British hands.

Although Campbell was out of the battle, Eyston was aware that John Cobb was getting ready to challenge him in a car that, on paper, appeared likely to be faster than his *Thunderbolt*. Eyston believed, though, that *Thunderbolt* had not yet reached its limit, so he decided to modify his car in order to beat his own record the following year.

Back in England, Eyston reduced the weight of *Thunderbolt*; coil springs, for example, replaced leaf springs; even so, the weight of the car was still about 6 tons. The driver's cockpit was completely enclosed, to protect him against the wind. Breathing equipment was also added, because he had experienced difficulty with the exhaust fumes in 1937. The usefulness of the tail fin was a point on which Eyston had not yet made up his mind, but the fin was modified so that it could be removed if desired.

When Eyston went back to Bonneville in 1938 he expected that he would complete his runs before the arrival of John Cobb. However, the failure of the flood water to clear held him up for five weeks. As a result, both Cobb and Eyston were present at Bonneville at the same time to fight their battle of speed—the outcome of which kept the world guessing for almost three weeks.

Eyston was alarmed on one trial run to see thick smoke filling the cockpit after the servo had put on the brakes too fiercely. He was only able to breathe because of his oxygen equipment, and his car left the course, since he could not see where he was going.

On 24 August 1938 he set up a speed of 347.16 m.p.h. on his first run—faster than his existing record. On his return run, though, the timing equipment failed to record a time: because of the bright light reflected off the metal surface of the car and off the glaring salt, the light beam shining on the photo-electric cell was not broken. No two-way mean speed was recorded, and no new record was set up. Afterwards the body of *Thunderbolt* was painted black—so that it would break the light beam on its next run.

On 27 August 1938 Eyston set up flying mile speeds of 347.49 m.p.h. on his run north and 343.51 m.p.h. on his run south—giving a mean two-way speed of 345.50 m.p.h. for the flying mile. He had beaten his own world's land speed record —and he believed he could go even faster, if need be, for his speed had been increasing through the measured distance.

John Cobb congratulated Eyston on breaking the record— then got ready to try to beat him. Eyston, meanwhile, did not leave the salt flats—in case it proved necessary for him to try to beat Cobb.

The car in which John Cobb challenged Captain Eyston at Bonneville was the *Railton*, designed by his friend Reid A. Railton—who had already designed the latest *Blue Birds* in which Sir Malcolm Campbell had broken the world's land speed record. The reason Cobb asked Railton to design his car was that his Napier-Railton, also designed by Railton, had performed even better than Railton had forecast at the drawing-board stage. Some indication of Cobb's modesty, and also of the confidence he felt in Railton, was his naming of his car after its designer.

Reid Railton designed the *Railton* from two given starting points. First, the weight that could be supported by each tyre was limited, and the size of the tyres was also specified by Dunlop. Secondly, the engines that were available were two supercharged Napier *Lion* VII D (WD) aircraft engines. The initial power of each of these two 12-cylinder engines, which had powered Betty Carstairs' speedboat nine years earlier, was about 1,250 b.h.p.; total power of the car was therefore limited to about 2500 b.h.p.—only about half the power of Eyston's *Thunderbolt*. Because of the limitations imposed by the tyres and engines, the weight of the Railton was kept low—and its weight, 3.15 tons, was something like half that of *Thunderbolt*. The need for maximum acceleration, because the length of the run to get up speed before entering the measured strip was shorter than ideal, even at Bonneville, was another factor that led to the emphasis on engineering efficiency.

Owing to the need to reduce wind resistance to a minimum, to make maximum use of the available power, Railton started by designing a body that was efficiently streamlined— and only afterwards did he give his attention to the design of the chassis. The testing of models in the wind tunnel at the National Physical Laboratory, Teddington, helped to obtain the efficiency of streamlining desired. Everything was enclosed, including the wheels, and indentations on the body that would increase drag were limited to little other than the covers above the four wheels, the canopy above the driver's head, and ports for the exhausts and superchargers. Streamlining was also improved by the elimination of a radiator, and the use, instead, of ice-cooled water to cool the engines.

Four-wheel drive was employed, to reduce wheelspin. The engines were mounted, in opposing directions and at an angle, on either side of a single girder down the centre of the chassis. The backward-facing engine, placed slightly farther forward, drove the rear wheels, and the forward-facing engine drove the front wheels. The opposing directions of rotation of the crankshafts of the two engines helped to balance out torque. A single gear lever and one throttle controlled both engines.

John Cobb, a methodical and calm man, generally liked to take his time, to make sure that everything was right; and, on 30 August 1938, three days after Eyston set up the record, he decided to make some more trial runs in order to get more used to the Railton before he actually challenged Eyston. The surface of the salt was poor, but on his second run he reached a speed of about 325 m.p.h.

In these early runs, including some made previously, the engines of the Railton were not working perfectly: the temperatures were below those required to give the best performance, and trouble was also experienced with carburation, partly owing to the thinner air at the 4,218 ft. elevation of Bonneville. A further annoying complication was that the engines stalled when Cobb changed gear owing to the absence of a flywheel and a normal clutch.

Cobb methodically continued to get the feel of the Railton, and on 12 September 1938 he made an official attempt on the record. George Eyston, who wanted to observe at first hand precisely what he was up against, watched Cobb's bid from an aircraft that followed the Railton down the course. Cobb was not yet completely satisfied with his car, and his mean two-way speed was only 342.5 m.p.h.—slightly slower than the record of Eyston he was trying to beat. However, he was by now coming to feel very much at home in the Railton.

On 15 September 1938 John Cobb made another attempt on the record. He walked along the plank that was placed across the body to avoid denting the aluminium alloy, then climbed into his cockpit; the fit was fairly tight for so large a man. Then the cockpit canopy was put in position.

Cobb grasped the wheel, that was not too far from the horizontal, and momentarily noticed again how close he was to the ground. His view from his seat in the nose was completely unobstructed: owing to the clear air, the mountains seemed much closer than they really were. The glare off the white salt was as brilliant as always, and he was glad of his dark glasses.

A lorry had to push him from behind to get him moving because he had no clutch, and the engines came to life at about 20 m.p.h. The stalling of the engines when he changed gear still worried him, so he started in second gear to eliminate one gear change. The distance available to get up speed before entering the measured strip was shorter that year than usual at Bonneville because the surface of the salt was relatively poor at each end of the course; consequently, he accelerated as fast as possible. The acceleration was fully as good as he had come to expect, and the lack of torque also continued to be impressive.

The absence of points of reference was very noticeable, and he had to concentrate all his attention on holding the car to the black line. His eyes became tired by having to refocus on points ahead that moved towards him with such astonishing rapidity. As he strained his eyes, changing focus, he noticed small specks of white salt flung up on to the windscreen. When he put on the brakes, he found difficulty in estimating the rate at which he was slowing down. When he stopped, he learnt that his speed for the first run, northwards,

was 353.3 m.p.h. for the flying mile.

The 4 cwt. body shell was taken off, new racing tyres and wheels were put on, then the shell was replaced on its chassis.

Cobb started his run back south well within the specified hour, and his speed for the flying mile on the return run was 347.2 m.p.h. His mean two-way speeds were 350.20 m.p.h. for the flying mile and 350.1 m.p.h. for the flying kilometre.

Cobb had beaten the world's land speed record set up by Captain Eyston on the same course just under three weeks earlier—and he had also become the first man officially to go faster than 350 m.p.h.

Captain Eyston had watched John Cobb beat his record, and he congratulated his rival. The very next day Eyston was out on the salt to show Cobb he could beat him.

George Eyston was not afraid to make changes as he went along, and he had already modified Thunderbolt in two ways since breaking the record: he had taken the tail fin off; and he had removed the radiator, substituting a water tank because he did not have time to obtain the thermostats needed for ice cooling. The object of both these changes was to improve streamlining.

One of the problems that worried Eyston as he sat in his cockpit waiting to make his reply to Cobb, on 16 September 1938, was how well Thunderbolt would hold to the black line in the absence of the stability provided by the removed tail. His worries about the way the car would perform were not lessened by having to wait until the timing equipment was prepared. Then, when he did get going, he found that his acceleration was not too good because the mixture had become weak while waiting. He made the best of his slow start, but at least his doubts about the removal of the tail fin were removed: the car held its course without trouble, and his speed for the run north was 356.4 m.p.h. for the flying mile.

The other problem that worried him, resulting from his second modification of the car, was that the water might overheat without ice. On the return run the heat blown back from the boiling of the water did, in fact, turn out to be overpowering, but Thunderbolt performed satisfactorily, and he survived the heat somehow. His speed for the return run was 358.6 m.p.h. for the flying mile.

His two runs gave him a mean two-way speed of 357.50 m.p.h. for the flying mile. He had beaten the world's land speed record set up by John Cobb the previous day.

John Cobb, who watched Captain Eyston beat him, reacted calmly to his defeat because he believed that his Railton could go faster than Eyston's Thunderbolt. But the surface of the salt was not perfect, and the supply of special tyres was running low. In addition, although the theories of Reid Railton had been proved triumphantly right, new lessons had been learnt which needed to be incorporated in the car. John Cobb was therefore in no hurry to show that he could beat Eyston, and he went back to England so that modifications could be made to the Railton.

The outcome of this battle of speed between John Cobb and Captain G. E. T. Eyston at Bonneville in 1938 was thus a victory for Eyston. However, although he had lost this first encounter, Cobb was by no means willing to concede ultimate defeat—and he got ready to go back to Bonneville the following year to beat Eyston.

At Bonneville in 1939, John Cobb found snags in the performance of the Railton when he made his trial runs before attacking the record again: the engines misfired, and the old trouble of the engines stalling when Cobb changed gear was also experienced. His first attempt on the record, on 22 August, was not successful. The following day he made another attempt.

He was out on the salt early, on 23 August 1939, because an unusually hot day was expected. He had to fight a wind from the side to hold the Railton to the black line, and the wind was so strong, and his speed so fast, that, when he decelerated, he lurched forward quite hard against the steering wheel. Despite the heat, the tyres stood up remarkably well— even though their speed of rotation at the record speed was 2,900 r.p.m.

His mean two-way speed was 368.86 m.p.h. for the flying mile and 369.70 m.p.h. for the flying kilometre—his speed for the flying kilometre being a new world's land speed record.

Afterwards he set up new world's records for other distances: 5 miles—302.2 m.p.h.; 5 kilometres—326.7 m.p.h.; 10 miles— 270.4 m.p.h.; and 10 kilometres—283.0 m.p.h.

He had just become the first man to go faster than 6 miles a minute. Now the idea of going faster than the round figure of 400 m.p.h. began to take shape in his mind. But war was about to break out.

Although Captain G. E. T. Eyston had ended the winner the previous year, the final outcome of the battle of Bonneville was victory for John Cobb. The world's land speed record had been broken for the last time before World War II. But John Cobb believed that his Railton could go even faster after the war.

1937 *THUNDERBOLT* SPECIFICATION

COUNTRY OF MANUFACTURE. Britain.
ENGINES. Two Rolls-Royce type "R" Schneider Trophy aircraft engines. Cylinders: V12 (total 24). Bore: 157.4 mm.
Stroke: 167.64 mm. Cubic capacity (total): 73,164 c.c. Max. power (total): 4,600-5,000 b.h.p. at 3,200 r.p.m.
One centrifugal supercharger. TRANSMISSION. Friction-plate clutch, solid drive in top (dogs). 1 gearbox, 3 speeds.
Ratio top gear: 1.23. Final drive: bevel, no differential. SUSPENSION All: independent, leaf springs.
WHEELS. Total: 8, disc type. Rear: 2 twins, driving. Front: 4, all steering. Tyres: Dunlop, 7.0-31.
Tyre r.p.m. at record speed (1937): 2,480 r.p.m. BRAKES. Disc, Lockheed hydraulic, front on shafts,
rear on propeller shaft extension. 2 air brakes, hydraulic.
DIMENSIONS. Length: 30 ft. 5 in. Width: 7 ft. 1^{1}/$_{2}$ in. Height: 3ft. 10 in.
WEIGHT. Dry: 6 tons 17 cwt.

1938 *RAILTON* SPECIFICATION
COUNTRY OF MANUFACTURE. Britain.
ENGINES. Two Napier *Lion* VII D (WD) aircraft engines. Cylinders: V12, broad arrow (total 24).
Cubic capacity (total): 47,872 c.c. Bore: 139.7 mm. Stroke: 130.2 mm. Total power: 2,500 b.h.p. approx.
Cooling: ice-cooled water. Supercharged. TRANSMISSION 4-wheel drive, each engine driving 2 wheels
independently through own 3-speed gearbox. No clutches or flywheels. Top gear ratio: 1.35. Final drive, front and rear: bevel.
SUSPENSION. Coil springs, damped by rubber discs. Front: independent, wishbones. Rear: normal.
WHEELS. Dunlop disc. Tyres: Dunlop, 7.0-31, tread thickness ^{1}/$_{50}$, in. Tyre r.p.m. at record speed (1938): 2,770 r.p.m.
BRAKES. Hydraulic, band brakes on gearboxes, drums cooled by water system.
DIMENSIONS. Wheelbase: 13 ft. 6 in. Track: 5 ft. 6 in. front, 3ft. 6in. rear. Length (over-all): 28ft. 8in.
Width (over-all): 8 ft. 0 in. Height (over-all): 4 ft. 3 in.WEIGHT. Dry: 3.15 tons.

1937 *THUNDERBOLT* SPECIFICATION
COUNTRY OF MANUFACTURE. Britain.
ENGINES. Two Rolls-Royce type "R" Schneider Trophy aircraft engines. Cylinders: V12 (total 24).
Bore: 157.4 mm. Stroke: 167.64 mm. Cubic capacity (total): 73,164 c.c. Max. power (total): 4,600-5,000 b.h.p.
at 3,200 r.p.m. One centrifugal supercharger. TRANSMISSION. Friction-plate clutch, solid drive in top (dogs).
1 gearbox, 3 speeds. Ratio top gear: 1.23. Final drive: bevel, no differential. SUSPENSION All: independent, leaf springs.
WHEELS. Total: 8, disc type. Rear: 2 twins, driving. Front: 4, all steering. Tyres: Dunlop, 7.0-31.
Tyre r.p.m. at record speed (1937): 2,480 r.p.m. BRAKES. Disc, Lockheed hydraulic, front on
shafts, rear on propeller shaft extension. 2 air brakes, hydraulic. DIMENSIONS. Length: 30 ft. 5 in. Width: 7 ft.
1^{1}/$_{2}$ in. Height: 3ft. 10 in.^{1}/$_{50}$, in. Tyre r.p.m. at record speed (1938): 2,770 r.p.m.
BRAKES. Hydraulic, band brakes on gearboxes, drums cooled by water system. DIMENSIONS. Wheelbase: 13 ft.
6 in. Track: 5 ft. 6 in. front, 3ft. 6in. rear. Length (over-all): 28ft. 8in. Width (over-all): 8 ft. 0 in.
Height (over-all): 4 ft. 3 in. WEIGHT. Dry: 3.15 tons.

EYSTON'S SPECTACULAR WORLD'S SPEED RECORD

SPEED AT UTAH

When Capt. G. E. T. Eyston set out on his successful attack on the world's land speed record, "Thunderbolt" was given a coat of black paint to ensure that the electric eye of the timing apparatus should not fail to record its passage. Although the "eye" functioned properly, the fantastic speed attained by the car was far too great even for the fastest Press camera to record clearly, as the top picture shows. On the right Capt. Eyston is seen being congratulated by Art Pillsbury, of the American Automobile Association, at the conclusion of his 345.49 m.p.h. triumph.

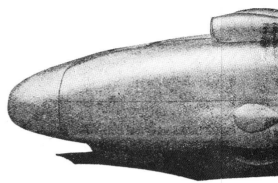

EYSTON'S

IN A DRAUGHT. The salt blast and vacuum caused by "Thunderbolt" on the run when the timing apparatus failed was so strong that it ripped the panelling over the wheels.

THE raising of the Land Speed Record step by step during the past few years has been usually a matter of lifting it by a fraction of time each attempt, equivalent to a gain of a few miles per hour. To lift it in one fell swoop by no less than 33 m.p.h. when the record already stood at well over 300 m.p.h. is a feat which is almost fantastic. Yet that is precisely what Eyston did. He regarded his previous record of 312 m.p.h. simply as an experimental run as a prelude to his 345 m.p.h. recently.

He was held up in Utah by bad conditions for a long and trying period, during which he remained as always calm and unflurried. Then, when the condition of the hard salt beds seemed about right, on August 24 he went out for the record. Annoyingly the timing apparatus broke down after one run at 347 m.p.h. but quite coolly Eyston started all over again on the 27th.

He took both the world's mile and kilometre records. The mile went at 345.49 m.p.h. mean speed and the kilometre at 345.21 m.p.h., so that the mile figures ranked as the World's Land Speed Record. His fastest one-way run was over the mile at 347.49 m.p.h. Interesting that in 1937 his car was slower over the mile than the kilometre.

As soon as Eyston had filed his claim for the record with the A.I.A.C.R. in Paris, John Cobb took out the Railton for a preliminary canter, after one or two previous runs at low speeds to get the feel of the car. On Monday, August 29 he went to and fro over the measured distances at speeds estimated at between 300 and 325 m.p.h. but no times were issued. Cobb had a little trouble with the gear-changing mechanism and stopped during one run. However, this was soon cured and he finished his day well pleased with the car and feeling much more used to the sensation of driving so unorthodox a machine at 300 m.p.h. The really terrific acceleration of the car which weighs less than half Eyston's car, was most marked. A few last-minute details of adjustment remained to be made, and Cobb announced he would not go out until the end of the week.

These Share the Credit

Engines: Rolls-Royce, Ltd. **Tyres:** Dunlop. **Wheels:** Dunlop Rim and Wheel Co., Ltd. **Bodywork** (and radiator, petrol tanks and piping): John Marston, Ltd. **General Assembly** (and manufacture of approximately 600 details): Beans Industries, Ltd. **Fuel:** B.P. Ethyl. **Oil:** Castrol. **Sparking plugs:** Lodge Plugs, Ltd. **Instruments:** S. Smith and Sons (M.A.), Ltd. **Magnetos:** British Thomson-Houston Co., Ltd. **Upholstery:** D. Moseley and Sons, Ltd. **Gearbox:** Beans Industries, Ltd. **Gearbox casing:** Birmingham Aluminium Casting Co. **Road springs:** English Steel Corporation, Ltd. **Valve springs:** H. Terry and Sons, Ltd. **Frame:** John Thompson Motor Pressings, Ltd. **Brake gear:** Automotive Products Co. and Ferodo, Ltd. **Clutches:** John Thornycroft. **Gear change and steering mechanism:** Burman and Sons, Ltd. **Steering wheel:** Bluemel Bros., Ltd. **Steering damper:** T. T. N. Patents, Ltd. **Bearings:** Hoffmann Manufacturing Co. **Pipes** (from engine to radiator): Petroflex, Ltd. **Parts of hubs and suspension:** Wolseley Motors, Ltd. **Various aluminium-bronze castings** for spring suspension: T. M. Birkett and Sons. **Friction metals** (for gearbox and clutches): Ferodo, Ltd. **Precision work:** Wolseley Motors, Ltd., and S. Coals. **Woodwork:** L. Bamberger and Sons. **Cellulose finish:** Nobel Industries, Ltd. **Controls:** Simmonds Aerocessories, Ltd. **Duralumin structure:** Duramin Engineering Co., Ltd. **Gits seals:** Charles Weston, Ltd. **High tensile bolts,** nuts, shafts, and final drive: E.N.V. Engineering Co., Ltd. **Universal drive joints:** Universal Power Drives, Ltd. **Final drive joints:** Laycock Engineering Co., Ltd. **Jacks:** Henry Miller and Co. **Castings in RR 50:** High Duty Alloys, Ltd. **Piping:** Gabriel Manufacturing Co., Ltd. **Stampings:** Firth Derihon. **Tecalemit** lubrication system. **Perspex cockpit cover:** Mouldrite, Ltd.

FRONT VIEW. The frontal aspect of "Thunderbolt" with its oval, slatted radiator vent and streamlined air intakes is suggestive of some fanciful monster

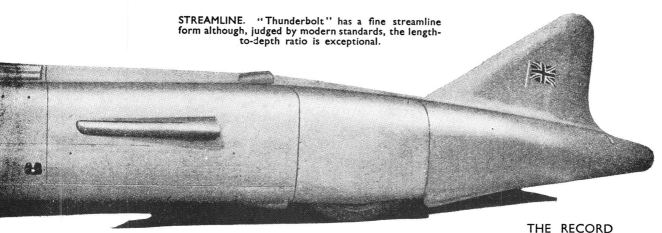

STREAMLINE. "Thunderbolt" has a fine streamline form although, judged by modern standards, the length-to-depth ratio is exceptional.

GREAT RECORD

Interesting Details of the Modifications to Capt. G. E. T. Eyston's Car Which Helped to Provide the Great Increase in Speed

THE RECORD

THE FLYING MILE

		secs.	m.p.h.
Northward run	...	10.36	347.49
Southward run	...	10.48	343.51
Mean	...	10.42	345.49

FLYING KILOMETRE

		secs.	m.p.h.
Northward run	...	6.45	346.80
Southward run	...	6.50	344.15
Mean	...	6.48	345.21

The 1937 Figures

Flying mile: Mean, 11.56 secs., 311.42 m.p.h.
Flying kilometre: Mean, 7.165 secs., 312.0 m.p.h.

The interest in George Eyston's car from the technical standpoint relates very largely to the modifications which have been made to the job since last year. As is generally known, these include modified streamlining with improved air entry to the blowers, coil in place of leaf springs and a general use of Lockheed servo systems for the brakes and other controls.

AIR INTAKES. Air is supplied to engines by these two streamlined intakes which pass a total inflow of nearly 200,000 litres per minute.

This type of brake mechanism enables a large area braking system to

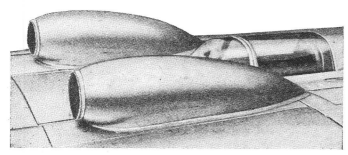

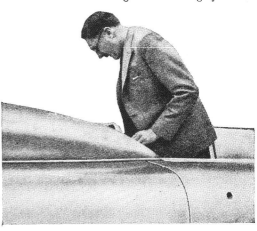

GETTING IN. Capt. Eyston lowering himself into "Thunderbolt's" narrow cockpit.

The designed maximum speed of the car was originally about 335 m.p.h. and it is interesting to know that the tractive resistance at this speed is just as important as wind resistance. This somewhat unexpected fact is, of course, due to the very good streamlined form of the car which, judged by ordinary standards, has an exceptional length-to-depth ratio.

As a result reductions in weight permitting changes in tyre pressure have a very beneficial effect on the maximum speed obtainable, and many of the improvements which have been made since the last run have been directed towards a saving of weight.

As is generally known, the car is powered by two 12-cylinder Rolls-Royce aero engines giving a maximum

output which probably exceeds 3,500 b.h.p. Each engine is blown by a turbo-type supercharger and the fuel consumption when running at full power is rather in excess of 400 gallons an hour, an amount which an ordinary 12 h.p. saloon would use in a normal running year. The engines are cooled by a radiator mounted ahead of the main streamlined form, the air now coming up through slots on the top of the body after it has passed through the radiator tubes.

As is now generally known, the car has four front steering wheels with six tyres, the rear pair having twin rims. They are independently sprung by wishbone systems with coil springs and include short cardan shafts which drive disc-type brakes.

be used with a minimum of unsprung weight and offers, therefore, important technical advantages as compared with the orthodox brake system. Ferodo material is used for the brakes and also for lining the clutches.

These latter components were somewhat maligned in the report of last year's attempt, in which it was stated that Eyston was having continuous clutch trouble. Actually the trouble arose in another part of the transmission system, and when this was modified all was well.

For initial stopping from really high speeds air brakes are used, but these are not very effective below 200 m.p.h., and from this speed until rest the whole mass of the car is largely retarded by the Ferodo friction brakes.

FASTER THAN T[...]

ON a November morning a year ago a little knot of men stood round a car. On every side of them stretched a flat, unbroken expanse of hard salt, across which damp mists were beginning to advance. Over the mountains in the distance massing clouds held a threat of early rain.

The record season was ending. In places the salt was already wet and slippery; the oncoming rain would go far to transform the place into its winter state. From a dried up lake-bed, iron hard and flat as a billiard table, it would become a vast sheet of sludge on which high speed was utterly impossible. If the record was to be broken at all it must be now.

Their eyes travelled from the oncoming clouds to the car. It was an ugly monster, severely purposeful from its blunt nose to its finned tail. Its thirty-five feet of length gave it somehow an unwieldy appearance, and indeed there were people who openly declared that it was too heavy to be controlled at full speed. Others said, with some justification, that it was not a car at all. Its seven tons, two engines and eight wheels certainly removed it far from the sphere of ordinary motoring.

The group broke up. Timekeepers went away across the flats to their apparatus, while mechanics woke the thunder of the two massive Rolls Royce power units. The man who was to drive the car, Captain George Eyston, lowered himself into the narrow cockpit and gripped the wheel.

Years of painstaking work and thousands of pounds of money were crystallised in this wheeled monster, yet its usefulness was intended to last for only twenty-four seconds. If it could cover a measured mile in both directions in no more than that and thus break the land-speed record, it would have achieved its purpose and rewarded the men whose ideas it embodied.

The course was clear now, though the mists still obscured the farther end of the thirteen-mile straight, and with an eruption of sound that justified the car's name, Thunderbolt, Eyston shot away.

The mechanics watched the car recede. They heard the driver change gear once at 100 miles an hour, a second time at 200. Then the car became hazy in the distance as it streaked towards the measured mile. The sound died away and presently news came through from the timekeepers that the car had clocked 305 miles an hour for its first run—not too large a margin over Sir Malcolm Campbell's record of 301 set up two years earlier. Much depended on the return run, for the land-speed record is worked out on the average speed of attempts made in opposite directions.

The minutes ticked away while mechanics at the farther end of the lake-bed changed the eight tyres. The thin rubber treads could not be expected to stand up to more than half a minute. Then the roar of the car's engines came again, growing louder every second, until the car itself appeared, hurtling towards

them with amazing rapidity. They saw the air-brake flaps open at the tail, catching the air-stream and helping the driver to slow, and gradually the car's speed dropped off until it was rolling evenly towards them.

Faster—or slower? The lack of anxiety in Eyston's face supplied the answer. He knew by the feel of the car, before the timekeepers arrived to confirm his triumph, that he had been travelling faster than anyone else had ever moved on land.

The return run had been made at 317 miles an hour, giving an average of 311 for the flying mile and 312 for the kilometre. Thunderbolt had beaten Blue Bird's best by exactly two-fifths of a second, and Captain George Eyston had added his name to the twenty-five speedmen who, since 1898, have held the land-speed record Blue Riband of motoring.

FASTEST

FIVE MILES A MINUTE. A fine speed study of Thunderbolt streaking across Bonville Salt Flats. The size of the driver will help you to gauge the size of the car.

IT is a curious thing that, in Thunderbolt, the history of speed has in some measure repeated itself. Ten years before Eyston took his car to Bonville Flats, Utah, for this record attempt, Sir Henry Segrave took a giant Sunbeam surprisingly similar to Daytona Beach for the same purpose.

Like its successor, the Sunbeam had two engines, the same shape—like a squashed cigar—and its driver had the same grim warnings flung at him by pessimists. The car was too powerful to be held at full speed—it would get hopelessly out of control and smash itself to scrap-iron and so on.

Moreover, the resemblance does not end there. For just as Eyston confounded his critics by doing exactly what he had set out to do, so Segrave proved his car by becoming the first man to attain the coveted speed of 200 miles an hour.

Actually there is a three-engined monster in the history of the land-speed record, though it is unfair to compare it with the other two. This was a lumbering brute of a car, devoid of streamlining, built with the idea that if there was enough power under the bonnet nothing could stop it going fast enough to capture the record—which, in theory, was perfectly correct.

The designer had taken a frame from an ordinary lorry and crammed three five-hundred horse-power Liberty aero-engines into it, and in due course it turned up at Daytona Beach under the name of the Triplex Special. They couldn't persuade an experienced race-driver to take the wheel, and in the end the builders were obliged to accept the offer of a man named Lee Bible whose chief asset was his pluck.

But it's one thing to build a car that will travel fast , quite another to build one that will steer at the same time. In theory the Triplex was fast enough. In practice it ran amok as soon as Bible let it out, digging a deep hole in a sand-dune and killing him instantly.

After that effort, designers went back to single-engined cars, and the record continued to climb regularly until ultimately Sir Malcolm Campbell touched the three hundred mark for the first time in his latest Blue Bird.

Blue Bird's Rolls Royce aero-engine developed nearly 2,500 horse-power at full revs. Eyston has two similar power units giving his car close on 6,000 horse-power, and you might reasonably have expected him to have beaten Campbell by a wider margin. You must remember, however, that over three hundred miles an hour quite a small increase in speed makes a tremendous difference to the wind resistance that must be overcome.

Put your head out of a railway carriage window when you are travelling fast and you will feel the wind pushing you back with surprising force. Thunderbolt has to push against a wind about five times as fast, and its frontal area is a lot larger than your head. Indeed, just because of wind resistance, it's probable that land-speed record-breakers in future will require more and more power and even then the increases in the record speed are likely to be small.

But Thunderbolt is very much more than two powerful engines in a streamlined chassis. In many ways it is the most unusual record-breaker that has ever been built.

Have a look at the heading picture. About the first thing that strikes you are the two curved pipes, like ventilators on a ship, that project immediately behind the cockpit fairing. They are the exhaust pipes from the inner banks of cylinders of the two V-type engines, which incidentally are placed side by side. The exhausts from the outer banks project from the side of the car.

Then, on each side of the cockpit, you can see the air-scoops leading to the superchargers. While, right at the back, under the fin, there is a panel that looks like a closed trap-door. There is one of these on the other side of the car, too. These trap-doors are hinged on the front edge, and they can be opened from the cockpit to act as air-brakes. Remember we mentioned them before ? Their action is simple. Opening them spoils the streamlining of the car and automatically increases the wind-resistance. Result, the car slows up.

There's something else you may not have noticed, and that is the placing of the cockpit itself. The driver sits *in front* of the engines, just as he does in one of the German Auto-Union racers of the older type.

But the most unusual feature of the car is its wheel arrangement. The back ones are double, like those on buses and lorries, since this gives the car a better grip of the ground when it is accelerating and also reduces the consequences of a burst tyre. In front, the car has a pair of bogies, very like a railway

FINISHING TOUCHES. *Assembling the record-breaker before packing it up for its trip to America. One pair of front wheels is already in position. The axle for the second pair can be seen just in front of the man on the ladder.*

TURNABOUT. *Checking petrol and changing the tyres after Eyston's first attempt. Part of the metal casing has been detached, revealing the front wheels. The car uses eight gallons of petrol per mile.*

engine. The first pair of wheels are closer together than the second pair, and they are so arranged that moving the steering-wheel turns all four in unison. The idea behind this is that the more wheels you have, the less weight each one has to support. Once again the strain on the tyres is relieved.

So much for the car. What about the course? Why was it necessary for Eyston to pack up his huge record-breaker and go to the immense expense and trouble of transporting it some four thousand miles to the middle of the North American continent?

He did it because nowhere else on earth is there space for a car of Thunderbolt's speed to be driven flat-out. Even Bonville Flats, with a straight run of thirteen miles, are not too big for a car that takes seven miles to reach its full speed.

The chief drawback to Bonville is, of course, its inaccessibility. The nearest town, Wendover, is twenty miles away, and to reach the flats you have to traverse a rough track that winds up into the Wasatch Mountains.

Imagine yourself standing at the top of this track. At your back the peaks of the mountains thrust upwards into the sky; and before you, reflecting the hot sun with dazzling intensity, a tremendous expanse of white salt stretches almost as far as you can see. It is flat as a sheet of water, absolutely featureless as far as the hills, blue in the distance, on the farther side.

There you have Bonville Flats. Thousands of years ago there must have been a huge lake there.

Then, for some reason, the waters seeped away or evaporated, leaving this fantastic bed of salt.

From the point of view of the designer nothing could be better, for the surface is so hard that you cannot drive a ten-inch nail into it, and any damage the wheels of speedirons may do is automatically repaired by Nature when the winter rains set in.

But from the driver's point of view there is, admittedly, room for improvement. He must put up with the glare of the sun and the sweltering heat, for the surrounding mountains shelter the flats from anything in the nature of a breeze. And thirdly, there are the mirages. Mostly the place is free from these queer optical freaks. The trouble is you never know when they are going to appear. Once before, when Eyston was attacking a long distance record, trees and houses which he knew were not really there started springing up all over the course.

By choosing November for his land-speed attempt, Eyston escaped the worst of these drawbacks. Nevertheless he nearly left it too late. He had not reckoned on having to make three attempts before he succeeded in breaking the record.

The first time he let the car out he clocked 309 miles an hour, and it seemed as if the record was safely in his pocket. Then, on the return run, the clutch of one of the engines started to slip, and the driver had to slow before he had completed the measured mile.

It took a week to remedy the trouble, and when he was ready for a second attempt he tried a novel way of starting up. Thunderbolt was backed until it was resting against the front bumper of a powerful motor-coach. The coach started, and, pushing the record-breaker ahead of it, accelerated up to fifty miles an hour. At that speed Eyston gingerly let the clutch in and Thunderbolt shot away on its own.

Soft patches had appeared on the course since the previous attempt and twice Eyston had to kill skids before he was properly under way. He rocketed across the timing strips, slowed and turned for his second run. Officials raced up; 310 they told him.

For the second time it looked as if he would achieve his ambition, and for the second time a clutch went back on him at the critical moment. It was no longer possible to repair the damage. Both clutches were taken out, re-designed and des-patched to Detroit for alterations, while the mechanics hung around, twiddling their thumbs and casting anxious eyes at the weather reports.

The weather was already breaking when the clutches came back. The car was hurriedly reas-sembled, and at the last possible moment, Eyston went out and broke the record. By nightfall it was raining steadily, but then no one cared.

It's exceedingly difficult, unless you have actually seen a record attempt, to get any idea what 300 miles an hour means. You can think of it as five miles a minute, or as a mile in twelve seconds, and reflect that on your bike you cannot cover the same distance in much less than three minutes. But figures do not really help.

The only way to get a really concrete idea is to consider the strange effects such a speed has. One of the strangest is that a driver moving at 300 is going so fast that he can see the roundness of the earth. Stand on Bonville Flats and they look as flat as a pancake. At 300 miles an hour, however, they seem slightly humped, and looking ahead, the driver can watch objects come up over the horizon.

From the spectator's point of view the thing that strikes one most forcibly is the strange way the car seems to leave its own sound behind. If you are broadside on to the measured mile and some distance from it, the roar of the engines goes on getting louder for several seconds after the car has passed. You have the odd experience of hearing the sound increasing at the same time as the size of the car is decreasing.

And think of the impetus of seven tons of car moving at that speed. It means this. That if the car were to be run at full speed up an inclined ramp that finished suddenly, its own momentum would shoot it right over the top of St. Paul's Cathedral.

Can Thunderbolt go any faster ? With a few modifi-cations Captain Eyston thinks it can, and perhaps, by the time you read this, he will have pushed his record still farther out of the reach of any other country which may feel like having a shot at it.

On the other hand he may have lost it, for as I write, a new car intended for the land-speed record is being completed for John Cobb. Cobb has been Eyston's rival in the record world all along, and if Thunderbolt must lose the record, there's certainly no one its owner would rather see gain it than Cobb.

It is only three years since Blue Bird touched the magical figure of 300 miles an hour for the first time ; and already the record is creeping upward towards a new goal. Over the horizon of speed the figure of 400 is appearing.

How long will it take us to reach that ?

FIRST ATTEMPT. *Captain Eyston gets up speed on his first go for the record—a photo which gives a good impression of the flats and the Wasatch Mountains.*

COBB at UTAH

In Practice Runs with the Railton Cobb Reaches 325 m.p.h.

THE RAILTON WITH ITS LID OFF—The body is a very lightweight structure and can easily be lifted off to give access to the power units.

FORWARD DRIVING POSITION—The driver sits right at the front of the car with the entire power assembly behind him. Here is Cobb at the wheel.

THE BEAUTIFUL STREAMLINE form of the Railton is shown to advantage here.

If Cobb breaks the record the news will be found with our week-end events reports.

368·85 M.P.H. !

John Cobb the New Land Speed Record Holder : Twin-engined Railton Averages Over Six Miles a Minute at Bonneville Salt Flats, Near Salt Lake City

From John Dugdale, of " The Autocar," who is with Cobb at Utah

MILESTONES IN THE HISTORY OF THE LAND SPEED RECORD

* 1904.	103.56 m.p.h.	(Rigolly)
* 1920.	156.04 m.p.h.	(Milton)
† 1927.	203.79 m.p.h.	(Segrave)
† 1932.	253.97 m.p.h.	(Campbell)
† 1935.	301.13 m.p.h.	(Campbell)
† 1938.	350.20 m.p.h	(Cobb)
† 1938.	357.50 m.p.h.	(Eyston)
† 1939.	368.85 m.p.h.	(Cobb)

* One way only.   † Mean of two runs.

Bonneville Salt Flats, August 23rd, 1939.

BY 6 o'clock this morning John Cobb, driving his special aero-engined Railton car, had broken the world's land speed record of 357.5 m.p.h. set up last year by George Eyston's Thunderbolt. His exact speeds for his two best runs were 370.75 m.p.h. and 366.97 m.p.h. He thus beats Eyston's speed by over eleven m.p.h.

Far away in England it is probably difficult for the reader to appreciate the magnitude of Cobb's achievement and to visualise the extraordinary scene out here on the Salt Lake.

The attacking of the land speed record is something unique in several ways. First, the white salt track itself is thrilling both in aspect and in history. Second, everyone concerned with the record has to arise with the dawn and there is the strangest hush over the gradually lightening desert. Third, one must face up to the great personal risk of this endeavour, this attempt to travel faster on land than any man has done before. Together, these impressions give a most exciting and expectant atmosphere.

This morning the officials of the American Automobile Association (familiarly known as the " Three A.s ") and the timekeepers were early at their posts.

Incredibly soon it seemed to be broad daylight and sooner still it was, as usual in August in the State of Utah, a bright sunny day. Presently that day would become almost unbearably hot (over 100 degrees in the shade), and so preliminaries were hurriedly completed.

Really that extraordinary two-engined Railton standing waiting on the salt ready to have its fish-like body dropped down on to the chassis (for the body

has to be removed for the wheels to be changed and the engines checked) looked for all the world as if it were just getting dressed ! Anyway, before the car's body is fitted the engines are started by a separate starting engine and warmed for the run to come.

Then the engines are switched off. The body is lowered on to the chassis, and Cobb climbs in. Getting a car like the Railton off the mark is not exactly a job that anyone might undertake. A lorry is driven up behind, a special bumper gear engages with a push-bar in the tail of the Railton, and the two machines start slowly away. After a while Cobb switches on, the four wheels turning, the two transmissions jerk and the engines cough, black smoke puffing suddenly out from the top and from beneath. There is more coughing, a roar,

and the engines are alive. The lorry slows and the Railton speeds away.

By now it is already uncomfortably hot in the sun and the glare from the white salt plays unpleasant tricks with the driver's vision. Apart from this sort of mirage effect the Bonneville Salt Flats are so vast that the curvature of the earth's surface is clearly apparent and to the 370 m.p.h. driver the ground seems to drop away before him. The black-paint line leading straight across the salt is his main guide.

One can follow the course of the car as a tiny black dot silhouetted against the mountains—a leg of the Rockies—many miles away. The roar of its engines rises and then falls away into the distance. Watching from behind the timekeepers' depot at the beginning of the measured mile one gets only a brief

Last-minute preparations.   Fixing the body, which has to be removed to change the wheels.

glimpse of this terrific 6-mile-a-minute progress; a glimpse, however, which, accompanied by the roar of the car and the long plume of white salt, is sufficient to give a most lasting impression.

The time is announced, "9.76 sec." That represents 370.75 m.p.h. Splendid! At that rate he should break the record by miles!

Six miles down the track the mechanics lift the body to change the wheels and to refuel, for the regulations

SUPPLIERS	
Ball and roller bearings	Hoffmann Manufacturing Co.
Body material ...	Northern Aluminium Co., Ltd.
Brake and shock absorber lining ...	Ferodo, Ltd.
Brake operating gear	Lockheed Hydraulic Brake Co., Ltd.
Cockpit window ...	Triplex Safety Glass, Ltd.
Frame	John Thompson Pressings, Ltd.
Fuel	Gilmore Oil Co.
Fuel controls ...	R. Tampier.
High tensile steel ...	Firth Derihon Stampings, Ltd.
Instruments, thermostats and Petroflex fuel pipes	S. Smith & Sons, Ltd.
Magnetos	Joseph Lucas & Co., Ltd.
Oil	Gilmore Oil Co.
Oil seals	Super Oil Seal Manufacturing Co., Ltd.
Paints and dope ...	Cellon, Limited.
Plugs...	K.L.G. Sparking Plugs, Ltd.
Special controls and wheel nuts ...	Simmonds Aerocessories, Ltd.
Steel tubes and light alloy extrusions ...	Reynolds Tube Co., Ltd.
Steering gear links ...	Automotive Products, Ltd.
Steering gear ...	Burman & Sons, Ltd.
Suspension springs ...	Tempered Spring Co., Ltd.
Transmission gears ...	David Brown & Sons, Huddersfield.
Tyres, wheels, seat cushion and rubber suspension... ...	Dunlop Rubber Co., Ltd.
Universal joints ...	Laycock Engineering Co., Ltd.
Steering wheel ...	Bluemel Bros., Ltd.
Fuel gauge ...	Simms Motor Units, Ltd.
Designer ...	R. A. Railton, B.Sc., M.I.A.E., M.S.A.E.
Builders ...	Thomson & Taylor (Brooklands) Ltd.
Engines ...	D. Napier & Son, Ltd.
Carburettors...	Claudel-Hobson Carburettor Co.

governing the record require that the runs in each direction must be made within the hour. The work is completed to time and in the distance one hears the hum of the accelerating car again.

The eye picks out its image. As steady as an arrow, the Railton comes. Not until Cobb is well past does one hear that sudden harsh roar, for he has outstripped the sound of his own engines.

The two Johns go sightseeing. John Cobb and John Dugdale of "The Autocar" arrive in Los Angeles in Mr. Gilmore's private plane.

There is an eager impatience for the time.

9.81 sec. That represents an average of 366.97 m.p.h., and Cobb has done it! At the same time the kilometre record was also taken at 369.74 m.p.h. The two kilometre runs were: North, 367.92 m.p.h. (6.08 sec.), and south, 371.59 m.p.h (6.02 sec.).

Reid Railton believes that the car still has speed in hand and that 378 m.p.h. is a conservative maximum. The Dunlop tyres are almost unmarked, and take a good share of the credit for the 11 m.p.h. improvement on last year's figure. Their treads are only $\frac{3}{50}$in. thick! Twenty covers were used up in test runs before the record was taken.

Cobb reports the car as being most tractable. He was not worried by the wind; the chief difficulty being in changing gear. The absence of flywheels and clutches makes it extremely easy to stall the engine, as, indeed, happened in Tuesday's unsuccessful attempt.

Cobb will try for the longer records on Friday. On each run twelve miles were

covered and there was a 25 min. pit stop at the end of the north run, during which the body was removed, four wheels changed, fuel and oil taken on, and some plugs changed.

The engines are supercharged Napier-Lion aeroplane units of twelve cylinders, arranged in three banks of four cylinders each. The capacity of each engine is 23,936 c.c., and the power from each is over 1,250 h.p. at 4,000 feet altitude. At sea level the power developed is 1,480 h.p. at 3,600 r.p.m.

It may come as a surprise to readers of *The Autocar* to learn that these engines are ten years old and were originally installed in Miss Betty Carstairs' high-speed motor boat Estelle, in 1929. By modifications to the supercharger a considerable increase of power has been obtained and other amendments have brought about a reduction of weight to 1,120lb. each, the weight per horse-power now being approximately 0.83lb.

So for the first time in history the land speed record stands at over six miles a minute.

An impression of the Railton at speed on Bonneville Salt Flats, by F. Gordon-Crosby.

Germany's Mercedes-Benz

In the year or two before the outbreak of World War II, Germany was planning to take the world's land speed record away from Britain. Germany had won much glory in Grand Prix racing, and she wanted to earn even more prestige internationally by winning a record held by Britain for so long. The German challenger was the Mercedes-Benz *T80*.

This attempt to win greater glory for Germany was conceived by an Austrian, Hans Stuck. He had won fame driving for Auto-Union, Austro-Daimler, and Mercedes—and he wanted to add the world's land speed record to these motor racing successes.

Stuck had already broken world's class records with cars, such as the *P-Wagen*, designed by Dr Ferdinand Porsche, and both had worked together. Thus it was natural that Stuck discussed his idea with Porsche, also an Austrian.

Dr Porsche had designed the *SSK*, the *36/220*, and the Auto-Union racing car, among other famous designs, and he had introduced supercharged engines at Mercedes. He believed above all in engines.

Porsche's faith in engines was fortuitous when he and Stuck sought a backer, for the *Luftwaffe* had just refused to support an aircraft engine developed by Daimler-Benz AG; and, when Porsche put forward the idea of a land speed record car to the men at Unterturkheim, Daimler-Benz agreed to finance the project because they wanted to show the *Luftwaffe* just how good their engine really was.

Daimler-Benz took a step towards the world's land speed record early in 1939 when Rudolf Caracciola broke the world's flying kilometre and flying mile records for Class D cars in the 2-to-3-litre category. Caracciola set up these records in a 3-litre, 12-cylinder Mercedes on an autobahn near Dessau. The lessons learnt at the Class D level influenced the design of the *T80* being built to capture the absolute speed record, in Class A, Unlimited.

The aircraft engine used to power the *T80* was the type DB 601, the inverted V12-cylinder engine having a cubic capacity of 44,000 c.c. and developing about 3,030 b.h.p. The engine incorporated a centrifugal supercharger and employed fuel injection.

The body, as well as the engine, reflected aerodynamic influences; this was partly because Baron von Fachsenfeld, the aerodynamics designer, was also connected with its conception. A horizontal fin was mounted near the rear at each side, for example, to endeavour to relate the load of the rear wheels to changes in wind resistance. The lightweight metal body was well streamlined, and even the parts of the body above the six wheels were shaped as fins to act as stabilisers.

The *T80* incorporated an important innovation intended to help reduce wheelspin, which had proved such a handicap in previous attempts on the world's land speed record: an automatic device throttled back the engine, quite independently of the driver's accelerator, whenever wheelspin of the rear wheels became too severe.

The car, which Daimler-Benz developed at Unterturkheim in 1938-1939, had three axles, and the driver sat at the front.

The original plan was to attack the world's land speed record at Bonneville. However, the German authorities later insisted that the attempts be made on a 7-mile stretch of autobahn near Dessau—so that the record would be broken in Germany. So short a length would, of course, have been dangerous. Difficulties were encountered, though, when it was proposed to mine brown coal discovered under the autobahn.

When war broke out, many of the parts had been assembled, but construction was not complete. As a result, the *T80* was never driven. Work on the project ceased on the outbreak of war.

In the early 1960s rumours spread that the *T80* was being prepared to make an attack on the world's land speed record. These rumours, however, were denied by Daimler-Benz AG.

To-day the Mercedes-Benz *T80* may be seen in the Daimler-Benz Museum in Stuttgart-Unterturkheim—all that remains of Germany's attempt to reach 400-450 m.p.h. that failed to come off owing to the outbreak of World War II.

MERCEDES-BENZ *T80* SPECIFICATION
(supplied by manufacturer)
COUNTRY OF MANUFACTURE. Germany.
ENGINE. Daimler-Benz type DB 601 aircraft engine. Cylinders: 12. Cubic capacity: 44,000 c.c.
Power: 3,030 b.h.p. approx. Centrifugal supercharger. WHEELS. 6 wheels, 3 axles.
DIMENSIONS. Length: 8.5 m. Body width: 1.80 m. Frontal area: 19 sq. ft. approx. WEIGHT. Dry: 2.8 tons.

HOME AGAIN!

John Cobb's War-time Homecoming : "The Autocar" Staff Writer Brings Back Inside Story of Britain's New Land Speed Record

(Above) A final photograph as the "Bremen" fled from New York.

(Left) John Cobb's farewell party to America in the Cotton Club, New York, with Beris Harcourt-Wood (centre) and John Dugdale of "The Autocar."

THE greatest motoring achievement of the year, the establishment of a new land speed record of 369.74 m.p.h., by John Cobb's Railton, looks like being the last landmark in the world of motor sport for some time. No excuse is necessary, therefore, for further reference to a wonderful performance which will still be history in spite of warfare.

I came back with John Cobb and ex-Bentley driver Beris Harcourt-Wood in the *Aquitania* last week. One could not but sympathise with Cobb on his personal aspect of the crisis and the outbreak of war. Once again he has been robbed of the full measure of acclamation which is duly his. Last year during the keen rivalry for the record between him and George Eyston he was permitted to hold the record for one day only. This year the outbreak of war rendered his homecoming virtually ungreeted.

The record was broken on Wednesday, August 23rd, and the longer distance records were set up on the following Saturday, August 26th. Four days later we sailed from New York, on Wednesday, August 30th. The *Aquitania* was due to sail early that Wednesday, together with the *Normandie* and the *Bremen*, the Nazi liner which had at last obtained its release from the harbour authorities. First it was announced that the *Normandie* would not sail, and a large number of French passengers transferred to the *Aquitania*; but, although we were due out at midday, by 6 p.m. the gangway had still not been lifted. We watched the *Bremen* steam out and at last at about 7 p.m. we followed.

By

JOHN DUGDALE

(The writer was with John Cobb in America)

It was an uneasy voyage, with all port-holes and windows blacked out, no navigation lights and a zigzag mystery course. The ship was alive with rumours; how the *Bremen* had dashed south for a neutral port to be armed as an auxiliary cruiser; how we, too, were heading south—and certainly the weather became hotter and hotter. At lunch-time on Sunday, September 3rd, a notice was posted that war had been declared and the next news was that the *Athenia,* another liner on the Atlantic route, had been torpedoed with over a thousand people aboard. The reality of the war could not have been brought home to us more quickly.

As one gazed at the horizon it was easy to imagine that one saw a tiny dot that marked a submarine. It may seem a strange comparison, but somehow I was reminded of the many times during the past few weeks in which I had gazed at the horizon of another sea, the white sea of salt from which we had just hurried 2,000 miles across the American continent. Owing to the complete flatness of the salt bed one used to get some strange effects watching for the first glimpse of the record car, since vision of objects on the surface is restricted to about four miles. From the starting depot, for instance, the time-keeper's tower, the tents and the car parks, which were about six to seven miles away, were quite invisible, although the mountains in the distance formed a background to which the salt appeared to lead uninterrupted.

I do not hesitate to say that the Bonneville Salt Flats, Utah State, U.S.A., form the finest speed track in the world. The only man-made track which might compare is the special *autobahn* at Dessau, Germany, which in spite of its 90ft. concrete width for six miles possesses the hazards of a race track compared to the Salt Flats. As I am probably the only person in the world who has seen record attempts on both tracks I feel qualified to give this opinion.

The Salt Flats, which have been formed by the drying-out of a lake 125 miles to the west of Salt Lake City, provide the most perfect surface imaginable, dead level for 100 miles in one direction and completely hard in large areas. The section surveyed for the records was 13 miles long. This year conditions were as good as anyone had ever seen them, and the salt was so hard that a small sliver would actually cut like a knife. Another effect of the salt is that it eats through leather shoes, so that rubber shoes must always be worn. Conditions are, however, very dependent on weather, as the disadvantage of the salt is that its flat surface provides little drainage and the slightest rainstorm turns it immediately into a lake. It can take many days for such a lake to dry out.

Sunshine and Rain

Thus, in respect of the weather, Cobb must be counted lucky, as the desert sun never ceased to shine till three hours after the final records were broken. Heavy rain clouds then rolled up from the plains of Nevada, and when we drove back into Salt Lake City the white salt bed had already become a glistening lake.

Following the breaking of the land speed record, I was naturally interested to note the reactions of Cobb and his crew. The record runs were complete by 6 a.m., and as we had all had to make a very early start we had returned to bed for some more sleep; I did not see Cobb until tea-time. H. R. Fletcher, the chief Dunlop technician, joined us and there was little doubt of the mutual satisfaction as Cobb and he positively beamed at each other. Indeed, the tyres had been remarkably good.

John laughingly said, "Now I am sure you can build me a tyre to go 400 m.p.h.?" Although the Dunlop expert was not to be drawn on this question, I share John Cobb's view.

What It Feels Like

Asked the inevitable question of how it feels to drive at 370 m.p.h., John himself answered that the nearest parallel which he could give was a power dive in an aeroplane. As to deceleration, so often said to be the trickiest part of the driving, he explained that this was so great on lifting his foot at 370 m.p.h. as to throw him forward in the seat. He began braking in bursts from 300 m.p.h., and finally would coast into the finishing depot with the free-wheel in action. Personally, I had not quite realised that the brakes were applied from such high speeds, and it certainly says much for the linings. The Railton has two transmission brakes only, hydraulically operated and cooled by the water in the cooling system. This does not have a circulation system, but actually ejects water on to the track. The car is designed for single runs only, so that the loss of water is not important.

It seems strange at first that heated water is used for "cooling" the brake, but so long as there is a medium for carrying away the heat generated, the temperature is not so important. Reid Railton pointed out the trail of steam under the car when later we watched the finish of the ten-mile record together.

As the designer of the car, Railton's impres-

(Top Left) Even the Railton in America had to have its diet of crushed ice. (Above) Western Union had a busy table on the salt flats, a quarter of a mile from the track. Altogether, 25,000 words were wired. (Left) For entering the car these planks were rigged up on the starting lorry, a powerful Dodge truck.

(All photographs taken by "The Autocar")

(Top) The Railton at speed, showing the course taken beyond the black centre line. (Below) Three hours after the final records had been taken a rainstorm turned the flats into a liquid lake.

sions are also of great interest. He, too, was just as pleased as Cobb and everyone else connected with the record, the tyres affording him the greatest satisfaction. Tyres are really the governing factor of the car's speed, and if Dunlops came to Railton and said they now had a tyre capable of 400 m.p.h. I do not think it would be long before the present Railton record car would be capable of that speed. But from the tyre angle it would not be advisable to make a big jump in the record. Tyre manufacturers have a grave responsibility, and in fairness to them it must be stated that they set Cobb a conservative limit in speed. Already this year they have proved that they can build reliable tyres for the astonishing speed of 380 m.p.h.

380 m.p.h. Reached

That the car reached 380 m.p.h. was shown by the chart from the speedograph. Railton showed me the circular disc on which was recorded a red line showing the curve of the car's acceleration and deceleration, speed being plotted against time. The pointer had moved for about four minutes (about 12 miles had been covered!) and the line climbed steadily up to 380 m.p.h. and dropped as steadily back. It was estimated that the car reached 300 m.p.h. in three miles.

No wonder that Railton was pleased with the tyres, since the only marks on the 1/50in. rubber treads were blisters, and these were caused as the car was swung round at the end of its run, giving the smooth treads a sideways thrust they were not meant to take. Following the runs, Reid Railton would go out on the track and examine the wheel marks with care. The car leaves four distinct lines owing to its crab track, and from the nature of the marks you can tell to a yard just where the driver changes gear.

The designer's job was not confined to recording data, since before the record run Railton had to do some hard thinking as to why one of the supercharged Napier-Lion aero-engines was over-heating. Eventually the header tank was dismantled and baffle plates modified.

The wheel marks on each occasion were absolutely regular, and a course between the black centre line and the outer edge of the 150ft. wide swept strip was purposely chosen. Cobb said that the cross wind did not affect his course, and the centre line was avoided as it might have been slightly rough, since in rescraping the track they had had to leave the black line intact. That he was able to keep a steady course on a track theoretically reduced to 75ft. in width shows how true the car ran.

Afterwards Cobb said, "She really is marvellous; absolutely tractable at 380 m.p.h."

He is convinced that he has the finest high-speed car in the world and never ceases in his praises of Railton. Also, he proved the tractability of the car by cruising up from the finish to the timing box under power, steering the long machine through a gateway which could not have been much more than 15ft. in width. Altogether, I calculate that he drove the car about 75 miles, during the record attempts and runs, and in so doing used—but did not wear out!—36 of the 48 tyres taken.

Few Troubles

Mechanical troubles were few, and when the water system had been altered a recurrence of misfiring was cured by carburettor adjustments. Carburation is tricky at the height of the flats (over 4,000ft.) and in an atmosphere where the temperature rises very rapidly.

The success of the Railton is a tribute to the foresight of John Cobb and Reid Railton in producing a thoroughly scientific design. The Railton has far less power than the previous record holder and has half the weight, but it took the record with comparative ease and safety.

Four-wheel-drive to give the maximum acceleration; a power-weight ratio better than the modern Grand Prix car; and the finest streamlined body ever produced, are perhaps the three points chiefly responsible for Britain's new 369 m.p.h. record.

Finally, success was clinched by as fine a crew of English engineers as you could wish. The way that Ken Taylor and his men worked so efficiently and unsparingly impressed even the most hard-boiled of Americans.

THE WORLD'S LAND SPEED RECORD

Date	Driver	Car	Place	M.p.h.
1927				
29 March	H. O. D. Segrave	Sunbeam	Daytona	203.79
1928				
19 Feb.	M. Campbell	Napier-Campbell	Daytona	206.96
22 April	R. Keech	White Triplex	Daytona	207.55
1929				
11 March	H. O. D. Segrave	Irving-Napier	Daytona	231.44
1931				
5 Feb.	M. Campbell	Napier-Campbell	Daytona	246.09
1932				
24 Feb.	M. Campbell	Napier-Campbell	Daytona	253.97
1933				
22 Feb.	M. Campbell	Campbell Special	Daytona	272.46
1935				
7 March	M. Campbell	Campbell Special	Daytona	276.82
3 Sept.	M. Campbell	Campbell Special	Bonneville	301.13
1937				
19 Nov.	G. E. T. Eyston	Thunderbolt	Bonneville	312.00
1938				
27 Aug.	G. E. T. Eyston	Thunderbolt	Bonneville	345.50
15 Sept.	J. R. Cobb	Railton	Bonneville	350.20
16 Sept.	G. E. T. Eyston	Thunderbolt	Bonneville	357.50
1939				
23 Aug.	J. R. Cobb	Railton	Bonneville	369.70
1947				